Stutthof Diaries Collection

For Truth & Honor

Tore Jørgensen

 FriesenPress

One Printers Way
Altona, MB R0G 0B0
Canada

www.friesenpress.com

Copyright © 2022 by Tøre Jørgensen
First Edition — 2022

All rights reserved.

No part of this publication may be reproduced in any form, or by any means, electronic or mechanical, including photocopying, recording, or any information browsing, storage, or retrieval system, without permission in writing from FriesenPress.

ISBN
978-1-03-910808-0 (Hardcover)
978-1-03-910807-3 (Paperback)
978-1-03-910809-7 (eBook)

1. HISTORY, MILITARY, WORLD WAR II

Distributed to the trade by The Ingram Book Company

Table of Contents

Introductions — 1
Prologue — 3
Chapter 1 – Norway at War — 5
    Reichskommissar of Norway — 6
    Police Uncertainty — 7
    Nazification of the Police — 8
    Unpopular Mandates — 8
    Winds of Change — 9
    Aktion Polarkreis — 10

Chapter 2 – Prisons in Norway — 12
    Ulven Internment Camp — 12
    Espeland Camp — 14
    Grini — 15
    Falstad — 17
    Police Prisoners — 18

Chapter 3 – Journey to Stutthof — 21
    Train Ride Eastward — 22

Chapter 4 – KZ-Stutthof Camp — 25
    Barrack 19 — 27
    Stutthof Leadership — 28
    Kapos – The Criminal Element — 29
    Food Rations — 30
    Camp Life — 31
    Danish Prisoners — 33
    Christmas 1943 — 36
    The Night Became Holy — 37
    A Dane in SS Service — 38

Chapter 5 – A Camp of Their Own	**40**
Lillestrumen	43
Letters and Packages	45
Camp Activities	48
The Man Who Defeated Germany	50
Chapter 6 – Out to Work	**53**
The Tone Has Changed	54
The Worst Work Detail	55
Farm Work Detail	56
Tears for Human Compassion	57
Haying Work Detail	58
Wood Detail	60
Joachim at Babylon	60
The Unterdeich Work Detail	61
BBC Radio	63
Chapter 7 – Orders from Berlin	**65**
The Rocket Factory	66
An Unexpected Visit	67
Serving as Guards	68
Temporary Reprieve	69
Police Discipline	72
Documents from Norway	72
Rumors of Evacuation	73
Library and Pastimes	74
Planting Vegetables	75
Mystery of the Herring Barrels	76
KZ-Stutthof Tragedy	77
Gas Chamber	77
Chapter 8 – Civilian Prisoners	**80**
Period of Chaos	82
An Act of Compassion	84
Finnish Prisoners	85
Cold Winter	85
The Hospital	86

Polish Uprising	88
Christmas and New Year 1944	88
Wise Leadership	90
Chapter 9 – End of Sonderlager	**92**
Typhus Outbreak	94
Packing Begins	96
Red Cross Packages	96
Preparation for Evacuation	97
Evacuation of Main Camp	99
Pleni Norwegia	100
Chapter 10 – The Death March	**101**
Napoleon	103
Column 8	104
The March Begins	105
Klein Zünder	107
Praust	108
Polish Prisoners	111
Kalpole	111
Nestempole	112
Maria Notwinski at Zukau	113
Pommersdorf	116
Streep	118
Chapter 11 – Evacuation Continues	**119**
Goddentow	121
A Close Encounter	122
Transport Leader Danesch	125
Chapter 12 – Evacuation Eastward	**127**
The Police Cooks	128
A Time for Reflection	130
Mrs. Tarnowsky	130
The Stingy Widow	131
Secret Organization	133
Farmer Patsowsky	134
Wagon from Kalpole	134

Red Cross Packages ... 135
August Walth ... 136
Russian Advancement ... 136

Chapter 13 – Germanic Column ... **138**
The Wagon Became Separated ... 140
Danesch Panics ... 140
Mingling with Other Prisoners ... 143
Seeking Accommodations ... 144
Putzig ... 145
The Jewish Women ... 147
Tjiremesin ... 148

Chapter 14 – Back To KZ-Stutthof ... **150**
Danzig ... 153
Troyl Labour Camp ... 153
New Transport Leader ... 155
Watching the Fireworks ... 156
Troyl to Stutthof ... 158

Chapter 15 – Main Camp Stutthof ... **161**
Returning Evacuees ... 162
Other Prisoners Return ... 163
Tischlerei ... 164
Bombs and Grenades ... 165
Russian Attacks ... 167
The Mole Holes ... 169
Water, Hygiene and Disease ... 170
Catering and *orge* ... 172
Two Norwegians and a Cow ... 175
Orge Horses ... 175

Chapter 16 – Daily Life at *Tischlerei* ... **178**
Visiting Werderhof ... 179
Fall of Danzig ... 181
Eastern Front Moving West ... 183
Looking Back ... 185

Chapter 17 – Second Evacuation   **187**
    Evacuation Begins   188
    Boats Arrive   189
    A Pitiful Sight   190
    Rumors Persisted   192
    Torpedoed   193
    The Corral   194
    Entering Hela   195
    Wolfgang   198

Chapter 18 – Voyage Begins   **202**
    The Jewish Women   203
    Man Overboard   203
    Danish Islands   206
    The *Anna Marie*   *207*
    The Old Woman   210
    Heading for the Bay   211
    Hitler is Dead!   212
    Full Evacuation Mode   213
    The *Thielbek*   *215*
    Heading for Lübeck Bay   216
    The Oberleutnant   217

Chapter 19 – Deliverance   **219**
    Something is Happening   220
    A Word of Warning   221
    Abandoned   223
    Pelzerhaken   225
    Seeking Accommodations   226
    Massacre at Pelzerhaken   228
    Neustadt   230
    Commandant Hoppe   232
    The *Athens*   *232*
    Liberated   235

Chapter 20 – Norway House   **237**
   Wine Cellar   238
   Neustadt in Chaos   239
   Cap Arcona and *Thielbek* Tragedies   241
   Role Reversal   243
   Alternate Route Home   244
   Prolonged Stay   245
   Norway is Liberated!   246
   Funeral for Linda   248
   Sevi Bulukin   250
   Going Home at Last   251

Glossary   **252**

Introductions

True adventure stories can make us better people. Not because we see heroes and villains in them – we can see those in fiction – but because they are true, we know we could be like the people in them. This World War II story of the Norwegian police is such a story. It is a story of the redemptive power in making a conscious choice against evil – a choice available to each of us.

On the morning of August 16, 1943, the Oslo chief of police was executed by a German firing squad. He had **refused** to arrest three young women who failed to show up for mandatory labor under Nazi occupation laws. The opposition to the police chief's execution resulted in the arrest of hundreds of **Norwegian** policemen deemed potential security threats to the German occupation.

Two hundred and seventy-one police prisoners were transferred to Stutthof, a concentration camp in Eastern Poland. Walled off in a small camp of their own, the prisoners submitted themselves to re-education, learning German and performing various tasks to assist the German cause. In other words, they were offered an opportunity to participate in the Nazi war effort without taking up arms. At the end of the process, they were asked to decide whether they would support the German cause or the Norwegian government in exile in London. The police prisoners unanimously refused to join the German war efforts and instead endorsed their government in exile.

By 1944, not even the Nazis had much confidence in victory. Still, their brutality towards their concentration camp prisoners continued without restraint. In Stutthof, the Norwegian police prisoners achieved real camaraderie with their fellow sufferers and were able to play a role in their survival. Their story is a reminder of the unmitigated evil of the Nazi regime that must not be repeated in our time. In this retelling of the story, we see psychopaths chosen from civilian prisons to torment and terrify helpless internees in concentration camps. We see Jewish men kept in dog kennels and led out on leashes to lick the boots of their masters. We see supervisors boast openly about the number of prisoners they have killed. We see Jewish and Slavic women worked to death and then incinerated. Finally, we witness the Nazi collapse and their defeat in a war of folly, based on the myth of racial superiority. During their ordeal in Stutthof, the Norwegian policemen's unity and discipline contributed to their survival and the survival of those they helped.

True to their training, the Norwegian police recorded the details of their experience in the Stutthof camp. These articulate, experienced witnesses provided a unique record, accurately documented in their diaries and memoirs, how personal sacrifice can triumph over ruthless greed and violence. In the first book of The Stutthof Diaries Collection series, entitled For Truth & Honor, their story enables the reader to experience the redemptive power of conscious choice against evil — a choice we may be forced to make one day.

Prologue

As far as I recall, it was 1952 when I first saw the book *Norsk Politi bak Piggtråd* (Norwegian Police behind Barbed Wire). I was five at the time and visiting my grandmother. The book caught my eye while playing hide-n-seek. Both the book cover and the title aroused my curiosity. While leafing through the book, one particular drawing struck me and left a lasting impression on me. It was a drawing of two young men being hanged, with what appeared to be soldiers standing around the gallows. I was intrigued and asked my father about the book and the drawing. Like many WWII veterans, my father refused to discuss the book or any of its content. A short time later, I learned my father had been a prisoner of war at a concentration camp called KZ-Stutthof in Eastern Poland. I didn't see the book again for another twelve years. In the meantime, we had emigrated from Norway to Canada. During one of our many moves in Canada, I saw the book again and quickly looked through it once more. That was the last time I saw it, as it was lost during our many moves in Canada. My family returned to Norway to live, but I decided to stay in Canada and finish my education. After meeting my wife in Canada and raising four children, there was no reason to return to Norway. The one memory that has been etched in my mind was the book on the police prisoners at KZ-Stutthof. My father passed away in 1998, without sharing much about his wartime experience. The year after my father passed, I started researching KZ-Stutthof and the policemen who, along with my father, were imprisoned at the camp. My research led me to diaries and memoirs written by police and Norwegian civilian survivors of KZ-Stutthof, including Olaf R Walle, Karl M Haugan, Gulbrand Nyhus, Sverre Lauglo, Erling Oftedal, Erik Aandahl and police historian Jørn-Kr. Jørgensen. I am particularly thankful to Erik Dahlin. His father, Finn Dahlin, kept detailed journals of the events and published them under the title *Di Trodde På en Bedre Dag* (They Believed in a Better Day). The drawings are by Anker Hafstadt and my granddaughter, Anna Jørgensen. Several words and titles that may not be familiar to the reader are bolded when they're mentioned for the first time. Definitions of the terms are found in the Glossary section of the book.

In researching the concentration camp KZ-Stutthof, I was led to reports written by the Institute for Historical Review. I began an email exchange with the organization, and they provided me with their official version of the KZ-Stutthof history. I soon discovered that the institute's information on KZ-Stutthof differed from that of the police diaries, especially when it pertained to the Jews. The Institute for Historical Review believes that any eyewitness report by the 'Zionist' (their word) was unreliable because the Jews had an agenda. To which I replied, "What agenda did the Norwegian police have? Their treatment was much better than other prisoners. Besides, they were trained to report the facts and review the evidence. Therefore, if the Norwegian police diaries support the eyewitness reports, would it not give strong evidence to those 'Zionist' reports?" The institute did not reply.

It has been my passion for the last sixty-eight years to publish an English translation of the events entitled *For Truth & Honor* under *The Stutthof Diaries Collection* series. It's a story of survival, of loyalty, and reaching across cultural barriers to share each other's burdens, to risk death and torture, to help utterly helpless people, who were without hope. It's also a story of man's inhumanity to man and how love and compassion can help people through some of the darkest periods of human history.

CHAPTER 1 –
Norway at War

The Beginning

In the tumultuous year of 1940, which saw the British driven from continental Europe at **Dunkirk**, the occupation of Holland and Belgium and the fall of France, the invasion of Norway on April 9, under the German code name Weserübung, received little attention. Norway had been confident its neutrality would be respected by the warring nations, Britain and Germany. Norway's confidence was based on a letter the government received from Berlin declaring Germany's intention to respect Norway's territorial sovereignty under all circumstances, provided that Norway maintains irreproachable neutrality. Therefore, Norwegians were surprised and unprepared when Nazi Germany attacked Norway on April 9, 1940.

Norway's neutrality was undermined by its own countryman, **Vidkun Quisling**, the leader of the Norwegian Nazi ideology party, **Nasjonal Samling (NS)**. While visiting Adolf Hitler in Berlin during the winter of 1939, Quisling informed Hitler that the Western powers were planning to establish bases of operations in Stavanger and Kristiansand. Quisling proposed that, if Germany chose to occupy Norway, he would take over the bases and hand them over to Germany.

Immediately after the invasion, on the morning of April 9, Quisling proclaimed himself the new head of the government and ordered the armed forces to surrender to the Germans. Quisling's intervention only served to stimulate the resistance movement, and Germany quickly realized that Quisling did not serve their interest. Quisling's leadership lasted only a week.

Reichskommissar of Norway

Two weeks after the invasion, **Josef Terboven** arrived in Oslo as the new **Reichskommissar** (national commissioner) to oversee the occupation of Norway. Terboven was answerable only to Adolf Hitler and ruled Norway with an iron fist. In early September 1941, Terboven received a visit from **SS-Oberst-Gruppenführer Reinhard Heydrich** (the architect of the Holocaust), whom Hitler called *Der Mann mit dem eisernen Herzen* (The Man with the Iron Heart), along with SS-**Brigadeführer Walter Schellenberg**, the German head of Military Intelligence. Terboven was told in no uncertain terms to keep a *hard line* against the Norwegian people and to firmly clamp down on the resistance movement in Norway.

Four days after Heydrich's visit, Terboven instituted severe measures seeking to eliminate all resistance in Norway. Terboven had ten civilians and twenty-four resistance fighters executed. He also ordered the arrest of all Jewish males over the age of sixteen.

In another example of the measures instituted, the quick and brutal annihilation of the coastal fishing town of **Telavåg** was personally overseen by the Reichskommissar. As the villagers watched, all buildings were destroyed, all boats were sunk or confiscated and all livestock were taken. The men of the village were either executed or sent to the concentration camp at Sachsenhausen in Poland or Grini in Oslo. Of the seventy-two who were deported from Telavåg, thirty-one were murdered in captivity. Women and children were imprisoned for two years. In addition, eighteen Norwegian prisoners (unrelated to Telavåg) held at an internment camp were also executed as a reprisal. Though smaller in scale, the Telavåg atrocity is often compared to similar events at **Lidice** in the Czech Republic and **Oradour-sur-Glane** in France. Telavåg was completely erased from the map.

Under the Regulation of Protection 1942, Terboven introduced the death penalty for a variety of crimes. Among them: leaving the country without permission, listening to illegal radio, being caught with illegal newspapers and helping prisoners of war or refugees.

Police Uncertainty

Amongst the Norwegian police, there was uncertainty under the Nazi occupation. The police had no instructions or regulations on what part they should play in war, much less under an occupation. The policeman's oath was to enforce Norwegian law. However, with Norway now under German occupation, in most cases the police wanted to avoid the impression they were servants of the Nazi political agenda. On the day of the invasion, many policemen left the force to join the resistance, thereby leaving the police force severely undermanned.

During the early days of the occupation, the Norwegian public was filled with uncertainty. Rumors that Oslo would be bombed led to large scale panic and mass evacuation of the capital. It became the police's responsibility to restore order and security among the Norwegian public.

King **Haakon VII**, and the elected government of Norway, had escaped to England to continue the resistance fight. This left Oslo Police Chief **Kristian Welhaven** as the top civil servant in the country.

The Germans wanted contact with the entire Norwegian population, which they were unable to establish through the strongly disliked NS party of Vidkun Quisling. Welhaven became a calming force to the public and was the representative the Nazis were looking for to instill order and confidence among the Norwegian public.

The Norwegian police were extremely loyal to Welhaven, and the Nazis found his influence among the police members to be too strong.

Welhaven's refusal to carry out certain orders forced the Nazis to remove him from office and replace him with a Nazi sympathizer, the much disliked **Carl Bernhard Askvig**. The police leadership had now taken on a definite political overtone, and the uncertainty and insecurity increased.

There were, of course, policemen who sympathized with the Nazis prior to the invasion and welcomed the occupation. They were few in numbers at first. At the time of the invasion, the total police force consisted of 3,000 men, of which 120 (or four percent) were members of Quisling's NS party. At the other extreme were policemen who sought to defeat and frustrate the Nazi occupation. The majority of police, however, were in the middle and seemed unsure which way to align themselves.

Nazification of the Police

Minister of Police **Jonas Lie** pressed strongly for every policeman to be a member of the NS party, with the goal to 'Nazify' the Norwegian police force. The police were divided on this issue, as initial membership into NS was voluntary with no apparent consequences. To many, NS membership was a way of relieving the uncertainty. They regarded membership as only a piece of paper, as things were no different than before and membership was just a formality.

Those within the police who were opposed to the Nazi occupation were well aware of who the collaborators were and who to avoid. Strangely, many of the NS police members were actively involved in the resistance themselves, or at least sympathetic towards their colleagues who resisted.

That began to change when Reichskommissar Terboven introduced unpopular orders the police were required to implement. In addition, the exiled Norwegian government regarded NS membership as being disloyal to Norway.

Unpopular Mandates

One month after the invasion, the police were ordered to confiscate all radios from Jewish residents. The order was then expanded to include all radios in Norway. When the Nazi salute was forced on the police, it met with whole scale resistance, and the orders were changed to become voluntary. In fact, the salute became an easy way to identify Nazi sympathizers within the police department.

Police membership in NS was now on a decline. The main reason for the decline was moralistic, violation of human rights and orders contrary to the Norwegian Constitution. Mandates to stamp all Jewish passports with a 'J' were very unpopular.

By March 1942, a further division within the police began to appear and would eventually lead to a chain of events resulting in a definitive action by the Germans against the police. Among the most divisive mandates was the arrest of teachers refusing to teach the new Nazi curriculum. The teachers' passive resistance became popularly known as the **'Paper Clip Resistance'**.

The police were now ordered to arrest their friends, and their children's teachers, for being loyal to their country.

The arrest orders, the issuing of gray uniforms to conform to the German dress code, and the orders to arrest all Jewish residents and confiscate their property resulted in a mass exodus of police membership in NS. Several members of the police force, at the risk of their lives, organized evacuation of Jews out of Norway and into neutral Sweden.

It was at this point that Reichskommissar Terboven put his foot down. The threats the Germans had previously given to the police had clearly not accomplished the desired result. Now the Germans intended to force the police to make a decision to either be loyal to the Nazi occupation or face the consequences.

Winds of Change

During the early stages of the war, Germany met with little resistance over its expansion policies. Then, towards the end of 1941, Germany began to experience setbacks, first in the air and then at sea and land. On the Eastern Front, the German army was stopped outside Stalingrad and forced to abandon its siege. This was followed by the defeat of the German stronghold in North Africa and Allied forces landing in Sicily. From Sicily the Allied invaded Italy.

Germany felt the pressures on all fronts, as their war measures met with stronger and stronger resistance. In an effort to bolster their position, Germany began a concentrated effort to clamp down on all resistance within the countries they occupied. The Norwegian underground had become better organized and presented a solid threat to the German occupation.

It now became expedient for the Germans to determine who was loyal and who would present a security risk. At the core of the German concerns was the Norwegian police. The Germans were aware that a large number of the police were unsympathetic to the German occupation. Germany feared the police would become a military threat. Several policemen had already been arrested for sabotage.

Faced with pressure from Berlin, and wanting to bolster his own image with Hitler, Terboven and his commanders formed a plan to eliminate the disloyal element within the Norwegian police. The plan needed to be carried out at the earliest opportunity. It included policemen and civil servants throughout Norway who were considered security risks. The strategy was to force them to sign a document stating their loyalty to the German occupation.

Aktion Polarkreis

Terboven saw his opportunity with the arrest of Chief of Civil Police, **Gunnar Eilifsen**. The president of the State Police, Bernhard Askvig, had ordered Eilifsen to hand over five constables. The constables reported to Eilifsen that they were ordered to arrest three girls who failed to report to mandatory work detail, known as ***Arbeidstjenesten***. The constables refused to arrest the girls and Eilifsen agreed with them. He informed Askvig that he would not support such a mission. Eilifsen was summoned to appear before Askvig at Møllergaten 19 (State Police headquarters) but was immediately arrested and put in detention. Terboven was informed of the case and became greatly incensed, claiming that such subordination was a direct defiance to his authority and must be punished. He demanded Eilifsen be sentenced to death immediately by a Norwegian court.

Eilifsen was first tried and acquitted by a panel of three judges. There was no constitutional provision to sentence Eilifsen to death for refusing to carry out orders. Under Norwegian law, disobeying orders was punishable by a jail sentence or dismissal.

Eilifsen was sent back to his cell, and the defense went home. Infuriated, Terboven demanded an immediate new trial. Later that afternoon, Eilifsen was brought back to the courtroom with only one judge and the prosecutor. Eilifsen was sentenced to death and was to be executed at the next sunrise (August 16).

Eilifsen didn't have the opportunity to contact family or a defense lawyer. Justice Minister **Sverre Riisnæs** objected at first and pointed out that there was no legal basis for Eilifsen's execution. Terboven pressured Riisnæs to write a law that stated that the police, NS and Germanic-SS Norway had the scope of the Military Penal Code, even in peacetime. The law has often been referred to as *Lex Eilifsen*. Police Minister Jonas Lie was also pushing for the death penalty. The fact that Eilifsen and Lie were childhood friends attracted attention.

Eilifsen was shot at sunrise on August 16, 1943. His execution was used as a ploy. The same day Eilifsen was shot, plans were implemented to crack down on resistance against the Nazi occupation within the police force. All over Norway, police were rounded up under the code name *Aktion Polarkreis*. The police prisoners were kept in detention at various Gestapo locations throughout the country. They were given an ultimatum: either sign a loyalty oath or face the same fate as Eilifsen.

The oath read:

> *Jeg lover at jeg samvittighetsfullt og etter beste evne vil oppfylle mine plikter som politimann I følge de bestemmelser som gjelder for min tjeneste, og følge de ordrer som blir gitt meg.*
>
> (I promise that I will conscientiously and to the best of my ability fulfill my duties as a policeman by the regulations applicable to my service, and follow the orders given to me.)

Those who had no conscience in the matter signed and were then sent home. Hundreds of police members refused to sign and stood as a collective protest against the Nazi regime. They understood that the time had come to no longer sit on the fence, but to take a stand.

CHAPTER 2 –
Prisons in Norway

On the morning of Monday, August 16, 1943, approximately 500 policemen and civil servants all over Norway were arrested and brought to the local Gestapo jails. After being interrogated at the local jails, the police prisoners were transported to various concentration camps throughout Norway. Those arrested in southern Norway were mostly interned at Ulven, Espeland or Grini, while those arrested in the northern half of Norway were imprisoned at Falstad, south of Trondheim.

One policeman wrote to his wife while en route to Gestapo jail:

> We har ennå intet fåt vite, men så vidt jeg fostår er alt politi I Sogn arrestert. Jeg tror det er arminnelig internering av politiet på Vestlandet, muligens mot politiet over hele landet.

(We have no information on what is going on, but it appears that all the police in Sogn have been arrested. I believe it is general internment of all police on the West Coast, maybe the whole country.)

Ulven Internment Camp

Ulven internment camp (Norwegian for *The Wolf*) was used by the Nazis as an interrogation camp. The original prisoners were Jewish or Communist, but soon a broader selection of prisoners arrived. Conditions were relatively complaisant until 1942, when **Untersturmführer** Otmar Holenia took command and imposed harsh conditions. Ulven was mainly used for executing prisoners for a variety of reasons. It's not known how many were murdered in the camp.

The arrested police members arrived at Ulven on Wednesday, August 18. The Nazis regarded the prisoners as the unreliable part of the Norwegian police force. In addition, there were civilian prisoners in the camp who were considered activists within the resistance.

Police were given the choice of chopping wood in the forest or working in the vegetable garden.

Camp commander Holenia was nicknamed *stormen* by the prisoners because he would *storm in* hoping to catch the prisoners in illegal activities.

Though the situation was quite serious, there were some lighter moments in the camp. On one occasion, Police Chief Alf Reksten was washing floors in the Gestapo quarters when an officer asked Reksten for his name and rank. Reksten replied that he was the police chief in Sogn and Fjordane and had the rank of Major. The Gestapo stood silent for a minute and walked away. The next day, word came that none of the Norwegian police prisoners were to wash floors for the Gestapo.

The camp's chief cook was let go on Friday, August 20. At roll call the next morning, it was asked if there were any cooks among the prisoners. Jomar Lie volunteered. Lie was a policeman whose family owned a hotel, where he would often help in the kitchen, teaching him culinary skills.

Lie observed that the field workers left every morning in a horse-drawn carriage and returned every evening with a carriage full of vegetables. Lie found an old wooden box for the field workers to hide under the wagon and fill with food. When the wagon returned and passed by the kitchen, the prisoners would hand the box full of vegetables to Lie. He promptly emptied the box and hid the vegetables in various places. The next day, Lie would put the vegetables in the soup. Soup was the main meal of the day for the more than ninety prisoners, so it was important that it should be nourishing.

On one occasion, Commander Holenia *stormed* into the kitchen right before supper, walked over to the large pot on the stove, and began stirring it. He continued to stir it for several minutes and complained there were too many vegetables in the soup. Lie, who spoke German fluently, said he tried to make at least two nourishing suppers a week to make up for the poor ones during the rest of the week. Holenia accepted the explanation and told him to continue.

Unfortunately, Lie's career as the chief cook came to an end a week later. Two trout, along with a generous supply of butter, were delivered to the kitchen to be prepared for the camp commander. Lie fried the trout and spread the browned butter over it. A lawyer named Morten von Krogh, representing Holenia in legal matters, proceeded to serve the fish. A few minutes later, von Krogh burst into the kitchen with Holenia on his heels. Lie was told off and escorted out of the kitchen because the camp commander takes butter on the side, not on top of the fish. As a result, Lie was sent to the internment camp Espeland, with Holenia ordering that he be given the hardest and heaviest jobs in the camp. Lie was put to work digging holes for fence posts and carrying heavy timbers. That was the penalty for not knowing that the camp commander should have his fish and butter served separately. The rest of the police prisoners were transferred from Ulven to Espeland on August 30.

Espeland Camp

Espeland was located in the county of Arna, east of Bergen. Surviving prisoners told of an extremely hard work camp. Because of its elevation, the camp was extremely cold at night.

The laundry was located in the cellar of the camp's commandant house. A set of stairs led to the rooms upstairs and a separate door leading from the laundry to the outside.

There were no water pipes into the laundry, so water had to be carried from a creek at the opposite end of the camp. Many trips were made during the day. The camp rule stipulated that whenever prisoners met a guard, they had to stay at attention, take off their cap, salute and give their name, rank, and serial number. That meant they had to repeat this process several times a day. Usually, the prisoners met the same guard, who they nicknamed *Chaplin*. After several times, Chaplin told them they only had to go through the routine once a day, in the morning.

The camp Commandant, **Hauptsturmführer** Herman Fuchs, liked to find ways to catch the prisoners doing something illegal. The laundry was a place where prisoners could warm themselves. But this was against the rules. The prisoners were never sure when Fuchs would be hiding on the stairs or lurking behind the door. On many occasions, Fuchs would burst into the laundry and make the prisoners stand at attention, ordering them to turn their pockets inside out, hoping to find something illegal. The prisoners were not allowed to have anything in their pockets and the lining had to be clean.

On one occasion, several prisoners stood smoking in a circle. *Chaplin* came upon the prisoners and began to curse them. The guard wasn't upset at the fact they were smoking, he was angry they didn't post someone to warn them when a guard was coming. Now he had to fill out a report. Failure to do so would have grave consequences for him. The prisoners promised to post a guard next time. *Chaplin* accepted that and didn't report them.

On Saturday, November 20, the police prisoners were ushered into trucks and taken away to the railroad station at Haugeland. From there they were ushered onto a train bound for Oslo. From the Oslo train station, they were transported by truck to Grini concentration camp.

Grini

Grini was originally built as a women's prison. Its construction started in 1938 but wasn't finished until 1940. It was never put to use as a women's prison. The German invasion of Norway changed all that, and the Nazis took over the camp. Initially, the Germans used it as a prison camp to detain Norwegian military officers captured during the Norwegian Campaign (Weserübung). The status was changed in June 1940, when it was used to house **Wehrmacht** soldiers. In June 1941, Grini's status was changed to a concentration camp. The camp was run by Schutzstaffel (SS) and Gestapo and was renamed *Polizeihäftlingslager Grini*.

As Grini's inmate population grew, more barracks were built to accommodate the increase of Norwegian political prisoners. Many were held at Grini before being shipped to camps in Germany and Poland.

The police were brought directly to the headquarters and were lined up single file in the hallway where they stood for several hours, without food or water, and with their noses pressed up against the wall. The police prisoners were registered by two young Nazi sympathizers from Trøndelag.

On one occasion, all prisoners were forced to stand at attention from 19:00 to 23:30 while guards searched for weapons and radios. Both Reichskommissar Terboven and Colonel General **Wilhelm Rediess** were present. With them was an execution squad that was ready to shoot ten previously selected prisoners if they found anything illegal. Fortunately, nothing was found.

The police were mostly put to work on the Holz-Commando, or the 'woodgang' as it was called. On the 'woodgang', the police worked alongside prisoners from Telavåg. Jomar Lie was picked to be in charge of a barrack consisting of forty newly arrived prisoners. He briefed them on what was expected of them, but they thought he was exaggerating and that things couldn't be as bad as he said. The following day, one of the cruelest Nazi officers, **Unterscharführer** Kurt Walter Kuntze, arrived for inspection. He was not at all pleased with what he saw, and let his displeasure be known. Lie received a vicious blow to his face, was shoved backward out of the barracks, and fell to the frozen ground where he was savagely kicked.

On Wednesday, December 8 at 12:30, the alarm sounded for general inspection. The police prisoners lined up just outside their barracks for roll call. Those whose names were called were escorted outside the main gate. The sixteen prisoners left behind were all sure they were to be shot for something they had done. The rest of the police prisoners were moved to the main courtyard, where they stood at attention for over three hours in freezing winter weather. A roll call was taken every other hour. Finally, the prisoners were ordered to hand in their uniforms and dress in their civilian clothes. They were not permitted to sleep. Around 03:00 they had their last roll call. The yard was now alive with Nazis shouting instructions to board several trucks and buses. The prisoners feared they were going to Germany but hoped they were going to another camp in Norway.

When the last bus was full, there were still fifteen prisoners left standing outside the bus. The German guards stood bewildered, not knowing what to do when Kuntze came along and looked at the situation. Taking a prisoner to the door, he kicked the prisoner in the back end several times until the prisoners in the bus made room for him. Kuntze did the same with each prisoner until they were all aboard. The additional prisoners were carried overhead hand over hand until everyone had a place on the bus, even though their feet didn't touch the floor.

The men were driven to Filipstadskaia (dock), where the steam ship *D/S Donau* was moored, to transport the prisoners to Germany.

Falstad

Falstad was founded in 1895 as a boarding school for boys. It was part of the general movement in Europe, and Norway in particular, to reform the penal system, especially for children. It was most notably established to serve the needs of "misguided" youths (rather than criminal youths) through education, labor and a "Christian spirit".

The buildings burned down in 1921, and new brick buildings were constructed based on the 19th-century prison designs, with a courtyard in the middle of a rectangular building.

German authorities originally visited Falstad in August 1941, with the intention of making it a center for the German **Lebensborn** program in Norway but found it unsuitable for that purpose. The Germans soon decided to put Falstad to use as a prison camp. The first prisoners, 170 Danes, had volunteered and then reneged to be part of **Organisation Todt**. They spent three months in the camp, using the time to start construction on the barbed wire fence and watchtowers.

Falstad fell under the authority of Reichskommissar Josef Terboven and **Heinrich Fehlis**. Fehlis commanded the Security Police and commanded a 200 member *Einsatzgruppe* of the security police. For all practical purposes, Falstad became the personal prison of SS-**Obersturmbannführer** Gerhard Flesch, leader of regional Einsatzkommando V based in Trondheim. Known by the title *KdS Drontheim*, Flesch regularly used the nearby forest (*Falstadskogen*) as a site for 'extrajudicial' executions of POWs and following special trials of political and Jewish prisoners.

The camp population grew steadily, and an expansion program was begun. Prison barracks were built southeast of the main building, utility buildings were built around the center and the commander's quarters were built just on the other side of the river. The grounds were monitored from three watchtowers.

The camp authorities burned and sabotaged what documents they could before the liberation in 1945, but it is estimated that at least 4,500 prisoners from thirteen countries passed through Falstad.

Police Prisoners

Policemen arrested in the northern half of Norway were first taken to Vollan Gestapo headquarters in Trondheim and interrogated before being transported to Falstad.

Upon their arrival at Falstad, the police were given prison uniforms with the letter "P" and a white dot on the chest. The white dot meant they couldn't go outside the camp area; the ban was strictly adhered to. The new administrator, Warner Jeck, who arrived a few months before the police prisoners, had eased the degradation and abuse of the prisoners instituted under the former commander, SS-**Hauptscharführer** Paul Gogol.

The police were given their own room and kept isolated from other prisoners, except during work detail when they worked with other prisoners in carrying and crushing rocks at the quarry. It was meaningless work that lasted between ten to twelve hours per day.

The police work detail was under the leadership of Obersturmbannführer Bøckman, who showed favor towards them, allowing the police to build a wall to rest behind and not be seen. Bøckman stood in the watchtower and warned the police when danger was near.

The police prison food consisted of cabbage soup for dinner, dry bread with jam for breakfast and supper and stewed mussels during evening meal. The local civilian citizens gave the police prisoners' milk, fish and bread in large quantities.

That was until a Nazi sympathizer became resentful of the police's favorable treatment and reported it to the Reichskommissar. Terboven immediately sent Gerhard Flesch from Trondheim to investigate. The camp Commandant Jeck was reprimanded and forced to treat the police like other prisoners. Flesch straightaway assigned Edward F. Lambrecht as the police's prison guard. Also known as "Gråbein" (Grayleg), in reference to wolves, Lambrecht was both cruel and evil, particularly towards Jews.

At various internment camps, the police prisoners learned to *orge*; to steal from guards to stay alive. The ability to *orge* became an important factor in their future survival.

> *Orge, verb = organisere = I tysk konsentrasjonsleire å tilvende seg noe av det som leirledelsen (vokterne) hadde fratatt eller unnlatt å levere til fangen I hans krav om å få leve.*
>
> (Orge, verb = to organize = In German concentration camps, to apply some of what the camp management (guards) had deprived or failed to deliver to the prisoner in his desire to be allowed to live.)

At night, a wagon would appear regularly to pick up the sick prisoners. Those prisoners were never seen again. Only one policeman became sick and later died, police constable Nygaard from Trondheim.

The whole time the police were incarcerated at Falstad, they received visits from their loved ones only on two occasions.

Christmas 1943 was fast approaching. Rumors circulated that there would be a Christmas amnesty and some prisoners would be set free. At first, not many took the rumors seriously. However, on one dark December morning, a few hundred men were called out to hand in their uniforms and put on their civilian clothes to get ready for a trip. They were hopeful. During the evening meal, Flesch walked in and removed some older prisoners. The prisoners then realized they were not going to be released but taken to another camp, possibly in Germany. All police prisoners were going, except a few older policemen who were sick. The police were awakened at 03:00 on December 7, 1943. Without their luggage, extra clothes, food or toiletries, they were transported on buses to Trondheim and into the unknown. All they received was half a loaf of bread provided by Jeck in the last minute. He seemed to think that the SS had treated the police unreasonably.

It was a bitter moment arriving in Trondheim. The police's own comrades were forced to accompany the prisoners from the bus to the railway station. The bright spot was that many prisoners' wives and loved ones had learned of their transport and were hiding in the rail cars as the police prisoners passed by. When the prisoners arrived at the station, their hands and feet were tied with thick silk cords. They were threatened with the penalty of death if they loosened the bonds. The police prisoners were given a bowl of porridge along with the half loaf of bread provided by Jeck.

The transport arrived at the Oslo train station at 02:00 on December 8, 1943. The station was virtually empty when they arrived, and the police were forced to face the wall for forty-five minutes. The prisoners then marched along Karl Johans Gate (Street) in their summer clothes, with their hands and feet bound, forcing them to hop like rabbits to Møllergaten 19; headquarters of the State Police. From Møllergaten, the prisoners were transported in a covered truck to Filipstadskaia.

CHAPTER 3 –
Journey to Stutthof

The steamship *D/S Donau*, docked at Filipstadskaia, was a 13,000-metric-ton German freighter converted to transport prisoners and military personnel. The police contingent totaled 204 from Grini, 37 from Falstad and 13 from other prisons in Norway. There were also 291 students and 955 other prisoners, for a total of 1,500 prisoners. It was the most extensive prisoner transport from Norway to Germany during the war. The guards forcefully boarded the prisoners at 08:30 Thursday, December 9, 1943, and set sail for Germany.

Prisoners were divided into compartments throughout the ship. Each compartment was split into three levels. Those who arrived first ended up in the top level, the next filled the second level then the third. When the third level was filled, the remaining prisoners were put on the top deck with the Wehrmacht soldiers on leave for the Christmas holidays. A short time after departing, the police stood on the outside deck. They watched the Norwegian coastline disappear over the horizon. When they saw the lights of Helsingborg (Sweden), several contemplated jumping into the water and swimming to shore. But the thought of the frigid waters made them change their mind. The main topic of conversation was their situation and the fear of running into a mine or being torpedoed by a Russian submarine. In that case, they would have no chance of survival. Suddenly, the alarm went off and the engines were put in reverse. A mine was discovered fifteen meters from the port side.

The Wehrmacht soldiers on leave had rigged up a field kitchen on the upper deck to boil pea soup. As fate would have it, the soup was scorched and the soldiers refused to eat it. A "friendly soul" then proposed that the prisoners could eat the burned soup, as a new batch was being prepared for the soldiers.

On the second day of sailing, a worship service was arranged. The sermon was delivered by Pastor Robertstad from Bergen, whose brother, Karl Robertstad, was one of the police prisoners. It was a service that most would never forget. After the sermon, they sang a hymn and then a silence fell over the entire assembly. Then, out of the silence, a lonely baritone voice began to sing *Norge mit Norge* (Norway my Norway). Olaf Walle had sung that song many times at Grini, but this time it had a much deeper meaning. Men were lying on their bunks, staring at the ceiling with tears running down their faces. The realization they may never see their families, or their beloved Norway, had overcome them.

When the ship sailed near Swinenmünde in Northern Germany, *Donau* passed a merchant ship heading towards Norway. The vessels passed so near to each other that one policeman recognized one of the seamen, who immediately acknowledged him. In that way, many of the relatives and friends back home would learn they were sent to Germany.

Train Ride Eastward

Donau docked at Stettin in mid-afternoon on December 11, 1943. The police were separated from the other prisoners and then lined up for roll call. After being counted, they were divided into five groups and ushered into separate railroad cars. Each car was designed for forty men without luggage. The first three cars were packed with sixty prisoners, including their belongings, forty in the fourth car and thirty-four in the fifth. One police prisoner, Torstein Herring, was taken away at Stettin and transported to KZ-Sachsenhausen. Herring was arrested in early 1943 as a member of the resistance.

It was too tight in the railroad cars, making it virtually impossible for everyone to sit. The prisoners alternated standing and sitting the entire trip. The only light came from a crack in the wall under the roof. An extra tall policeman, Rolf Henry Granlund, was stationed under the gap and reported what he observed. After nearly ten hours of waiting, the train finally began its trip eastward. The police would not be able to leave the train for the next twenty-four hours. To relieve themselves, they passed a jar around to urinate in. Afterwards, they gave it to Granlund to empty through the crack. In another railroad car, the prisoners used a gap in the door just large enough to urinate through, and in another, a prisoner used

Cramped Railroad Cars

his pocketknife to take out a few floorboards. When the train took a scheduled stop, the police would disembark and relieve themselves.

The locomotive broke down in Belgard (Stargard). There they remained for six hours while waiting for a new locomotive, but that locomotive broke down at Stolp.

The police had nothing to eat until they arrived at Gotenhafen near Gdynia in Poland. A group of women from the German Red Cross served the police prisoners soup. They remained in Gotenhafen for six hours.

D/S Donau docked at Stettin on December 11. From there they travelled for fifty-four hours until arriving at Gotenhafen on December 13.

From Gotenhafen the train travelled eastward to Tiegenhof, where the police disembarked and were met by a contingent of heavily armed Wehrmacht and SS soldiers. Several prisoners couldn't help but smile at the humorous situation, seeing the police were unarmed, exhausted, hungry and in no condition to resist. The Germans, on the other hand, were armed with machine

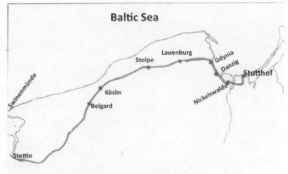

Train Ride Eastward

guns, rifles and hand grenades. The prisoners stood at attention while being counted over and over again. After a considerable wait, the prisoners boarded a small train with open railroad cars. The SS guards were hostile and would shout at the police while hitting them with their rifles and kicking them. Leif Tackle was hit in the back of the neck with a rifle and fell to the ground; the SS guard proceeded to kick him with his heavy boots. Tackle lost several teeth in the exchange.

The train ride took several hours before arriving at their final destination, Waldlager. In the moonlight on December 14, 1943, 253 Norwegian police prisoners, surrounded by German soldiers, marched the 300 meters from Waldlager station to Stutthof camp. The police had never heard of the camp before. Their first impressions were somewhat confusing. They had come to a camp with electric barbed wire, guard towers with armed guards and barracks laying very close to each other. Yet the camp smelled of flowers; there were flower baskets everywhere. Their first impression was, "this looks ideal!"

CHAPTER 4 –
KZ-Stutthof Camp

Stutthof concentration camp lay thirty-five kilometers east of Danzig. It was connected by a broad and well-kept highway named Danziger Strasse. A small and narrow track railroad called Kleinbahn went southeast to Schiewenhorst, where there was a primitive ferry that crossed the Weichsel River to Nickelswalde. From Nickelswalde, the Kleinbahn went to a small town named Steegen and further to the small village of Stutthof. The camp lay one kilometer directly east of Steegen, and five hundred meters west of the village of Stutthof. The camp lay on a delta separated from saltwater (Danziger Bucht) and surrounded to the north by a small two-kilometer forest of fir trees. Approximately 500 meters east of the village of Stutthof was an inlet called Frisches Haff. The area was damp and cold and relatively unhealthy. The wind blew constantly, and several places were underwater, in some places by as much as four meters, at high tide. The area was traversed by several canals where some large ships travelled.

The camp was initially built as an internment camp for potential opponents of the Third Reich. Afterwards, it would provide workers for the German war effort. The increasing number of Germans being called into military service caused a severe manpower shortage.

Construction began in July 1939, using prisoners from Danzig prison under SS **Sturmbannführer** Max Pauley's command.

Stutthof had approximately 4,500 inmates at the end of January 1940. These inmates consisted almost entirely of Polish men, including numerous priests, teachers and other intelligentsia members deemed politically unreliable. A small number of women also arrived at Stutthof during the middle of the same year. They were housed in Barrack I, which received the designation "Women's Block". When prisoners first entered the camp in September 1939, there were already several tents, a kitchen, a washroom and a latrine. Felling trees was considered the most demanding job.

Up until October 1941, there were only three inmate barracks in the camp. At approximately the same time, sewer installations were completed and washrooms were installed in the barracks. Previously, inmates had to wash in troughs in the open air. Another barrack was used as an inmate infirmary. It contained, among other things, an operating room, a first aid room and a pharmacy. There was also a kitchen barrack and a laundry. A former old folks home served as headquarters. Barracks for camp workers were built in early 1940. There was a paint shop, a furniture workshop, joinery, an electrotechnical workshop and a forge when completed. Outside, the camp had stables for livestock, a slaughterhouse and cages for raising Angora rabbits. In addition to the so-called *Erziehungshafline* (educational inmates), there were nationals of occupied territories, Germans who violated their labor contracts or neglected to comply with the call-up for labor service.

Reichsführer-SS **Heinrich Himmler** visited Stutthof on November 23, 1941 and decided to change its status to a regular concentration camp **Konzentrationslager (KZ)**. The decisive factor was economics, as Himmler argued:

> "*Niemand schenkt mir das Geld; es muss verdient werden, und es wird verdient, indem man den Abschaum der Menschheit, die Insassen, den gewöhnlichen Verbrecher zur Arbeit setzt*".

> (No one gives me the money as a present; it must be earned, and it is earned by putting the scum of humanity, the inmates, the habitual criminal to work.)

At the end of 1942, Max Pauly was recalled to KZ-Neuengamme, which he commanded until the end of the war. Pauly's successor was SS Sturmbannführer **Paul-Werner Hoppe**. Hoppe was no longer fit for service due to being wounded on the Eastern Front. Therefore, he was recalled into the concentration camp service. He had already been a member of KZ-Dachau camp staff from 1937 to 1941. Hoppe commanded KZ-Stutthof until the end of the war, but left the camp at the beginning of April 1945. At that point, it was unofficially commanded by SS-Hauptsturmführer Paul Ehle.

East of the main camp lay several large factories that belonged to *Deutsche Ausrustungs Werke*. They were affiliated with *Focke-Wulf-Verkene*, where airplane parts were made. Adjacent was another factory building where submarine parts were made. The camp provided the factories with cheap labour.

KZ-Stutthof had forty-five *Aussenlager* (work camps) east towards Königsberg and westward towards Stettin and provided these camps with cheap labour. In 1944, many of the work details were involved in expanding the camp. In this kind of work, the police prisoners came into the picture. They would also be involved in work projects west of the camp, including repair shops and workshops. The police would mainly be used for road construction and bridge-building.

Barrack 19

The Norwegian police prisoners had no knowledge of all this as they marched through the main gate early that December morning. The prisoners stopped in front of a barrack that was entirely surrounded by electric barbed wire. On the front of the barrack was No.19. Here the police were to be quarantined indefinitely. Barrack 19 was divided lengthwise into two equal wings, Block A and Block B.

Upon entering the barrack, the prisoners first found a small common entrance area. From there, they were separated into the two wings, with 150 men in each wing. The first room in each wing was for washing. A door led into a large room used as a dining room that also served as a meeting room. Past the

Entering Stutthof

room was a large sleeping room with bunk beds, three high on each side and a narrow passage between the two rows. Each prisoner had his own bunk, and there were still empty bunks. Sounds were absorbed by the large meeting room, and those that lay farthest away could not hear any activity in the main meeting room. Therefore, it was necessary to institute a communication system that included verbal calling from bunk to bunk.

Stutthof Leadership

The police had hardly found their beds when the camp commandant, Sturmbannführer Paul Werner Hoppe, followed by a long line of officers, showed up. The Commandant gave a speech in the courtyard, which emphasized the prisoners' responsibilities. Hoppe mentioned several times that there was only one way out of the camp, each time pointing to the crematorium's chimney.

The Commandant asked if there was anyone who spoke German, whereby Sigurd Skjolden was pushed forward. Hoppe heard that Skjolden had been a marine officer and gave him the title of *"Korvettenkapitän"* (Corvette Captain).

Hoppe asked why the Norwegian police would not join Germany against their common enemy. He sarcastically declared, *"Was kann das kleine Norwegen im Kampf der Zivilisation gegen die Barbaren tun?"* (What can little bitty Norway do in civilization's fight against the barbarians?).

Skjolden, never afraid to speak his mind, quickly engaged in a sharp exchange of words with Hoppe. During the exchange, it was learned that Hoppe's civilian work was as a gardener. That explained the flower baskets at the entrance and the large garden around the commandant's residence. Hoppe's residence was a two-story brick building surrounded by an extensive garden that was, of course, maintained by prisoners.

Second in command was a tall individual the Danish prisoners called *Stork*, SS-Hauptsturmführer **Theodor Meyer**. He also went by the name *Murder Meyer* because he was in charge of executions. The police recognized Meyer as the officer that counted them earlier at the Waldlager station.

The camp supervisor was Otto Selonka, an unsympathetic type who paraded around the camp in a black silk shirt, riding pants and shiny black riding boots. Selonka would always carry a leather whip with him. He used it regularly on prisoners who didn't immediately do what he wanted or how he wanted things done. Selonka was a German criminal convicted of rape and murder who regularly practiced his brutality. A watchdog followed him and, like his master, tore into prisoners at will. There weren't many prisoners who had escaped either his whip or the dog's teeth. Selonka was constantly in possession of alcohol and was regularly drunk. During his drunken spree, he would frequently pick out a young girl for himself to violate.

Kapos – The Criminal Element

The Block Chief of Barrack 19 was the criminal Emile Kinkowski, who lived in Block A in a corner by the dining room, where he also had his office. Kinkowski bragged that he was number three among **Kapos** when it came to executing prisoners. During his post-war trial, it was proven that he killed 375 prisoners. His prisoner number was 13,921 and he wore a green triangle (criminal). Kinkowski was arrested for his participation in the 1933 burning of the parliament building in Berlin (**Reichstag fire**).

An eighteen-year-old Russian soldier named Dimitrov was the Cabin Chief in Block A. He was captured behind German lines. The police wondered how a Russian could be a Kapo at a German concentration camp. A few days later, the police witnessed Dimitrov climb through the barbed wire fence between Barrack 19 and the Lithuanian Barrack to beat to death a Lithuanian prisoner who had fallen because of fatigue.

Dimitrov Beating a Lithuanian Prisoner to Death

The Cabin Chief in Block B was Gutlob Kübler. He had served earlier in the German marine but was convicted of some criminal activity. The police never did find out what his crime was. Kübler walked around with a cat on his shoulder.

As the camp population started to grow, the Germans found themselves short of personnel to run the camp and resorted to using criminals from Danzig's prison. These criminals were schooled in idealism, fanaticism and sadism. They went through extensive training to undermine their personal and moral values. Then they were given leadership over the prisoners in the concentration camp and were given the title **Kapos**.

Kapos were not automatically placed into these positions, they first had to be a prisoner for some time. They also had to demonstrate that they were qualified to take responsibility and carry out the SS leaderships' wishes. The Kapo leadership was the most barbaric period in KZ-Stutthof history. These criminal leaders carried out unimaginable brutality towards the prisoners, especially towards Jewish women. Among all the German concentration camps, brutality towards prisoners was commonly rewarded by the SS.

The Kapos often fought amongst themselves and were equally as cruel to each other. They reported each other to the SS and would even kill each other. Between these insane criminals and the SS, the prisoners lived in constant fear. The Block Chiefs and Cabin Chiefs wielded a lot of power among the SS leadership. Within the camp, the Kapos were more powerful than the SS.

The Kapos saw it as their right to lord over the prisoners and steal from their meagre rations. The SS administration was aware of their barbarism but didn't care. The police's immediate leaders were criminally insane, and did what they wanted towards them. If these criminals had not been told by the camp administration to not handle the Norwegian police prisoners like other prisoners, several of the police would no doubt have been beaten to death. This was a picture of a world turned upside down, a world where the police were the prisoners and prisoners were the police. The Camp administration was very much aware of this. Still, they turned a blind eye that gave the criminals *carte blanche* to steal, which they did at every opportunity.

Food Rations

The police were given a ration of 200 grams of bread (four pieces a day), with a little margarine and some cheese. This was not enough food, and they were continually hungry. Each prisoner watched closely to make sure he didn't get less than the others. There was much disagreement over the size of the bread pieces. Some pieces were heavier than others as it was virtually impossible to cut each piece exactly the same size. It was agreed to set up a committee in charge of ensuring each prisoner would get equal amounts. For supper, they usually had soup made from kohlrabi or red beet peelings. The peelings were not washed, resulting in a lot of sand in the bottom of the soup bowl. The soup was delivered to the barracks from the main kitchen in two twenty-five-liter buckets called Kübler. The prisoners would then carry the buckets to their dining room to be distributed. On one occasion, in Block A, two police prisoners tripped over the doorstep. They dropped the buckets, spreading soup all over the floor where 125 men had walked. Suddenly there were 125 men on all fours, each jostling to scoop up his portion of the soup.

The food the police received was not nearly enough. They learned later that the prisoner's food portion would only keep a healthy person alive for three months. Hunger became the main topic of conversation. They would often recount the excellent meals they had at home, especially during the holidays. In many cases, they would hallucinate and see mirages of lavish tables spread with all types of food.

A few days after the police arrived, they were ordered to surrender their belongings and civilian clothes. The Germans took their luggage, backpacks and all valuables, including rings, watches or anything else of value. Several policemen hid their rings and watches at the bottom of their backpacks and other places. Once they surrendered their valuables, the prisoners would never see them again.

It was common knowledge that the Germans would search and ransack the prisoner quarters to find valuables. The Germans also searched for gold in the prisoners' teeth. If they discovered gold, they would pull the teeth without anesthetics. One policeman had a gold bridge in several of his teeth. He pulled them out himself and hid them in a place outside the barracks. When the police moved to Sonderlager a few weeks later, he dug them up and reburied them at the new camp. When he went home again, he had his gold bridge with him.

Camp Life

Their first roll call was December 14 at 06:30 in the dark outside Barrack 19. They had only fallen asleep at 03:00 after fifty-four hours of travelling from Norway. When the guards had finished counting them several times, they were commanded to take off their hats, *Mutchen ab!*

This was the greeting that all prisoners had to do before their superiors. When roll call was over, the police heard the unfamiliar command *Ein Lied* (a song). This was one of the main differences between concentration camps in Norway and Germany. In Norway, they were forbidden to sing during roll call, but in Germany they were commanded to do so.

That morning, standing in front of Barrack 19, they sang songs they knew well but which the Germans didn't. They sang *Vi vandrer med freidig mot* (We wander boldly forward), *Kjaerringa med staven* (Old Lady with a stick), *Ola Glumstolen* (Ola Glumstolen) along with others. There were many fine voices among the police, and when they sang together in harmony they sounded like an accomplished choir. Their singing was followed by a moment of silence; undoubtedly, the Germans hadn't heard such singing behind the barbed wire before.

A few days after their arrival, the police were given writing materials and told what they should write.

> *"Ich bin gut angekommen und bin. Die aller herzlichen – und Neujahgrusse!*
>
> *Dein......"*
>
> (I have arrived, and I am well. A very cordial – and New Year greetings!
>
> Yours......)

This was a source of much joy for the police since it would allow their families and friends at home to know they were alive. The cards were mailed on December 18 and arrived in Norway in early January.

This period was a difficult one for the police prisoners, imprisoned so far from home and in a foreign and hostile country. Electric barbed wire surrounded the main camp, but a second electric wire surrounded their barrack, making them feel even more isolated. They were not allowed to walk about in the main camp. They had nothing to occupy their time, other than what they initiated themselves. The hunger pains were beginning to take their toll, and their physical and psychological well-being steadily declined. Their hunger was so intense that some chipped pieces of wood slivers from their bedpost to chew on. This, at least, gave them the feeling of munching on food. Several police fainted from lack of nourishment.

There was, however, a small blessing of being fenced in from the rest of the camp; they didn't see the brutality perpetrated by the guards on other prisoners. In this respect, they were spared seeing the whipping, beating and other barbaric punishments. They heard of a small boy who had tried to take a small piece of bread. He was tied to a tree stump and given twenty-five heavy strokes with a stick to his back. If anyone tried to interfere, they would be given the same punishment. The police were also spared seeing prisoners hung from lampposts with their hands tied while the SS-guards burned their feet with cigarettes. They didn't see the cruelty, but they certainly heard the screams. The police did observe walking skeletons half-dead, being beaten and chased, dying at the hands of their guards.

Morning Wakeup Call

Danish Prisoners

The Danish prisoners became their friends, and a deep friendship developed between them, especially with their leader, **Martin Nielsen**. The Danes were Communists and arrived at Stutthof three months before the Norwegian police; they were located in Barrack 13. The Danes were the first prisoners that did not receive the customary twenty-five lashes with a stick to their backs. However, their body hairs were shaved, and they were given prisoner uniforms.

The prisoner uniforms were *zebra* striped with white and blue. The uniform was made of very thin material and consisted of a jacket and pants with a round *kallot* for the head. In winter, the prisoners received a coat of the same thin material. The undergarment was a standard blue striped shirt with pants that were to be renewed every six months. Of course, they were never renewed; neither were the wooden shoes. The prisoner's number was on the left side of the jacket and the right thigh of the pants. Under the number was the national identity (e.g. N for Norway, D Denmark, P Poland, R Russian, RD German, F France). Under the letter was a triangle that identified the type of prisoner and why they were arrested. Red for political prisoners, green for criminal prisoners, violet for different Bible groups and black for sexual criminals. If the triangle pointed upwards, the prisoner was serving life in prison.

The majority of the prisoners were, of course, political prisoners. All Russians, along with the RD German, were considered criminal prisoners. Russian prisoners consisted mainly of civilians between the ages of twenty and sixty years of age. When German troops met with resistance, they gathered all the men between those ages and sent them to concentration camps. Consequently, the concentration camps filled up very quickly and emptied almost as quickly. These Russian prisoners were given civilian clothes belonging to Norwegians, RD German, Danish, French and some Polish and Lithuanian prisoners.

The civilian clothes were mainly ragged, as the best clothes were reserved for Kapos or guards. Once the clothes were picked over, the leftovers were given to the Russian prisoners. The clothes were dilapidated and hung as rags on them. They made a pathetic sight as they marched each day to their work command. The very fact that only a handful froze to death with such meager clothing was surprising.

Prisoners wearing civilian clothes had their prisoner number and a red cross on the back of their jacket and pant leg. The red cross on the back varied in sizes. If a prisoner had a small cross, he was most likely a Kapo or a Block Chief or similar. Kapos always had the best clothes. One police prisoner saw a Kapo wearing his sport suit. This was not really surprising. Worse was when a Kapo tried to sell back photographs to a Danish prisoner of his own wife and family.

The Danish prisoners were very friendly and helpful towards the Norwegian police. From the very beginning, Danes provided the police with the newspapers *Berlin Times*, *Politics* and *Finnish Times*. Later, those newspapers were much appreciated, even when the police would receive newspapers from Norway; the Danish papers were always more recent.

The police were constantly lined up for roll call. If they didn't line up fast enough, the guards would hit them with whatever was in their hand, including whips, sticks or lead pipes. The roll call was regularly prolonged due to counting errors, especially at night. The guards were often drunk, which hindered their ability to count. The prisoners would stand for hours looking up into the stars as the guards counted over and over again. Except for roll calls, there weren't many police activities, except to walk about in the fresh air and discuss their future. The barracks were surrounded by electric barbed wire, isolating them from the rest of the camp. In some places, the barbed wire was only a couple of meters from the barrack walls.

The barrack next to the police was the Lithuanian barrack. It was designed for 300 prisoners, giving each prisoner a bed. There were, in fact, 1,200 Lithuanian prisoners, or four prisoners per bed. They wore the thin *zebra* striped uniforms made from cotton and always looked as if they were freezing. The Lithuanians would huddle together along the barrack walls to keep warm and sway back and forth while singing their despairing songs. Their melancholy songs had an adverse effect on the police. Many police prisoners didn't go outside anymore.

Even within the isolation of their barracks, prisoners were not safe. Regularly, bullets came flying through the barrack walls from indiscriminate shootings by the guards carrying out their executions. The guards, often being drunk, showed little concern where the bullets went. Often the bullets penetrated barrack walls, killing or injuring prisoners.

Executions were regular occurrences in the camp. Almost any excuse was given to execute prisoners. Generally, executions were carried out with a pistol shot to the back of the neck.

In light of their gloomy conditions, the police needed to find something to occupy themselves; being active was the best antidote for apathy and depression. They were fortunate to have many younger men who were full of humor and laughter. A choir was formed with Trygve Løkke as its director; they practiced often. The choir enabled them to focus their thinking away from their circumstances and brought them a much needed distraction. Among the police were many fine voices, and after a few practices they became an excellent choir. Concerts were arranged, which helped draw them together during this dark period, and gave them a sense of unity and fellowship that they had almost lost. Those among the police who were Christians held regular worship services and offered sermons of encouragement.

Christmas 1943

Christmas was close at hand, and despite their situation, the police were determined to celebrate Christmas as they would in Norway. On December 23, Emile and Kübler brought them two small fir tree branches, one for each wing. They decorated it the best they could with what they had on hand.

Christmas 1943

On Christmas Eve, the police were at attention as usual at 07:30. It was cold and icy, making it difficult to walk or stand at attention. After he finished counting, Emile, in his annoying hoarse voice, commanded them to sing. Løkke asked, *"Hva skal vi synge?"* (What shall we sing?). No one responded. Then a westerly wind broke the silence. They were cold and hungry when someone in the back row called out, *"Hva med fantastisk er skapelsen?"* (What about Wonderful is Creation?). It's difficult for those of us who were not there to understand their feelings when they sang. Although the police were hoping, they did not receive extra rations for Christmas, except for fifty grams of cheese, mashed beets and a couple of cigarettes.

Despite it being Christmas, the police were becoming increasingly depressed and physically weaker. In spite of all this, they grew closer as a group, and their comradeship gave them the will to hang on.

The police stood in a semi-circle with the little Christmas tree on the table while someone read the Christmas story out of the Gospel of Luke. There was a moving sermon by Willy Langerude, followed by several Christmas songs. As they sang, their thoughts went to their families at home, and by the time they had finished singing *Stille natt* (Silent Night), there wasn't a dry eye among them.

> *"History is lived forwards, but it is written in retrospect. We know the end before we consider the beginning, and we can never wholly recapture what it was to know the beginning only."* CV Wedgewood

The Night Became Holy

Barbed wire kept the police from going out from Barrack 19. The Danish prisoners, on the other hand, were free to walk about the camp. Martin Nielsen wandered from his Barrack 13 and walked around the camp to be by himself with his thoughts. He went towards the camp's Christmas tree that was covered with coloured lights. Nielsen stopped when he saw the drunken SS-guards and the criminal leaders dancing and carousing around the Christmas tree. He turned away and walked into a dark part of the camp. In the dark, he heard deep and strong male voices. Their voices were clear in the cold night air. Polish male prisoners sang as a choir, one of the season's loveliest songs of peace on earth. When Nielsen got closer, he saw several hundred Polish prisoners standing by the barbed wire singing a greeting to the women barracks. It was then silent for a moment. The silence was broken by a choir of female voices responding to the men, then silence. The barbed wire couldn't stop their singing. After a moment, the silence was again broken. This time a chorus of Russian men singing to the Russian women in the women's camp, followed by silence. After a short moment, the silence was again broken by Russian women singing back to the Russian men. Their voices died, and for a moment, there was silence. It was as if the night had become holy.

Suddenly, the silence was broken by the beam from a spotlight and a guard yelling from the watchtower, *"Holen Sie sich innerhalb Sie verlausten, schmutzige Schweinehunde, oder ich schieße!"* (Get inside you lice-infested, dirty swine dogs, or I'll shoot!).

In Barrack 19, the Christmas celebration came to an end, and the police were ordered to go to bed two hours earlier than usual. The Kapos and the block leader were going to have a party with accordion music and sing long into the night.

On Christmas Day, the police prisoners received a little extra in the form of thin stew. They also got a dessert of cooked red beets.

A Dane in SS Service

Commonly, at the evening roll call, the Germans did the counting of prisoners. However, on this occasion, a soldier went between the rows and counted in Norwegian, *"en, to, tre, fire, fem" etc.* (one, two, three, four, five etc.). This surprised them. Later, they learned that the mysterious soldier was a Danish volunteer in SS service named Peter Lodahl Petersen, the Danish prisoners Block Chief in Barrack 13.

The police were told that they would soon be moved to another camp, Germanenlager, or Sonderlager as the police would name it. Sonderlager lay two kilometers south of the main camp and was under the administration and leadership of KZ-Stutthof. This news was received with enthusiasm. The thought of moving to their own camp had an uplifting effect on them. Petersen had been removed from his leadership of the Danish prisoners because he had informed on a Kapo who had stolen food and other items belonging to prisoners. The camp administration was more or less aware but would not deal with the situation. The criminal leaders were given their positions because of their criminal tendencies. But when Petersen brought it to their attention, the administration was forced to do something about it. The Kapo was arrested and punished, and Petersen was removed from Barrack 13. It was fortunate for the police that he was assigned as their leader. After all, he spoke and understood their language and customs.

By New Year's Eve, the police were getting frustrated again. They were bumping into each other, and the tight quarters were getting on their nerves.

Small differences seemed to become large problems and often caused name-calling and even shoving matches. It helped to think they would soon be in a new camp, and their living conditions would improve. But presently, the situation was the same and small issues exploded into large problems. The police leadership tried to defuse the tension by keeping them busy with concerts and practices.

Olaf Walle started the New Year's Eve entertainment with a song. Arne Domben read poems and police inspector Erling Oftedal held informal talks about the *Kamp om Sydpolen* (Battle for the South Pole). At 20:00, the police were ordered to go to bed. The Kapos were having their own New Year's party and didn't want prisoners to disturb the festivities.

On New Year's Day, the police received two cigarettes in celebration of the New Year. The men were like little children receiving presents; it didn't take much to get them excited.

The police were issued an Italian uniform called "**Badoglio**" uniforms. These uniforms were green in color with long pants and jackets, frock and a hat in a boat shape. Boots were to be given to them later, but they wore wooden shoes like other prisoners until then. They felt like fools in the uniform, but at least the uniforms kept them relatively warm.

On January 8, the police leadership was called to a meeting with Commandant Hoppe. At the meeting, they were told that the next day they would be transferred to *Germanenlager* (Sonderlager), with Petersen as *Blockführer*. They learned that they would be taking courses for the next thirty-six weeks at Sonderlager. The fact that concentration camp prisoners were to take courses was most unusual.

The police arrived at Barrack 19 on December 18, 1943, and left on January 9, 1944, exactly twenty-six days.

Badoglio Uniforms

CHAPTER 5 –
A Camp of Their Own

On the morning of January 9th, 1944, 253 Norwegian police prisoners marched in the mud and rain out of the quarantine barrack with Kapo Emile Kinkowski leading the way. Kinkowski was in fine form that morning, thinking that he would play a significant role in the new camp and believing he had secured himself a fortuitous future. They marched to the administration headquarters that was swarming with SS soldiers and stood at attention as Commandant Hoppe came out to speak to them. Hoppe looked over at Kinkowski and told him, *"Verschwinde!"* (Disappear!).

The prisoners watched as Kinkowski's shoulders sank, and the smile disappeared from his face. Humiliated and embarrassed, Kinkowski left. The police were all thrilled and felt no remorse for him whatsoever.

Hoppe looked over the Norsemen and saw that most of them were taller than him. Then his eyes rested on Anders Eckhoff, who was the same height as him. Eckhoff had curly blond hair and blue eyes, an ideal specimen of the *Aryan* race according to Nazi eyes. Hoppe gave Eckhoff a black armband with *Lagerältester* (Camp Spokesman) written on it. He then went over to Lars Backer and gave him an armband with Block 1 written on it and Finn Dahlin one labeled Block 2.

Police constable Magnus Kristensen was given an armband with *Verwaltungsschreiber* (Administration Secretary) written on it. Next, twelve room chiefs were chosen. SS-Hauptsturmführer Theodore Meyer warned them to listen when these men gave orders.

Marching to Sonderlager

Finally, the police prisoners marched to Sonderlager, which lay two kilometers southwest of the main camp. On the way to the camp, about five to six hundred meters from Sonderlager, they passed a brick factory named Ziegelei (Brickyard). The factory was relatively large and had earlier employed 450 men. The factory had its own electrical generator and provided both Sonderlager and Stutthof main camp with electricity. The factory's raw material was dug out of the earth from a large farm called Werderhof. A canal went 10 to 15 meters from Sonderlager's southeast corner, where some reasonably large boats sailed.

A few months before the police arrived, the camp was used as a quarantine camp for Lithuanian prisoners who had contracted typhoid. When the Norwegian police arrived, the camp was set aside for them, as an education camp. The camp consisted of four barracks built on a section of the Werderhof farm.

Sonderlager was surrounded by an electric barbed wire fence with two guard towers, one on each side. The prisoner barracks lay beside each other with their entrances off the assembly courtyard. The third barrack held the hospital at one end and workshop at the other, with a large hall called the *Kostebinderiet* used for large assemblies in the middle.

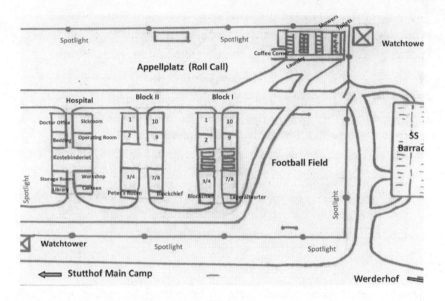

Sonderlager Camp

The fourth barrack, outside of the barbed wire, was for the SS guards. Hauptsturmführer Theodore Meyer was the highest authority over the camp. He lived in the director's building in Ziegelei, rode his motorcycle into the camp and held regular inspections.

Block 1	Room Manager
Room 1	Rolf Krosshaven
Room 2	Gisle Ianke
Rooms 3 & 4	Sverre Bjørgum
Rooms 7 & 8	Per Tingstad
Room 9	Arne Sundvor
Room 10	Gulbrand Nyhus
Block 2	Room Manager
Room 1	Carl Frøseth

Room 2	Olav Risøen
Rooms 3 & 4	Per Lorentzen
Rooms 7 & 8	Robert Danielsen
Room 9	Marcus Verling
Room 10	Fritdjof Skipperud

When the police first arrived at Sonderlager, they were mostly able to do as they pleased. Those who came from the same regions in Norway were able to room together. The block chiefs were each given a five-meter room that slept two. Blockführer Peter's room was next to the chief of Barrack 2.

The police were pleased to have the Danish Peter Petersen, as Blockführer, be their closest SS contact.

Lillestrumen

Unfortunately, another individual who the police nicknamed *"Lillestrumen"* wanted to have authority over them. Lillestrumen was a small, elderly spitfire of an individual. He had three stars, the highest rank of an under officer in the SS. He was Master Sergeant, which they understood was a rank no longer used in the SS. However, it was occasionally used for individuals who, like Lillestrumen, were old and faithful soldiers but the SS didn't know what do with. His residence was in the SS barrack immediately outside the camp's barbed-wire fence. Lillestrumen was in charge of the guards, a detachment of eight to ten men.

Lillestrumen had two more stars than Petersen. He quite often wanted to have his say in what went on in the camp, which caused conflict between Petersen and Lillestrumen. Petersen was outranked and would often say under his breath in Danish *"Du gamle djævel!"* (You old devil!).

Lillestrumen was proud of having the tall *Norweger* under his authority. *"Mein Grose Norweger, sind alle Norweger diese hoch?"* (My great Norwegians, are all Norwegians this tall?), he would ask. Lillestrumen was the first German to ask the question, but not the last. The police responded to him like they did to the rest. *"So groß!"* *"Wir sind die Kleinen, die durchschnittliche*

Körpergröße in Norwegen 190 (6'3") bis 198 (6'6") Zentimeter. (So tall! We are the short ones, the average height in Norway is 190 (6'3") to 198 (6'6") centimeters). This impressed the Germans, and as the police would often say, *"Det er mer enn en grunn, tyskerne ser opp til oss, nordmenn!"* (There's more than one reason the Germans look up to us Norsemen!)

Sonderlager was built as an internment camp for SS who did not obey orders or other disciplinary reasons. It was these prisoners that Lillestrumen was to be in control over. In that respect, he probably felt snubbed when it was the *Grosse Norweger* that came to the camp, and he was not able to lord over them the way he wanted.

On January 13, seventeen more police prisoners arrived from Norway and were housed in Barrack 1. They were detainees from the Haugesund area and were arrested at the same time as the others but were left behind at Grini for some reason. The police count at Sonderlager now stood at 270.

Four months later, Torstein Herring was transferred to Sonderlager from KZ-Sachsenhausen. Herring was the policeman taken when the prisoners arrived at Stettin in December 1943 and sent to KZ-Sachsenhausen. With Herring's arrival, the total Norwegian police prisoners at Sonderlager was 271.

The police remembered well the date of January 12. It was the day Peter brought a radio to the camp. Rumor had circulated that radio was part of the educational course, but they didn't put much weight to the rumor. How likely was it that prisoners would be allowed to listen to the radio in a German concentration camp? But that's what happened! The radio was stored in Blockchief Eckhoff's room, with loudspeakers in each barrack meeting room. They listened to Danish broadcasts through the radio, mostly from Kalundborg, where they heard many familiar and well-loved melodies that awakened thoughts of home.

Letters and Packages

Mail Wagon

In mid-January, the police were allowed to write letters under Petersen's censorship. This meant they were able to write letters in Norwegian rather than in German like before. There's no doubt that Petersen was much more flexible in his censorship than the Germans were. However, they were still not allowed to write anything about the camp or conditions within the camp. If they did, the letter was censored with a line through it and had to be rewritten. The police could convey to their friends and loved ones at home that they were hungry. One policeman said he longed for smoked herring, even though his family knew very well that he didn't like smoked herring. The family reasoned that if he longed for smoked herring, he must be in tough shape. In this way, policemen received packages with food from home.

The letters allowed their families to know where they were and that they were having difficulties. Towards the end of January, packages and letters began to arrive. At first, the packages were small. When their families realized that the packages were getting through, the size and volume increased.

The first twenty-six packages from the Danish Red Cross came on January 26, followed by thirteen Swedish Red Cross packages. Soon the prisoners would receive monthly packages in their own names from Denmark and Sweden.

Packages arriving at the camp could only be delivered if the prisoner's name and address were clearly on the package. It was crucial, therefore, that all charities received the police's information accurately. This allowed packages to arrive from all known and unknown charities.

The arrival of the packages helped the police to steadily gain strength, and their demeanor turned brighter. The volume of mail and packages increased continuously. On one occasion, eighteen sacks of mail and packages arrived at the post office in Stutthof village. Packages were handed through a window in the post office and loaded onto a hand cart pulled by the police post commando. The post commando also brought packages to the Danish prisoners in the main camp. The post office at Stutthof village recorded that 38,512 packages and 32,200 letters were delivered to the Norwegian police prisoners at Sonderlager in 1944.

The Danish Red Cross packages weighed five kilograms (eleven pounds). They contained one package of Ovaltine, one container of cheese spread, three boxes of melted gouda cheese, a box of powdered milk, one can of ham, two smoked sausages, thirty tablets of B vitamins, thirty tablets of C vitamins and a box of beef bouillons. The Swedish Red Cross package weighted eight to ten kilograms (eighteen to twenty-two pounds) and was highly regarded by the police. All items were in original packaging. The sender of the packages was *Help War Victims* through the YMCA in Stockholm, Sweden.

Ambassador Peter Ankor, a member of the International Red Cross in Geneva, Switzerland, was approached by many police prisoners' families for help. Ankor managed to get a Red Cross representative from Berlin to visit Sonderlager. The International Red Cross had access to internment camps such as Sonderlager, but not to concentration camps such as the KZ-Stutthof main camp. The Red Cross received regular information on the police at Sonderlager. That information was forwarded to the Norwegian Prisoner Help Organization in Sweden that delivered packages to Norwegian prisoners through the YMCA. As a neutral country, Sweden could not send parcels to prisoners in a country at war or to their families in an occupied country. Sending parcels were the same as to break their neutrality, which accounted for the packages being sent under the YMCA. The package project was financed by

> *John R. Mott, the world director of YMCA, received the Nobel Peace Prize in 1946 because he facilitated packages to prisoners during World War II.*

the Norwegian government in exile in London. The YMCA had direct contact with the Red Cross in Denmark, France, Portugal and Switzerland. The packages were sent from these countries to Switzerland, then forwarded to prisoners all over Europe.

Swedish packages the police received in September were particularly prized. Of course, they contained food items, orange juice, marmalade and more. However, the best items were leather boots. The boots were hand sewn and stylish. The prisoners paraded proudly around in their new boots; the German guards were visibly jealous of the prisoners' new footwear.

During their previous stay in Barrack 19 where the food was scarce and they were isolated behind barbed wire, the police nearly surrendered themselves to depression and apathy. They recognized that their depression affected their physical and emotional outlook and started to affect them mentally as well. Under such conditions, it would have been disastrous had the police leadership not diverted their minds into activities such as choir concerts. There is little doubt that the police leadership, with their constant doggedness about discipline, saved many police prisoners' lives. This resulted in creating a deep comradeship and loyalty among them. Their fellowship and devotion would play a significant role in their survival during the difficult times that lay ahead. The police had become, in every respect, a *band of brothers*.

At Sonderlager, the police were issued three wool blankets, a pillow and a mattress stuffed with wood filings. The wood filings were far easier to sleep on than straw. Each room had cupboards and a table with chairs. After their daily routine, the rooms allowed them to write letters, read a book or sit and enjoy some tobacco. During their month in Barrack 19, the prisoners were given the cheap Machorka tobacco that suppressed their hunger pains. It was an era when smoking was considered the norm. It would have been an excellent time to quit. Still, they kept on regularly receiving tobacco and cigarettes from the Red Cross. The Red Cross's real tobacco made them dizzy, as they were not used to real tobacco. The police ended up mixing real tobacco with Machorka tobacco. There was no more question of trying to quit smoking.

> The Machorka tobacco was waste from Die Tabakwerke in Grodno eastern Poland and consisted mostly of shredded stalks

Camp Activities

The police activities were limited and consisted mainly of roll calls from early morning till evening. The first roll call was at 06:10, then at 10:00 and 14:00, ending with the evening roll call at 18:10.

Time	Activity
06:00	Wakeup
06:10	Roll Call
06:10-08:00	Breakfast
08:10	Morning gymnastics
08:10-09:00	Exercise
09:00-10:00	Break
10:00-10:10	Roll Call
10:10-11:00	Exercise
11:00-12:00	German lessons
12:00-14:00	Dinner, followed by rest
14:00-14:10	Roll Call
14:10-15:00	Exercise
15:00-16:00	German lessons
16:00-16:45	Singing in the blocks
17:00-18:00	Supper
18:10	Roll Call
21:15	Lights out and complete quiet

Before dinner, the police had two mandatory activities: exercise and sport. After dinner, they were required to attend German language instruction, given by Gunnar Jørgensen, and lectures on policy matters. This continued until Easter when they began work details.

Understandably, there wasn't total harmony at all times. There was constant tension among specific individuals that broke out into verbal and physical jostling. The leadership intervened on several occasions, especially among the younger men who found it difficult to contain their energy. The leaders showed patience, understanding and diplomacy to resolve the tension and return to a sense of rational behavior. Homesickness was likely the most common reason for short temperedness, and it could strike at any time. Many preferred to be alone. It wasn't uncommon to see mature adult men shedding tears of loneliness during this period. Several policemen went for walks in the evening along the barbed wire fence with thoughts about home.

Kåre Ingvaldsen walked along the barbed wire with his trumpet and skillfully played tunes that were meaningful to the police, such as *Jeg vet om et land* (I know of a land) and *Norge mitt Norge* (Norway my Norway).

Roll Call at Sonderlager

Outdoor activities in the camp were hindered by the poor conditions of the yard. The yard was consistently muddy and wet, especially around the barracks where the water would gather in large pools.

In late March, the conditions became quite deplorable after a heavy snowstorm. The prisoners' wooden shoes (they wouldn't receive their leather boots from Sweden for another six months) made it extremely difficult to walk. When the snow melted, the grounds flooded and created a small lake. When Hauptsturmführer Meyer rode in on his bike for inspection and found the barracks acceptable, he asked Eckhoff if there was anything they needed. Eckhoff responded by pointing out the deplorable conditions of the yard.

Meyer agreed to provide gravel and **Navvy Jack**. The next day, tools and material arrived. The police constructed a three-meter-wide gravel walkway lined with bricks from Ziegelei. The walkway went from the laundry to both barracks, and another went from the barracks to the hospital. The construction lasted five days. Eventually, the Navvy Jack and the gravel formed a hard surface.

At the same time, the police were determined to do renovations on the inside, including painting murals on the daily meeting room's walls. Anker Hafstad painted **Håkonshallen** and **Valkendorftårnet** and a Viking holding a torch, representing the police from Bergen. Hafstad also painted a Viking ship in bright colors. The Germans were very impressed by the murals. They were very much intrigued by Viking history.

On several occasions, the police were promised they would march to the main camp to take showers. Finally, on the last day of January, they marched to the main camp to one of the warm water showers. After the showers, they marched back to Sonderlager. Several Russian prisoners came walking wearily towards them carrying their daily ration of bread – two hundred grams (two slices). The police must have looked pitiful to the Russians, for several Russian prisoners ripped off a piece of their bread and tossed it to the police. Others looked around carefully and, when the SS was not watching, did the same. The act of kindness shown by those poor prisoners was never forgotten. It was the spark that kindled the fire of compassion in the police prisoners. In the months to come, many Russians would be paid back, but some of them would not survive until then.

The Man Who Defeated Germany

When the police column approached the gate to Sonderlager, they were stopped by Commandant Hoppe. He was accompanied by an officer with lots of stars, followed by several officers of lower rank. Hoppe ordered for Reidar Kvammen to come forward and be introduced to the SS officer. Hoppe introduced Kvammen as *der Mann, der Deutschland schlagen* (the man who beat Germany) in 1936.

Kvammen was on the Norwegian football team that defeated Germany 2-0 during the 1936 Summer Olympics, knocking Germany out of the medal rounds. Norway finished with a bronze medal. It is interesting to note that both goals were scored by Magnus Isaksen, who was of Jewish descent. It soon became known among the SS that Kvammen was among the Norwegian police prisoners at Sonderlager. Several SS officers arrived between February and March to see the man who helped defeat the "unbeatable" German team. The fact that little Norway had defeated the mighty German team was unthinkable. Kvammen was often called forward by Hauptsturmführer Meyer during roll call and was proudly introduced by him. The Germans would walk around Kvammen admiringly and feel his legs as if he was a racehorse.

Football Matches

No question that Reidar Kvammen was a magnificent physical specimen. The result was the police being promised a football. Still, like other German promises, the police didn't hold much hope in this. But to their surprise, the football came. From mid-March, it became popular to hold football matches if the weather allowed. The football pitch was quite uneven, with mole holes over the entire field. Karl Robertstad *orge* a cat, and after a short time, the cat became quite apt at catching rats and moles.

The police occasionally marched to the main camp to take showers because there were no shower facilities at Sonderlager. Later, after bribing the guards with some choice food items, they were able to have a hot water tank and five showers installed, enabling the police to take showers every Saturday.

The police internment felt more like detention rather than imprisonment in a concentration camp. That sentiment caused the police to wonder what the Germans were up to. They were arrested because they were police officers. Still, they weren't convicted of any illegal activity against Norway's German occupation or activities against NS. The question on everyone's mind was "what was the purpose in making them take long term courses?"

CHAPTER 6 –
Out to Work

In late February, it became clear. Petersen carefully questioned the police on their attitudes towards Germany and their thoughts about entering service for Germany. Petersen informed them the Germans held the Nordic race in high esteem, and it was Germany's desire to have them on the German side.

The Germans intended for the police prisoners to serve as policemen in Belgium and Holland (Netherlands). The police answered firmly that the Norwegian police were not military police to be deployed in any European country. They emphasized that their purpose was not to fight, but to keep the peace and order by upholding Norwegian law. Their sole purpose was to defend civilian rights, and they were ready to continue to administer law and order. They were not willing to go into service for Germany.

Their arrest in Norway was meant to purge the police departments of members deemed disloyal to the Nazi occupation and who could cause possible resistance to the German occupation. Their deportation to KZ-Stutthof had the intention of converting them for service to Germany. That was why the police weren't registered as regular prisoners, given prisoner identification numbers or shaved bald. It was also why they did not receive prisoner uniforms, instead being given Italian "traitor" uniforms. Additionally, it accounted for why they were transferred to an internment camp and being taught German.

The twenty-six-day isolation in Barrack 19 was an attempt to break their resistance.

The Tone Has Changed

By April, the Germans' friendly attitude towards the police had changed entirely. Hauptsturmführer Meyer came riding into the camp on his motorcycle to meet with Eckhoff. He asked Eckhoff straight out if the police were willing to enter into service for Germany and serve as guards. Eckhoff informed him that they couldn't. Meyer then inquired if the police were willing to work on the local farms. Eckhoff agreed to bring the question to the police members and respond as soon as possible. That evening Eckhoff, the block chiefs and room chiefs met in Petersen's office to clarify the work details.

Petersen explained that Berlin had agreed to provide the police with the same food as the soldiers, if the police decided to go on work details and not just play football and do exercises! The work consisted of various jobs on the local farm Werderhof, in large commandos under guard supervision. The Germans, however, were willing to discuss smaller commandos of three or four workers without any guards. The commandos would work a nine-hour day instead of the twelve-to-fourteen-hour days that other prisoners were required to work, and they'd work only when there was work for them to do. Petersen kept emphasizing that this was a great privilege Berlin was giving them and the police needed to be 'worthy of the privilege'. Petersen explained that Germany's work pace was slower than in the Nordic countries, so the police shouldn't have any problems. The sick and the elderly police members would stay in the camp and carry on with camp work such as cleaning, repairs and gardening. A decision had to be made by that same evening. Many stories were circulating about the work commandos that the police were familiar with. The commandos were divided into several groups, some had simple and minimal work and others had hard work that made the prisoners work until they collapsed. Danish prisoners told the police of being on a work commando to enlarge the rabbit farm where the SS had twelve hundred beautiful Angora rabbits. The rabbit farm was next to the crematorium and had wide cement walkways between the pens. Underneath were cement pads. The work consisted of laying a foundation for additional pens that would accommodate another eight hundred rabbits. The Danes didn't have any tools or technical instruments but measured everything by eye, which wasn't very accurate. To prolong the work, they would move the dirt to one side and then move it back again.

The Worst Work Detail

The worst was the breaking of rocks. For that work, the Germans used prisoners that were going to die. Many of them were brutally whipped because they were exhausted and didn't keep pace with the rest. Others were beaten to death by the Kapos because the Kapos had something against them or weren't in good humor.

Tragically, several large farm owners were given Jewish women workers for various work details. Several of the large farmers would go to the Jewish women's camp where the SS had the women parade in front of them. The farmers would pick out the women they wanted and march them to work on their farms. The women were made to work at strenuous jobs from sunrise to sunset, with practically no food or rest. When the women could no longer work because of exhaustion and starvation, the farmer would march the women back to the camp and straight into the gas chamber. Afterwards, the farmer would go back to the Jewish women's camp and pick out new workers.

The question regarding police members working was then presented at an assembly in the *Kostebinderiet*. Reasons for and against were given. Those who were against objected for conscience's sake and felt work should be of free will. The discussions were lively and highly emotional. Some police members ended up yelling and pounding on the table. Even though they were in the minority, they were determined not to do any work at all. Those who agreed to work made one condition that they wouldn't work for factories producing war materials.

In reality, work proved useful for the police and helped maintain both their physical and mental well-being. Only 15 voted against work details. Eckhoff then reported the count to Meyer.

The police were anxious to find out what the soldiers' food was like. The first supper consisted of rice soup with meatballs. Other items were added later, such as varieties of soups, mashed potatoes with gravy, porridge and juice. The new menu helped build them both physically and psychologically and would be critical in assisting them in the difficult times that lay ahead.

Farm Work Detail

The size of the farms in East Prussia varied greatly from an estate with 750 acres, 70 dairy cows and 32 horses, to the madam Roskowski with a small cow and a pig. The cows were always white with black markings. Some were also big meat animals and significantly larger than the usual animals in Norway. The annual milk yield was said to be 4,000 liters per cow.

Compared with farms in Norway, the most distinctive livestock was flocks of ducks, which were everywhere. The ducks would even frolic in the canals.

Their work commando began on the Werderhof farm, a large farm of about 360 acres. The director of the farm had earlier been the owner of a pub in the village of Stutthof. He was bow-legged and walked with a cane. He was placed in command of the farm after the SS took the farm from its rightful owner. The director had a black mongrel that was proficient in catching rabbits, then eating them.

Farm Work

On the opposite side of the road that went right past the camp was a field of green plants. These plants were rapeseed, which the Germans derived oil from. Towards the west and south lay fields as far as the eye could see. To the north lay a forest of fir trees that separated them from the ocean, and to the east lay an inlet called Frisches Haff.

To the police, the farmhouse seemed small and in need of repairs. To a Norwegian, the local houses looked dirty and small. But the farm had splendid animals. There were large cows all white and black, a drove of pigs of all sizes, turkeys, chickens and ducks, several beehives, a German Shepherd under leash and several other yappy dogs.

Behind Werderhof was a girl's camp. This was a **Reichsarbeitsdienstlager (RAD)** camp for girls age sixteen to eighteen. The girls had their own leaders and were involved in various jobs in the area. The police didn't have much contact with them but met them occasionally on their way to and from their work commandos. Later, a number of the police were stationed at Werderhof and helped the girls repair some of their bicycles. The girls were always polite and considerate towards the police prisoners and often sang for them as they passed by Sonderlager. The songs were generally marching tunes, but occasionally they would sing Nordic songs such as *Per Spelmann* and *Vi går över dagstänkta berg* (We cross dewy mountains). One of their leaders confessed the songs were meant as greetings to the Norsemen. She had often seen several Norsemen standing behind the barbed wire, wiping their eyes.

The majority of the work details were on Werderhof and the surrounding farms. Lillestrumen served as the guard on most of their work details, but the police did go on several small commandos without guards. On several occasions, the police had their own members as guards and were responsible for making sure the job was done before returning to camp. German civilians often also served as guards. There could be up to one hundred and fifty men out on work commandos on any given day. The remaining police members in the camp were involved in camp maintenance. Work done outside the camp was considered work done on behalf of Stutthof, and payment was made to the camp administration. The paid wage was three **RM (Reichsmark)** per day per worker. The police hoped the money would be used to help fellow prisoners, especially in the main camp. But that was not the case!

Tears for Human Compassion

The police commandos often came in contact with work details from the main camp. This allowed them to give from their rations to those less fortunate, especially the Jewish women. They were firmly instructed to not have anything to do with other prisoners, especially Jewish women, under any circumstances. But on several occasions, they witnessed prisoners crying for joy after finding extra food that had been hidden for them under a haystack or left for them in the fields. A tear of joy for being shown human compassion.

The police work detail was sent to do all types of farm work, some involved planting trees and cleaning the canals of grass and straw during different times of the year.

Weeding and thinning of rows between rapeseed and red beets were spring and summer jobs. They were issued picks and shovels. Half of the workers raked between the rows while the other half weeded between the plants. A distance of one foot was between the plants.

Weeding was a never-ending job, and the rows went on for what seemed like miles and disappeared on the horizon. The hot summer sun made it even more unbearable. The farmers and their foremen regularly complained to the camp administration about the lack of work the *große und starke Nordmänner* (big and strong Norsemen) accomplished. The farmers expected much more for what they had to pay for the *große Nordmänner* (big Norsemen). The police reasoned that it was essential for them not to set a fast tempo that the other prisoners could not keep up with, being in a much weaker condition than themselves.

Hauptsturmführer Meyer, on the other hand, made sure he brought the complaints to the police, followed by demands they work faster and more effectively. The police agreed they should work diligently, but never at a pace that would cause their fellow prisoners to suffer from the main camp. The excuse the police offered to the administration was that the work they were expected to perform was utterly foreign to what they were accustomed to performing in Norway.

Work details began at 06:00 when they marched, for forty-five minutes, to their workplace. The work started at 07:00, with lunch from 12:30–13:30 and a thirty-minute coffee break, then finished at 18:00. Marching back, they frequently didn't return until 21:00.

Haying Work Detail

Towards the end of the summer was the haying work. The haying was backbreaking work, and the police found it necessary to relieve each other on occasion.

Among the worst haying jobs was tossing bales into the top of the hay barn and then stacking them. The sweat would pour from every pore in their bodies, with dirt and dust clinging to their bare tops. They were given an hour lunch break and a twenty-minute coffee break. The only other time they got a break was when the electricity went, or the belts started to smoke and something broke.

The result would be unexpected, but a much-welcomed rest.

At every opportunity, the police tried to sabotage the threshing machines by feeding them wire, glass, rocks or anything they could get their hands on to wreck the machines. Unfortunately, most of the equipment was German-built and of a higher quality than other equipment and the attempt to sabotage failed.

On one particular work commando, the police were threshing using an old-fashioned cane harvester. They got dust and plant parts in their mouths, noses and eyes, and it was difficult to get any breaks because the guard was always watching them. They needed to distract the guard while one sneaked off to get some rest, then alternate. On duty one particular day was a guard nicknamed *Grytulven* (angry wolf) because he looked like an angry wolf. *Grytulven* was from Danzig and not mentally all there. Karl Haugan struck up a conversation with him and asked him about his family. *Grytulven* replied he had a son who would be a gymnast because his body was so supple, and he could make the most complicated moves that adults couldn't. Haugan, showing great interest, asked how old his son was. The boy was eighteen months, *Grytulven* replied. Haugan said this was quite interesting and asked the guard to put his name on a piece of paper so he could remember it later. *Grytulven* was more than willing to accommodate him and brought out a fountain pen and started to write. When Haugan saw this, he burst out, *"Glaubst du nicht, dass wir Nordmänner dumm genug sind, uns davon täuschen zu lassen? Es ist unmöglich, mit einem Stift zu schreiben, ohne den Stift in ein Tintenfass zu tauchen!"* (You don't think we Norsemen are stupid enough to be fooled by this? It's impossible to write with a pen without dipping the pen in an inkwell!) *Grytulven* smiled proudly and began to write.

"Gutter komme og se," (Boys come and see), said Haugan, *"Vakten her har en penn som skriver uten blekk"* (The guard here has a pen that writes without ink). The others came running and stood around the guard with looks of astonishment. The guard repeatedly demonstrated that the pen could write without having to dip it in ink. And so, they were able to get a much-needed break.

Wood Detail

Wood Work Detail

After the harvest season, the police began woodwork detail in the forest. That work consisted of cutting trees and chopping wood as well as pulling up stumps. The forest work was the most grueling work they had done to date. Large logs had to be carried out from the forest. On top of the hard work, the police received little food or water on these commandos, making the labor even more challenging. The work also proved dangerous, and there were several accidents.

During one woodwork commando, Torgeir Gjerde was hit by a falling tree and knocked unconscious. He began to bleed from his nose and mouth and was promptly brought to the hospital in the main camp on a makeshift stretcher. Gjerde was in the hospital for several months and had several operations on a fractured skull. Thankfully, he recovered. Several also suffered back injuries, which affected them for the rest of their lives.

Joachim at Babylon

Fridtjof Erlandsen was a police prisoner who was a born optimist. Erlandsen, no doubt, was one of God's elects when it came to good humor and attitude. If he thought something was good, he would say in his northern accent, *"Dette er 'graciosa'!"* (This is "grasiosa"!). Hence the nickname *'Grasiosa'*.

During a work commando on a farm called Babylon, Grasiosa wanted to take a break. The farm had a German owner named Max Joachim, a former captain in the German Luftwaffe. Among the prisoners, the work detail was called *Joachim uti Babylon* (Joachim out in Babylon).

Babylon was managed by a Polish volunteer with Polish male laborers who were often miserable creatures that came strutting or riding in landlord clothes pretending to be managers of all Eastern Poland. The police often had difficulties in getting along with these *herrer* (Lords). Joachim himself was a callous and cold-hearted individual who surpassed even the most hated SS guard at KZ-Stutthof. He demanded full value for the money he had to pay and watched the police like a hawk.

Grasiosa had managed to sneak a visit to the toilet, which was actually a small plank over a manure pile. When Grasiosa decided it was time to return, he ran into Joachim. The farmer angrily asked Grasiosa what he was doing and why he was not working in the fields. Joachim then proceeded to give Grasiosa a vulgar verbal assault. Grasiosa, who was quick thinking, immediately told a story about his valuable gold watch that he lost while going on the toilet. The reason he stayed so long on the toilet was that he was desperately trying to find it *"Haben Sie eine goldene Uhr verloren?"* (Have you lost a gold watch?) asked Joachim, who could hardly believe his ears.

There were two things that every German would exchange for, if only they could get it. They were: first, gold (preferably in the form of watches or rings) and secondly, sardines in oil.

"Ja," (Yes) replied Grasiosa with an angelic voice.

"Aber wir müssen es nur finden" (But we just have to find it), said Joachim.

Together they began kicking around the manure pile.

Grasiosa thought the joke had gone far enough and said that it was just as well to give up. *"Es ist sowieso egal"* (It doesn't matter anyway), he added, *"denn ich habe mehr zu Hause"* (for I have more at home).

Marching back to Sonderlager at dusk, the prisoners saw Joachim and his wife and children, along with some farm helpers, in full swing with a flashlight turning the manure pile in hopes of finding the gold watch. The most unsympathetic farmer they had ever met during their imprisonment got taken!

The Unterdeich Work Detail

The most popular work detail was the canal detail called 'Unterdeich' which went from July and into the fall. The land in that part of Poland was flat for many kilometers, and the area had several canals that traverse the countryside west of KZ-Stutthof. Along the canals grew willows and reeds, and in the channels grew grass. The canals had to be weeded continuously and came under the administration of a private company called Daichverband. The company used prisoners from KZ-Stutthof as laborers. The canal commander was a sixty-seven-year-old civilian (Communist from Steegen) and former seaman. The police nicknamed him *Der alte major* (The Old Major), which he liked very much. During his early years, The Old Major had sailed with Danish boats and met Norwegian and Danish seamen. As a result, he knew a few Norwegian and Danish words. If the police shared food with The Old Major, he grew to be more humorous and often would rant against Hitler, which they found amusing.

Canal Commando

The Old Major had built himself a raft he named *Sturmvogel*, which he would stand in front of and give commands from: *"a bischen vorwärts"* (a little forward), *"a bischen rückwärts"* (a little backward), "steady so," but on occasion, he shouted in Norwegian: "*Videre!*" (Further). The raft would move forward by pushing the oars off the bottom of the canal. The rest of the work commando would stand on either side of the canal. First, one person came swinging a sickle, followed by others who would rake the cut grass and reeds. The Old Major would stand on the raft and cut the grass and reed using a large sickle. He swung in a wide arc on the right and the left in a continuous motion, all with remarkable skill. The reed that he cut floated to the top and was then collected.

The work was strenuous, and the workers found it necessary to take short breaks every fifteen minutes. The Old Major would often command them to slow down and take it easy, *"Immer langsam!"* (Always slowly) he screamed, and echoed, *"Eine fünfzehn Minuten Pause"* (A fifteen-minute break). According to him, the police were working too fast and too hard. The police named one of the many canals that went past Sonderlager after him and gave it the name *Immerlangsam-kanal* (Slow Canal). At first, the police wondered if it was because of his consideration for the Norwegians that he made them go slow, but they soon realized it was for his own concern. It was very strenuous work, especially for a man in his late sixties.

The work details continued without any significant problems, even though there were complaints the police were lazy. That complaint was consistently brought to the police's attention, especially by Hauptsturmführer Meyer. It was understood that the work they were told to do was unfamiliar, but a small contingent of police refused to work, which didn't help their reputation. Even though they were sent on work details, they refused to do any work and just sat and watched. The Germans viewed this as laziness.

BBC Radio

On several of the commandos, the police prisoners came in contact with civilians who were not supportive of Germany and would give them food and provide them with the latest news of the war. There wasn't much work on one such farm, and they would often sit with the farmer in the living room listening to the news from London over the radio, while the farmer's daughter and wife stood guard.

The police considered it vital to develop a trusting relationship with the farmers. They intentionally behaved in a polite and honorable manner, which was in contrast to many other prisoners who looked for any advantage of stealing anything they could lay their hands on. The police learned that most civilians did not approve of what the Nazis did or what they stood for. They developed an open relationship with many of their employers based on mutual trust because they were allowed to work without supervision. Many of their guards permitted the police to do what they wanted, and their presence was a mere formality.

CHAPTER 7 –
Orders from Berlin

In late September came orders from Berlin that the workload had to increase, and all had to work. There were to be no exceptions! This implied a twelve-hour working day, with a fifteen minute break in both the morning and afternoon and a thirty minute lunch break. The police were now also required to work on Sundays for six hours. The main camp had become overcrowded with 30,000–35,000 new prisoners. The new work commandos were tied into the expansion plan of the main camp. Bauleitung was the architectural company responsible for the goals of the camp expansion project. Every concentration camp had its own Bauleitung (construction management organization).

The commando did not start on a good note. The work was hard with no break until 14:00 when the workers received only a small portion of the SS food. Two heavily armed SS guards and two civilians guarded them. One of the SS guards kept yelling *los! los!* (hurry! hurry!). Finally, Rolf Krosshavn, the police work commando foreman, told the guard to shut up! He told the guard that the Norsemen knew what they were doing! There was no more yelling. However, it didn't take long for Bauleitung to complain about the work tempo being too slow. The police were given a one day reprieve to increase the tempo, and if there were no changes they would be punished. However, Petersen told Eckhoff not to worry about the threat. If the police increased their tempo, it would affect the other prisoners who were not in good shape. The police decided to work at a medium pace. There were no more run-ins with the Bauleitung or complaints from other prisoners.

As the days grew shorter from the beginning of November, the workday was reduced by two hours. Many police workers were assigned to other commandos, and the work force was reduced to thirty men per work detail.

Towards the fall of 1944, there was an increase in the goods sent by railroad towards the west. This resulted in work commandos being forwarded to the Weichsel River to unload railroad cars at Nickelswalde and Schiewenhorst, on both sides of the river. There was no bridge, only a flat-bottom ferry. The Germans requisitioned several barges and tugboats to accommodate the increase in traffic. The work included unloading the railroad cars at one end of the river and placing the goods on the barges to be towed across the river. The goods were then loaded onto a different train on the other side of the river that took the goods west. This was really hard and tiresome work. Several work details were organized to go to Danzig to unload ships and load the goods onto railroad cars.

The hard line the Germans took towards work details continued.

The Rocket Factory

New work details were continually being introduced, and one of them was called **Epp**-Work Commando, which began in early September. That work detail consisted of forty policemen and other prisoners from the main camp chosen to do construction. The work consisted of digging and pouring cement for the foundation of barracks to house workers for the Focke-Wulf factory located southeast of the main camp.

On one occasion, the police were ordered to repair equipment inside the factory buildings. The workers in the factory were specialists deported from the Czechoslovakian (Czech Republic) Skoda factory. The workers said they were manufacturing top-secret high-quality precision parts used in the combustion chamber for the V-1 and V-2 rockets. The parts had to be precision made and were inspected by German technicians using magnifying glasses before they were accepted. Then the parts were carefully packed in felt cloth before being sent westward. The Czech technicians were able to sabotage the production by introducing an imperfection the Germans could not detect. This was believed to be a reason for the V-1 and V-2 rocket's failure. The rocket's guidance system's imperfection caused the rockets to crash a few kilometers from the launch site. Other factories manufactured ammunition and parts for submarines along with other war materials.

On Sundays, the older police prisoners went to work. This allowed the younger police to have a day of rest. Around the beginning of September, the work had lessened and returned much like it was initially. From the time the police entered Sonderlager, they were called out for work details. They believed this was initiated by Hauptsturmführer Meyer as punishment for not joining the German side, but in September Hitler initiated his 'total war involvement' program, where all prison camps had to comply.

An Unexpected Visit

To persuade the police to join the German war effort, arrangements were made to "educate" the police through German ideology courses.

In mid-May, the police were surprised by a visitor from Norway, Untersturmführer Sverre Lie. Lie informed them that he had arrived to see if there was anything he could help them with. Lie's profession was actually a photographer, and he was a well-respected football umpire. Lie lived in Vinstra in Gudbrandsdalen and was considered one of the hometown *store gutter* (big boys). He joined the NS party of Vidkun Quisling and travelled to KZ-Stutthof to convince the Norwegian police to join the Germans. He started right away by interviewing each policeman in Peter's office, on the pretense of wanting to get to know them better. Lie asked direct questions about their thoughts on being co-operative with the Nazis, among other personal questions. He made notations but promised that their answers would not be used against them. Later, they learned that the questions were part of Lie's report to the Police Department in Norway. There were no misgivings about his intentions.

During the time that followed, Lie carried on lectures. Some days he arranged for all work detail to remain in the camp while he lectured morning and afternoon. Other days he lectured either in the morning or in the afternoon. Lie's visit also included showing films in the main camp from a German *Schulungsleitung* (Leadership Training), which showed films comparing German art and race to the Jewish and Russian art and race. The film was followed by a lecture. Lie was not the rigid type. His approach was more as a comrade, and his classes were idealistic and naïve. After a period of reservation by the police, they eventually developed a good relationship with him. Lie also got involved in several internal situations. After Fredrik Ketilsson died from a stray bullet during a work commando in the main camp, Lie tried to get Ketilsson's body home along with several of the sick prisoners.

Serving as Guards

With the invasion of Normandy on June 6, the Germans felt the urgency to take firm action with the police. In a speech on Saturday, June 29, Commandant Hoppe made it clear that Germany was no longer at peace with the police and that the police would be treated like other prisoners.

The Germans now demanded the police be sent directly to the front or serve as guards in the camp. If the police refused, they would be transferred directly to the main camp, be treated like other prisoners or go to the gas chamber. Petersen had warned the police of consequences if they didn't make a decision quickly. He repeated they would be treated like any other prisoners in the concentration camp and may face execution. The police were familiar with the German tactics used on other prisoners, including the Ukrainians. The Ukrainians were given the option between execution and service for Germany. The Ukrainians were tempted with privileges and with their own whorehouse of female prisoners. The result was that many Ukrainians volunteered into German service and were given an unfamiliar black uniform. They acted as helpers to the German guards and often were just as cruel. It was as if they had to demonstrate their new value.

The police's tactic was to delay making a decision. Service in a German police battalion or service on the German front was not an option for them. They were painfully aware that they would be required to give their response one day, but each day delayed would bring them one day closer to the end of the war. Discussing the German request, the police agreed that they would be willing to serve as policemen in Norway and protect their citizens, but that was all. That option was not acceptable to Hauptsturmführer Meyer, and he warned them that if he didn't get more of a positive response, the police would be punished. After a thorough discussion among themselves, the police presented a second option. Those who had earlier served in the marines were willing to serve in the coast guard in Norway. Others were willing to take police positions in Norway or serve as criminal guards in northern Norway. This, they suggested, would not compromise their conscience. The new options were not acceptable to Hauptsturmführer Meyer, and the situation had now become tense.

Temporary Reprieve

The failed assassination of Adolf Hitler on July 20 at his bunker near the city of Ketrzyn, on the border to Lithuania (250 kilometers east of KZ-Stutthof), gave the police a temporary reprieve. The incident couldn't have happened at a more opportune time. The Germans now had other things to divert their attention. The *obstinate* Norwegian police in Sonderlager were forgotten and were temporarily left in peace. There was no more talk of going into service for Germany or punishment if they refused. Life in the camp returned to normal, though there was a lot of tension in the air.

On August 22, the police assembled in the Block 1 meeting room to bid Sverre Lie goodbye. Lie informed the police that he had been ordered to return to Norway but didn't know why. Lie promised that when he returned to Norway, he would bring up their situation and work for their release. He had fond memories of the months he spent together with the police, he said, and it had left a lasting impression on him. There was a sense of disappointment among the police that Lie was leaving. He was a well-meaning idealist and was well aware that his teaching had not influenced them.

Their temporary reprieve lasted until November 16, when they were again given an ultimatum. Hauptsturmführer Meyer informed them that the Russians had broken through and were now in northern Norway. The police must now decide if they would join Germany in its fight against the *Bolsheviks* or not. He needed a decision by Monday (November 20). Meyer could, to some degree, understand the police's previous stand, but now he indicated that it would be impossible for them to be loyal to their King Haakon VII and the exiled government who have sided with the Russians against their own country. The Germans would accept nothing less than a commitment to pick up arms and join Germany. If the police refused, they would be relegated to regular prisoner status. That meant the police would lose their troop food as well as their privilege to receive packages. Petersen added that if the police continued to support the king, it would be the same as picking up arms and fighting for the Russians. They were given two questions to answer:

Question 1.

Bereit, zu den Waffen zu greifen und sich Deutschland im Kampf gegen Russland anzuschließen?

(Ready to pick up arms and join Germany in its fight against Russia?)

Ja (Yes) *oder Nein* (No).

Question 2.

König Haakon und die Exilregierung anerkennen?

(Recognize King Haakon and the exiled government?)

Ja (Yes) *oder Nein* (No).

They met the following Sunday in the *Kostebinderiet* hall to vote. The first question's answer was a unanimous 'no'. The second question's answer, a unanimous 'yes'. The following afternoon, Hauptsturmführer Meyer came riding on his motor bike and was given the results. He was extremely disappointed and angry and declared this ended their favorable status. Meyer then went over to Gisle Ianke and gave him a slap on the cheek with his glove. Ianke stood straight at attention and never blinked an eye.

On the following morning, Eckhoff and Petersen were summoned to appear before camp Commander Hoppe to learn what would happen to the police. The next morning, Hoppe's new conditions would be initiated:

1. The police would go back to regular prisoner food.

2. Only one letter would be written per month and only fifteen lines.

3. Only two letters with a total of sixty lines could be received a month.

4. All Norsemen to move into one Barrack in the main camp.

5. Remove their hats when meeting a superior.

6. The work details will be organized by a Work Leader, and all Norwegian police were required to report for work. They will be ruled over by Kapos that have the authority to use whips.

7. No smoking while on work commandos. If caught smoking, they will be whipped twenty-five times on their backs.

8. Listening to the radio or receiving newspaper was forbidden.

9. Red Cross and packages from other countries will be seized, but packages from home will be accepted.

10. The camp shoemaker, tailor, transport commander and Herman Heggenes, as the hospital administrator, will be retained.

11. Two hundred and fifty Estonians to move into Block 2 at Sonderlager.

12. No canteen outside of special bonuses.

13. The uniform stays.

When these conditions were presented in the *Kostebinderiet* meeting hall, there were many straight faces. The police had fallen from having a favored status to an ordinary prisoner status.

Their main question was if they were to remain at Sonderlager or transfer to the main camp. Petersen informed them that Commandant Hoppe sought to have them transferred to the main camp. Fortunately, a week before Christmas, Berlin's official news stated the Norwegian police were to stay at Sonderlager. The official statement also must have included information on Red Cross packages, for the packages continued to arrive as before.

The police, however, were to receive prisoner food rations, not troop food.

Letters the police had already written were not sent. The radio was seized, and newspapers were banned. Kapos from the main camp served as their foremen, and the work details continued as before. There were continually 160 men out during the week and a 110 on Sundays. Discipline was given by hand.

Police Discipline

In early December, during the general roll call, the police were informed they were to be disciplined with two hours of exercise for poor behavior. An **Oberscharfürer** called the sick and the police members over fifty to come forward and sent them back into their barracks. The exercise was caps off, jogging back and forth and, at the end, marching in a parade. All went well, thanks to all the exercising the police had done in the camp. The Oberscharfürer, an old infantryman, was visibly impressed and held a short speech and talked favorably.

The discipline was because a couple of the police did not take off their caps when they met the camp commander.

The harsh restrictions imposed on the police began to slowly lessen, and after a short period, things were pretty much the same as before. They started to receive letters again and write as often as they wanted and as long a letter as they wished.

Documents from Norway

On an evening roll call in mid-January 1945, Hauptsturmführer Meyer came striding into the yard carrying documents under his arm. It was quite evident that he had been drinking. He informed the police that the Police Department in Norway had dismissed them, and they were all fired.

The documents were from Police Minister Jonas Lie telling each police member they were removed from their position as policemen, placing them at the disposal of the Germans according to the Minister-President Quisling's resolution of December 23, 1943. The police found this quite amusing.

In Norway, both the Germans and their puppet government underestimated the police's determination to remain loyal to their king, country and government. The police wondered if the Germans were not aware that the police were arrested because they did not want to be disloyal and refused to work with the Germans or their puppet government. The police took their stand even under the threat of execution. How could they now believe they would change their convictions and join Germany in their war effort? The Germans themselves defined their position by bringing the police to

KZ-Stutthof and placing them under such foul conditions. In Norway, the police were defenders of law and order, of rights and justice. The Germans had brought the police to KZ-Stutthof, where murder, brutality and crimes against humanity were the norms, and then tried to coerce them into participating in it! Germany's intent was a "no go" from the start.

On the other hand, the police were able to manipulate the Germans for a time by giving them the expectation that they would conform. This stall tactic allowed them to receive better conditions in the Sonderlager camp. It also enabled them to receive packages with food sources from the outside. These packages helped the police to stay alive and relatively healthy to assist the unfortunate prisoners in the main camp. Often the police saw the expressions of joy from prisoners that found food they had left for them. During the upcoming typhoid epidemic, the police's relatively good health helped them fight the disease and give food to the sick in the hospital.

After the Germans understood the police would not conform, they were given ordinary prisoner status.

Rumors of Evacuation

The Eastern Front came continually closer, and rumors of evacuation began circulating. Papers became readily available and were a key source of information as the police followed the war's progress. The German paper, *The Danzig Vorposten*, was read with great interest, especially over the fall. The obituary pages with headings such as *Mit Ehre an der Ostfront gefallen* (Fallen with honor on the Eastern Front) were of particular interest. Even though much was censored, they understood what was happening on the war front by reading between the lines.

On several occasions and with the help of friendly farmers, the police would listen to news from London. John Bœvre recorded all the information. He kept a large map in Block 2 and kept it updated on where the eastern offensive lines were. Bœvre met regularly with different police prisoner groups to keep them updated. The progress of the war was of great interest, especially after the Eastern Front had come so close that they could hear the sounds of artillery.

Library and Pastimes

Soon after the police arrived at Sonderlager, they began receiving books from home. Books they had read were then donated to a growing library. The library became very popular, and Kahrs Peterson was the librarian. The library grew steadily, and by the end of Sonderlager there was a significant selection of books.

The police were prohibited from keeping a diary. Therefore, diaries had to be written in secret and only during free time. Most noted in point form using secret code and abbreviated description for specific events. They lived under the constant fear their diaries would be discovered.

Playing bridge became a favorite pastime, and tournaments were held regularly. There proved to be several good bridge players among them. When there was no tournament, there was a competition between the blocks or between the rooms. Bridge served as a useful diversion – it allowed the police to forget their situation and develop camaraderie. Singing was their favorite diversion. It wasn't the songs they were ordered to sing during roll call that gave them joy, but the songs spontaneously coming through their fellowship. These songs helped lift their spirits.

Songs such as *Det går bedre og bedre dag for dag* (Every Day Gets Better) and *Mellom bakker og berg* (Between Hills and Cliffs) were favorites. These songs became associated with their stay at Sonderlager, especially when Walle sang them. Walle's singing was always followed by a silent reflection of home. Most of them got a lump in their throat and wiped away tears after he had finished. The national anthem *Ja vi elsker* (Yes we love this country) was sung only occasionally, as the police wanted to save it for when they were liberated.

There were several talented musicians among the police. They included directors, composers and many talented vocalists. Surprisingly, there were also many gifted instrumentalists. Soon one instrument after the other showed up: violin, flute, guitar, trumpet and mouth organ. They composed their own song, *Vi kommer fra Norge* (We come from Norway) with the melody *Fjellsangen* (Song of the Mountain).

Vi kommer fra Norge landet der nord
fra høyreiste fjell of fra smilende fjord
I dag paraderer og takfast marsjerer

vi alle I Deutschland og synger I kor
Refreng:
Wir sind Polizisten med sang og humør,
Vi holder på gnisten,
Den gnist som aldri dør!
Alt mismot forsvinner til sollyse minner,
Til framtidens håp for hverandre vi strør!

(We come from Norway, the land of the north
from the majestic mountain and smiling fjords
Today we march in unison
And sing in harmony
In the land called Germany)
(Refrain)
(We are police officers
with song and humor
We hold on to the spark that never dies.
Discouragement disappears in sunlit memories.
Of the future hope, we have together)

Towards the end of May, the police endeavored to try to beautify the campgrounds. Julius Hordnes, Alf Johnsen and Finn Dahlin carried six wheelbarrows full of compost from the Werderhof farm to the camp and planted flowers at the barracks' entrances. They took the flowers from the garden in the main camp. The work was organized by Kristoffer Sœbø, who was himself an experienced gardener.

It wasn't difficult to find volunteers for the work. Even one of the guards volunteered, being a gardener in civilian life.

Planting Vegetables

In mid-June, orders came from Berlin that all camps were to grow vegetables and prisoners were required to dig and plant the rows. There were more than twenty police volunteers to pull the plough. The volunteers were accompanied by a flute, trumpet and song from an enthusiastic cheering section. The work was hard, and it didn't take long before the "horses" got tired. The cheering also drew to a close. Hordnes then went to the Werderhof farm with ten salted herring to trade for the use of two horses. With the help of the horses, plowing the cabbage garden was done in one morning. The following day the police planted 15,000 cabbage and kohlrabi plants. The summer was spent tending the vegetables. In the fall it was amazing to see how large the plants had grown.

The vegetables were given to the prisoner kitchen in the main camp. The plants were full of worms that crawled all over the kitchen and into the barracks. They crawled on chairs and tables and up the walls and fell from the ceiling.

Mystery of the Herring Barrels

Contacts in Norway had sent the police barrels of salted herring. A policeman from Haugesund was a partner in a fishing boat and arranged to have barrels of herring sent to Sonderlager. Fortunately, the barrels were permitted to be delivered. The contents were divided among all the police regularly. In June, three barrels of salted herring arrived. In late fall, five barrels were delivered, though some barrels were stolen on the way to the camp. The police learned that Hauptsturmführer Meyer and camp Commandant Hoppe stole one barrel each. Salted herring was in great demand, the police could trade almost anything they wanted for a herring. The guards were particularly craving herring, and it became the chief tool for bribing them. The police thought it would be prudent to save as much of this valuable commodity as they could. After considering where to hide the barrels, they decided to hide them under the *Kostebinderiet* meeting room floor. The police dug a small basement under the floor to hide the barrels. The work had to be done at night to not arouse the suspicion by the German guards. They did shift after shift until they had dug a large enough basement to store the barrels. The police were able to secure a few pets, including cats and a small puppy. The puppy (Germa) was a gift to Eckhoff, and the dog followed him everywhere he went. During the roll calls, Germa sat beside him. She became everybody's favorite.

In a fenced pen were six geese and two turkeys, stolen from the Werderhof farm, to be plumped for Christmas. There was also a dog pen for three German Shepherd puppies. Thorleif Lie, who was a police dog trainer, was given the task of training the dogs. Early and late, Lie walked about the fields training the dogs in both German and Norwegian. Towards the end of Sonderlager, Mrs. Meyer gave their small family dog to Petersen for the police to look after during the camp evacuation.

KZ-Stutthof Tragedy

On the evening of June 22, 1944, artillery shots were heard coming from the main camp. It was later learned that the previous day, 100 Polish prisoners were locked in their barracks. That evening all other prisoners were ordered to stay in their barracks; otherwise, they would be shot. Fifty Polish prisoners were pulled out of their Barrack and marched with a large contingent of guards. Even the guards in the watchtowers were doubled. Near the gate, the Germans began to tie the prisoners, who quickly understood what was happening and tried to escape towards the center of the camp. The prisoners were seized and brutally beaten and bound, then driven towards the gate. A father told his son to try to escape, but that proved virtually impossible with both hands tied behind his back. The Germans began to shoot at him while the other prisoners panicked. The shooting continued for five minutes. Bullets went in all directions, and prisoners in their barracks dove for the floor to avoid being hit by stray bullets. A prisoner in Barrack 1 had his arm shattered by a shot, and two prisoners in Barrack 5 were killed.

Half of the Polish prisoners were killed during the shooting. The remaining fifty prisoners were marched to the gas chamber.

Gas Chamber

During this period, the gas chamber's capacity was not adequate to handle the number of prisoners being executed. Railroad cars were then brought into the train station at Waldlager. Prisoners were marched into the railroad cars under the pretense of being transferred to another camp. The SS was dressed in railroad uniforms to fool the prisoners. The doors were locked from the outside and gas was dropped from a vent in the ceiling. The wagons then moved to the side tracks leading to the crematorium, and the bodies would be piled up in front of the crematorium.

Jewish Women and Children Transport

Large transports of Jewish women and children came to the main camp in July 1944. They arrived in long trains with open and closed cattle wagons. After the German offensive was halted at Stalingrad and the subsequent Russian offensive westward, evacuation transports from several places such as Riga, Kaunus, Königsberg and Bialystok arrived regularly. The Russians forced the Germans to move their prisoners towards the west. Most of the transports were destined for KZ-Auschwitz and KZ-Birkenau, but soon there was no more room to accept the refugees there. Now KZ-Stutthof came into the picture, and it was the primary reason for the German expansion of the main camp. KZ-Stutthof was called the front garden to KZ-Auschwitz, but the police called it the backyard of KZ-Auschwitz.

One of the transports that came from the ghetto in Kowno (Kaunus) was a fifteen-year-old Jewish girl named **Trudi Birger**, who arrived with her mother. They lived in the ghetto for three years and did hard labor for the Germans. Birger tells her own story in a book about the exhaustion and hunger, suffering and death among the Jewish women in the Thorn's labor camp (a subcamp of KZ-Stutthof). The book elaborates on the conditions in the *Vernichtungslager* (Extermination Camp) in the main camp KZ-Stutthof. It tells of her degrading treatment and her battle to resist the indifference to death, not to accept the fatalist view that it's inevitable she would be consumed by the flames in the crematorium. To die was better than to live. There was no future, and the present was hell!

CHAPTER 8 –
Civilian Prisoners

In August, Norwegian civilian prisoners from Grini arrived in the main camp. There were forty-four men and eighteen women. The civilian prisoners were transported on the French ship *DS Margasche* directly to Danzig. At Danzig, the men and women were separated, and each group was driven by truck to KZ-Stutthof. When the women arrived at the main camp, they were degraded by being forced to undress and stand naked while SS soldiers walked around and looked at them. The women's heads were shaved, and they were given prison clothes that were too small. The women were then registered and confined to a barrack in *Altes Lager* (Women's Camp).

The men followed in a separate truck, and when they arrived they were locked in a wet laundry room overnight. The following day, the men were put through the same degrading situation as the women but were allowed to keep their hair. They were given the standard striped cotton uniforms. Ottar Haugland was the prisoner's spokesman. Haugland was an engineer who studied in Germany for four years before the war, spoke fluid German and understood the German mentality. When Haugland was informed by the barrack leader that the Norwegians were to have their heads shaved, he went directly to Lagerältester Otto Selonka to convince him not to shave the Norwegians' heads. What he did was not without danger. Selonka was inebriated at the time and could have just as quickly turned on Haugland as the criminal that he was.

Selonka could have sent his guard dog on him or shot him on the spot. Similarly, the *Blockältester* (barrack leader) could have sought vengeance on him. The Norwegian civilian prisoners received a hard welcome to the main camp. This was the period when the transportation and liquidation of Jews from KZ-Auschwitz was at its peak. The morning after the Norwegian civilian prisoners arrived, they witnessed 200 Jewish women, both young and old, lined up stark naked in front of the adjoining Barrack in the Jewish women camp. The women stood there several hours before being marched to the gas chamber.

The civilian prisoners also witnessed Jewish women being kicked and beaten until they were unconscious and eventually till they died, for no other reason than they were Jewish. The Norwegians were themselves ill-treated and harassed day and night by their criminal Blockältester. The men were made to sleep on their backs. Their hands outside the blanket and straight down in military attention.

It was strictly forbidden to have contact with other prisoners. It wasn't long before Hauptsturmführer Meyer complained that individual policemen had winked at the Norwegian women. It took the police two days to smuggle food and vitamins to their fellow countrymen.

The Danish and Norwegian prisoners were confined to Barrack 5. Several of the Norwegian prisoners had to work on the EPP Commando, building an ammunition factory. Others were put to work in factories east of the camp. The Norwegians lived for some time in very tight quarters with three men to a bed, but they were still allowed to write letters home in Norwegian. Like all the other prisoners, they were given poor and little food, and their weight was plainly going down. They also received packages from home after some time, including Red Cross packages from the YMCA in Switzerland. The camp's already overcrowded condition became steadily worse as the prisoner population grew with every prisoner transport. The Danes came to Stutthof in the middle of October 1943 and were given registration numbers beginning at 25,660. When the police came to KZ-Stutthof on December 14, 1943, they were given a number starting with 6,000. If they had been registered as other prisoners and given numbers, their KZ-Stutthof numbers would have started slightly over 27,000.

The last official prisoner to be registered was given the number 105,302 on January 17, 1945. In total, the number of prisoners registered at KZ-Stutthof was 112,600 – but numbers were used over again as they became available.

This does not include prisoners that were not recorded but were directly sent to the gas chamber or executed in the forest.

The main camp was designed to hold a total of 45,000 prisoners. With the arrival of another 43,000 prisoners in the space of 3 months, systematic executions and elimination of prisoners were carried out to make room for the influx of new ones.

Period of Chaos

At first, many prisoners were not registered but taken directly to the crematorium. By August 1944, with the arrival of prisoners from KZ-Auschwitz, the situation became very grave. It was a period of chaos. No one knew how many prisoners died unregistered in the forest. The dead were stacked in large piles and burned. Also, prisoners who were not considered good workers were culled and sent directly to the gas chamber.

SS-Hauptsturmführer Otto Haust was the chief in the hospital. If he saw a prisoner put something in his mouth and swallow it, Haupt would jump forward and shoot the prisoner in the forehead with his pistol. He would then drag the prisoner to the hospital, to the prison doctors Wojewski and Gärthner, to perform an autopsy on the prisoner. While the autopsy was being performed, Haust watched. During a moment of distraction, Dr. Gärthner hid the ring deep inside the prisoner. The ring went with the prisoner to the crematorium.

Crematorium

One day in October, while working in the main camp, a police prisoner witnessed a Polish prisoner attempting to escape. He saw six soldiers with bloodhounds chasing the prisoner. Escaping from Stutthof was extremely difficult. There is a short distance to water both to the north and to the south, and the river Weichel lay ten kilometers west, but it was challenging to cross for escapees. The land towards the south was filled with long canals.

The main camp had several bloodhounds, and German Shepherds were trained in tracking down prisoners. Most of the escapees were captured. The prisoners were then taken back to the camp and executed as a warning to others. Often the SS guards allowed their dogs to tear into the prisoners and kill them. Despite this, there were several that tried to escape, and some were successful.

There was once a ransacking, in the main camp, of the Polish wood cutting commando. Bread was found in the possession of a German Kapo who had also hidden some pork in the forest. For this, the Kapo received a savage beating from the SS guards. During a roll call, Eckhoff took this opportunity to warn the police to be careful about showing charity to other prisoners. This was hard for the police to accept. They saw the prisoners' needs, and they had it so much better. Unfortunately, the police would learn that reality.

The Jewish barracks were ransacked, and a box of sardines was found in a Jewish man's possession. A sergeant ordered the police to turn over the policeman who gave the Jew the box. None came forward. The sergeant demanded that they give over the policeman later that same day. All the police knew that Julius Hordnes had shown compassion and given the Jew a box of sardines. But the Germans would never know this. Arne Sundvor talked with the sergeant and pointed out that the Jewish prisoner did not have the Star of David on his prisoner uniform, and therefore the policeman was excused. The case was then dropped.

An Act of Compassion

Once again, the police experienced an unusual show of human compassion while marching from Sonderlager to their work detail in the main camp. The detail was met by a column of Russian prisoners on their way to a different workplace. The Russians were carrying their daily allotment of bread. As the columns passed each other, the Russians broke off their bread pieces and tossed them to the police. This was the second time a Russian work detail showed compassion towards the police. They repaid the Russian prisoners' kindness by smuggling several salted herring packages into the Russian barracks. This, of course, was very dangerous. If the police were caught, the Russians would be severely punished, but the police would only have their package privileges taken away for a while.

It was inconceivable that such an act of kindness could have such negative consequences. The police struggled with this on several occasions. It was ingrained in the police to help the needy and defend the weak. It became challenging to refrain from helping people with little clothing, without proper shoes and without adequate food and drink.

On several occasions, the Germans indicated that every person of Slavic race was to be exterminated, along with Jews, Gypsies and several other ethnic groups. The Nazis warned that helping these poor creatures had the effect of making one an enemy of Germany. They were, thank God, able to help some.

Finnish Prisoners

At the end of October, Finnish prisoners arrived at Sonderlager, sixty-one men and ten women. Among them were young boys aged fifteen and sixteen. The Finns were crew on three Finnish ships *Bore VI*, *Mercator* and *Wappu*. The boats left Finland in September with German evacuation supplies bound for Danzig. The crew was promised return passage but was instead forced to choose between serving in the German marines or being prisoners at a concentration camp; they chose the latter. The Finns had three weeks of internment in Danzig before arriving at Sonderlager. Originally, ten ships sailed together; the other seven understood the situation and diverted into Swedish ports. Later there came still another Finnish crew of two women and seventeen men from the ship *Ellen*. The Finnish men were housed in the mailroom. The women were housed in a hospital room inside the sewing room. For the most part, the Finns kept to themselves initially, as most of them spoke only Finnish. It was fortunate that policeman Aksel Stefansen understood and spoke Finnish.

A week before Christmas, it was discovered that several Finnish men had lice, and this created quite a stir. Lice are carriers of typhus. The lice's source was found. The guilty party knew he had lice but didn't reveal it. As a result, ten men were sent to isolation, everyone in the camp had to shower and their clothes were sent to the main camp for cleansing. The clothes came back with more lice than before, and a new shower had to be taken. The responsibility for sending clothes to the main camp for disinfection and making sure everyone showered fell on Herman Heggenes and Otto Kristiansen. This needed to be taken seriously. Later, one policeman reported he had lice, and it was dealt with right away. Any potential problem was averted. The Finnish prisoners remained with the police until the liberation.

Cold Winter

When the police arrived at Sonderlager, they were rationed coal briquettes for January. The rations became less and less. By April, the quotas ceased. During the night, the police would put four or five briquettes in the stove to last till the morning. The police could have as many tree roots as they wanted if they would fetch the roots themselves outside the camp. Outside the main camp lay large piles of roots that were cleared during the original camp construction.

The older policemen carried out the tree root work commando with Einar Bjelland as the work chief. The woodwork detail was the only one allowed to distribute the wood. If anyone took wood without permission from the wood gang, the Germans regarded it as theft and the thieves would be punished. Towards the end, there was little to no wood to be found near the camp. The wood detail then began searching for wood elsewhere, but they didn't find much. During December 1944, the temperature dropped several times to -17°C. KZ-Stutthof's main camp used an enormous amount of wood, and the roots were quickly used up. The 'root detail' had to pull out new roots, which again were quickly used up. After New Years', the temperature became milder, but the wind blew often. The barracks were not insulated, and the need for wood was constant.

German meteorologists reported in a local paper that the winter of 1944-45 would be the coldest in 30 to 40 years, with -30°C at the most frigid period. The cold weather began before Christmas. It was so cold that John Trøen, in Block 1, received a piece of coal for his fiftieth birthday on January 15. It was most likely the best gift he or his room could receive under the circumstances.

During the first week in January, the work details stopped, but the work detail to Nickelswalde continued.

The Hospital

Herman Heggenes ruled the hospital, and he ruled it with an iron fist. There was no use for the police to try to feign illness to get out of work. One would need a sick note from Heggenes, who knew who the fakers were. Police who were sick for a few days would stay in their barracks. If it was for an extended sickness, the patient was admitted to the hospital at Sonderlager. Those who were seriously ill were transferred to the hospital in the main camp.

Heggenes was totally committed to his responsibility during the polices' stay at Sonderlager. There weren't many who hadn't gone to him for treatment of one thing or another.

When several policemen lay in the hospital in the main camp, Heggenes would visit them every day. Heggenes and Magnus Kristensen were the ones most engaged in the polices' wellbeing. The hospital at Sonderlager had its first outbreak in February 1944, when the police were at their weakest. There were periods of diarrhea, bronchitis and influenza. Just after New Year 1944 came the deadly typhus epidemic. Everyone was fearful of communicable diseases, but especially typhus. During the fall of 1944, the police wrote to the Oslo General Hospital to beg for desperately needed medication and vaccines. Sulphur tablets and the typhus vaccine were most crucial. It was met with great joy when Doctor Alfons Wojewski (whom the police nicknamed Dr. Tablettski) was able to give them the vaccine at the end of November.

On May 5, 1990, the police prisoners from Stutthof held a forty-five-year reunion after their liberation. The reunion was held in Oslo, and the special guest was Dr. Wojewski, who was located through the Red Cross in Poland. It was an excellent experience for Wojewski, who remembered the majority of the police by name. He received Norway's highest civilian medal from Major General Bjørn Egge. Several of his incredible accomplishments were outlined with the limited tools at his disposal. When Major General Egge indicated some doubt about the accuracy of the details that were read, three KZ-Stutthof police prisoners stood up. They lowered their pants to show the scars of the operations Dr. Wojewski had performed.

The police received three injections, with the last one given on December 9. They were also vaccinated against diphtheria and stomach Para typhus. This was administered just in time as typhus had already broken out in the main camp, and two barracks were quarantined. The medicine no doubt saved the lives of many of the police. Dr. Wojewski was, without a doubt, a great doctor and surgeon. In the camp, he performed several operating procedures. He removed, for example, several infected appendixes. Between Christmas and New Year, he removed an infected kidney. When Torgeir Gjerde was hit in the head with a branch from a falling tree, Wojewski removed the damaged bone and replaced it with a steel plate. This was not short of a miracle when one considers that Dr. Wojewski had nothing to work with, only a razor blade and no anesthetic.

Polish Uprising

In the last days of August and into September 1944, artillery fire was heard from the southeast. It was assumed it was the Eastern Front, but it was, in fact, the battle over Warsaw they heard. The Polish underground began an uprising at the beginning of August 1944. One-hundred-thousand men fought against the Germans for sixty-three days under the command of General Tadeusz Komorowski. The battle lasted until October 2, 1944, when the uprising was defeated by German tanks, artillery, and bombers. The Russian army stood on the other side of the Weichsel River and watched without interfering. Towards the end of November, fighting was heard from the Eastern Front, and it became louder and louder during December. The police observed the skies being lit up with magnesium torches to see the armies on the ground.

Christmas and New Year 1944

Christmas was approaching, and preparations needed to be made. The police were not sure if they would celebrate Christmas at Sonderlager, much less if they would celebrate Christmas at all.

They did, however, continue to live in Sonderlager and celebrated both Christmas and New Year's there. All work commandos ended at noon on Christmas Eve day. The Christmas theme of "peace on earth and goodwill to men" was virtually nonexistent. There was only the sound of artillery bringing death and destruction.

In reality, it was an extraordinary Christmas. Material wise, the police didn't have any need, and socially they were a united large family determined to make their Christmas celebration full of optimism.

At 16:00 was the Christmas party. A large Christmas tree full of lights stood in the middle of the floor, decorated with Norwegian flags and glittering icicles. On the walls around the room hung Hafstad's decorations of little elves and Christmas bulbs. Around the windows were decorations of garlands made of fir branches. The tables were against the walls and under the windows, pointing towards the center of the room. On the tables were small decorated Christmas trees.

On each table was a paper tablecloth and paper napkin. Each room had its own table filled with items from home. Petersen was visibly impressed and said, *"Hvis en tysk familie ind i stuen, ville de står med deres mund åben"* (If a German family entered the room, they would stand with their mouth open). He continued, *"De voksne på grund af al maden og børnene på grund af pynten"* (The adults because of all the food and the children because of the decorations). None of those things could be purchased in Germany at that time. The police accomplished all of this because of their creativity and using what was available in the concentration camp. There they were, grown men hardened by sixteen months in the concentration camp now sat in anticipation like wide-eyed little children. None of them had ever experienced, before or after, a Christmas Eve like this one. And none of them would ever forget it. After the program, they returned to their own rooms to lay thinking of their loved ones at home.

At roll call in the main camp on December 27, two Russian brothers were hanged on a gallows beside the Christmas tree. They were seventeen and nineteen years old. The brothers had attempted to escape from a work camp in Danzig. Before being hung, the eldest brother yelled "Скоро Красная Армия освободит вас всех и отомстит за нас". (Soon, the Red Army will free you all and avenge us). After this, he shouted, "Да здравствует Советский Союз" (Long

Two Russian Brothers Hanged

live the Soviet Union). They were left hanging until the next day as a warning against trying to escape.

The New Year's Eve meeting was held for all in Barrack 2. They arranged for a podium next to the stove. The door at the east entrance was removed and a wool blanket was hung to cover the opening. In front of the veil a scene was set up. A large mural made by Anker Hafstad was hung over the western door leading to the meeting room. It represented the old and the New Year, with the familiar motif of old *father time* and a child with an hourglass. The celebration began at 16:00 and delicious stew was served. During and after dinner, there was nearly four hours of entertainment, which was funny and well-received. It ended at midnight.

At midnight, to ring in the New Year, the police grabbed anything that would make a noise. If they couldn't find anything, they would slam the doors to make noise. After the revelry, they retired to reflect on the year that had just passed and thought of the New Year that lay ahead.

Over twelve to thirteen months, the police prisoners lived in close quarters, more or less. It can be said that it had gone exceptionally well and that the unity among them was extraordinary. For this, the police could thank their relative fortuitous conditions and their self-discipline. Police officers are trained to be disciplined and self-restrained under adverse conditions and circumstances.

Wise Leadership

At Sonderlager, the police were under the leadership of a wise and capable leader, Anders Eckhoff. Eckhoff had the Germans' appeal because he was blonde with blue eyes, an ideal representative of the Aryan race according to the Germans. Eckhoff was creative and always acted wisely and professionally. The respect and goodwill he earned from the Germans greatly benefited the police during their imprisonment. Eckhoff is the first to be credited for helping the police through their thirteen-month stay at Sonderlager. Unfortunately, the police lost four of their comrades during those thirteen months. Sverre Selheim died from *diphtheria* and *krupp*. Jostein Knapstad died from heart strain after a football game due to undernourishment. Jahn

Kornbrekke died in the hospital in the main camp from stomach sores. Fredrick Ketilsson was shot by a stray bullet on work detail in the main camp.

Police constable Einar Kvalheim was transferred to KZ-Sachsenhausen in January 1944 and remained there until the end of the war. Police constable Arne Jørstad from Trondheim was removed from Sonderlager by the Germans in February 1944. Jørstad was incriminated in sabotage and was transferred to a prison in Berlin for further interrogation by the Gestapo. Police constable Leif Reusch Berg was released from Sonderlager in August 1944. Of the original 271 Norwegian police officers, there were now 264 left.

CHAPTER 9 –
End of Sonderlager

The year 1945 began dramatically, with bouts of diarrhea in Sonderlager. In the main camp, the typhoid epidemic that started before Christmas was now rampant.

Over the New Year's weekend, one after the other police prisoners came down with stomach pain and nausea, followed by fever. One by one, they became bedridden. By the evening roll call, fifty men were in sickbay, with several more complaining of the same ailments, including several Finnish prisoners. Strangely, there were few sick in Block 1.

By the next day's evening roll call, eighty men were bedridden. The majority recovered after a few days, but several took a long time to recover. These men could not hold their food down and ended up in the main camp hospital. At the hospital, the men received shots with a medicine called *Neosalvarsan*. In January, the police were given a doctor from the hospital in the main camp, a Lithuanian prisoner named Antanas Starkus. He would remain with the police until the sickness was over. They nicknamed him the *professor*. In a relatively short period, he was able to learn conversational Norwegian.

Starkus explained that the cause of this stomach disease was bacteria that he called *spirochæter*. The bacteria belonged to the same strain as the syphilis bacteria. The *spirochæter* had entered the blood and attacked the walls of the major intestine with diarrhea and constipation. This resulted in slime and blood in the stools, a common phenomenon in concentration camps called *Lagerscheisse* (Diarrhea). In some concentration camps, the disease had a mortality rate of nearly 90%. The professor indicated that the disease was more severe than typhus, but he believed the excellent condition the police were in would help them. The *professor* said that the bacteria enter the body through the mouth. He left no doubt that the bacteria came from the main camp via one of the buckets used to carry the stew. Those who ate from one specific bucket became stricken, while few who ate from the other bucket became sick. The professor mentioned that ordinary hygiene and teeth brushing once a day were vital to avoid catching the disease.

Lagerscheisse (diarrhea)

The police maintained that poor food preparation and hygiene in the central camp kitchen was the reason for the disease. Eckhoff tried to get the police their own kitchen in Sonderlager, but he was refused because the administration believed the conditions were good in the main camp kitchen.

Tore Jørgensen

Typhus Outbreak

Typhus Outbreak

The typhoid epidemic in the main camp spread rapidly, and numerous prisoners died daily, especially Jewish women. Many guards also came down with the disease. Several fires were lit to burn the bodies, but it was not enough. The capacity of the fires was not sufficient for the number of prisoners dying each day. Outside the crematorium, the heaps of bodies steadily grew. There lay 1,000 to 1,200 bodies in long rows, piled several deep. In the Jewish women camp alone, 500 women died every day. In one month, it is estimated that 8,000 died of Typus. The old crematorium burned down in October 1944, but new ovens with a higher capacity were built in the new camp. The new crematorium had three ovens and was in full operation by Christmas, with a capacity of 500 bodies per twenty-four-hour period. During a short period, the crematorium was not fully used; the available capacity was used to pick out thirty of the weakest and sickest Jewish women daily. These women were put in a wagon and transported to either the gas chamber or the crematorium. The majority of these prisoners were so weak they didn't protest. They said nothing and had little will to live. The women knew they wouldn't survive anyway and looked to death as a means of freedom. One doomed Jewish prisoner said,

> *"Es geht bei mir genauso wie bei unseren Vorfahren im Alten Testament. Sie konnten das Gelobte Land sehen, durften aber selbst nicht eintreten"* (It goes with me the same as our forefathers in the Old Testament. They could see the Promised Land, but were themselves not allowed to enter).

The Jew had a last wish that his children would survive the war, all the suffering would be over and they would live happily in their homeland. He did not utter a word of hate or vengeance.

Even the new crematorium could not keep up with the number of prisoners dying as the pile of bodies continued to grow, in spite of its higher capacity. The camp leadership realized that something more had to be done. The Danish prisoners were commanded to go on a work detail one hundred meters north of the main camp and dig deep holes in the sand. Railroad tracks were brought in and placed across the holes. After a while, the Danes understood what was going to happen and, to their credit, refused to continue. The Danes were excused without being punished. Their work detail was given to Russian and Polish prisoners who were given a good ration of alcohol and tobacco for their services. On the railroad tracks were piled layers of wood and 800 dead prisoners in each pile. Gasoline was poured over the piles and then ignited. Bodies were burned in this way every other day to assist the crematorium.

Ottar Haugland was the camp electrician. He had clearance to go into areas others could not. On one occasion, Haugland was doing an electrical installation in the crematorium and observed the morbid work that went on there. He observed that the bodies were laid in groups of five, to be easily pushed into the oven. Haugland also noticed that the bodies lay there with their mouths wide open and asked why. He was told that the SS officer who was in control of the crematorium pulled the prisoners' jaws to check if there were gold or silver fillings in their teeth. If so, the teeth would be removed with a pair of pliers.

On January 9, 1945, the main camp was quarantined. No one could leave or enter the camp. As a result, all commandos to the main camp were cancelled.

Rumors of evacuation began circulating, but the police didn't know if they could believe the stories. However, during the evening roll call on

Friday, January 19, Petersen did confirm that evacuation could happen at any time and that the evacuation would be towards the west.

Packing Begins

The police began packing right away. Several had backpacks they received from home, and others had seaman's packs. Others had the camp tailor, Lars Dale, make packs out of materials in the camp. The Finns made leather ties for many of the police and were paid with food items.

A Finnish prisoner suggested it would be easier to pull the backpacks on a sleigh, and the Finns proceeded to build small but wide sleighs. There was a substantial wood supply from the wooden Red Cross food packages the police had received. There were sleighs in no time in the rooms, halls and lined up against the outside barrack walls.

It was strongly emphasized that they were to keep up with the columns. The SS would shoot anyone who fell behind. The police became concerned about their sick comrades. Would they be able to keep up? What would happen to their members who were really sick and in the hospital in the main camp?

From Saturday, January 20, and over the following few days, there was a heavy snowstorm, and the temperature dropped to -13°C. There fell more snow than over the entire previous winter. In the Sonderlager camp, the police were kept busy shoveling snow.

On Monday, January 22, the news came that they would not be evacuated by train, but they'd be walking the whole journey. On the map, they discovered the journey was a minimum of sixty-five kilometers. That night they went to bed with the anticipation of being awakened at any time.

Red Cross Packages

The following morning, several new work details left the camp, and some returned without having had any work to do. One detail left by truck for Danzig. A second detail of forty men was sent to pick up Red Cross packages sitting in a railroad car parked near the main camp, next to the crematorium. Another detail of ten men was to carry large cases of medicine to the main camp. This proved to be heavy work, involving carrying cases in deep snow. The workers surveyed the problem and decided that Jacob Jacobsen would go to Werderhof and borrow a horse and wagon. This went well, and with Jacobsen driving the wagon they quickly transported the cases to the main camp.

When the same work detail arrived in the main camp, they were ordered by a sergeant to shovel snow from the railroad tracks. It didn't help to protest and tell the sergeant they had other orders. The group then went to get some shovels. On the way to pick up the shovels, the police met another work detail of forty men who had received the same orders. The police went back to the sergeant and explained the situation and were excused from shoveling snow. They also learned that the mail detail hadn't yet picked up the Red Cross packages from the railroad car by the crematorium, so they picked up the packages. Jacobsen delivered ten sacks of parcels to the Danish prisoners in the main camp and took five bags of packages back to Sonderlager.

The police noticed an increase in Russian airplane activities. For several days they heard artillery to the south and saw the skies lighting up like Christmas tree lights. The *Danzig Vorposten* read that Deutsch-Eylau and Toruń had fallen to the Russians, and fighting had spread eastward towards Allenstein. The Russians were moving towards Elbing and Marienberg. The front was now only forty kilometers away.

Preparation for Evacuation

On Wednesday, January 24, Petersen declared that the commandant and several SS officers had forsaken the camp and chaos in the main camp. He predicted the Russians would be in the camp by the morning and told the police to be ready to evacuate. They were to catch up with the evacuees from Werderhof. There was great joy and smiles on everyone's face. In the morning, the police were filled with anticipation, but no matter how hard they looked, they couldn't see any Russians. A work detail of fifty men left at 01:30. They were to meet outside a railroad checkpoint, by Danzig Strasse, at one of the roads that lead to the main camp. There they encountered another police work detail that had left the previous evening. Together they waited until 03:30, when a drunk sergeant recognized several of the group and invited them inside a workshop where they could warm themselves. At 05:00, a fifty-man work detail found themselves at the ferry terminal at Nickelswalde, where they unloaded railcars and placed the goods on barges. When the commando returned to Sonderlager, they told of many kilometers of German civilian evacuees, with tractors, horses and wagons, waiting to board the ferry to cross the Weichsel River. A steady stream of evacuees kept coming from the east, with vehicles loaded with all sorts of household goods. Most had been waiting all night. Many evacuees were lightly dressed, especially those from the Elbing district, who were forced to leave their homes in a hurry. Several women were without outer clothing and with only slippers on their feet. The evacuees told of four Russian armored cars that drove into Elbing and began shooting indiscriminately, killing many civilians.

The police had great expectations of being rescued by the Russians, but there was no news that would've let them know that their rescue was imminent. Mid-morning on Wednesday, January 24, the evacuation of Werderhof and the small work camps in the area began. A tractor pulling a large wagon came first. In the wagon sat people, an assortment of furniture and four horses tied to the back. Even though they were Germans, they were civilians with whom the police had worked for over a year. The police waved to them with the greeting *"Gute Reise!"* (Have a good trip). That afternoon, twelve policemen and two polish prisoners headed to the farm to salvage the goats and pigs. All that was left behind was theirs, and it was clear that most of the food would go to their sick friends.

Hauptsturmführer Meyer and his family evacuated that night.

On the evening of January 24, powerful explosions were heard to the south in the direction of Elbing. The explosions were so powerful that the barracks shook and the walls bowed from the air pressure. On the morning of January 25, Eckhoff received orders that the main camp evacuation would begin that evening, and all needed to be ready to go. Sonderlager would be evacuated at the same time. They had heard that many times during the last several days, but this time it seemed to be genuine. The police hurried to get their sleds ready and pack for the last time.

Evacuation of Main Camp

From Sonderlager, the police could see the road all the way to Steegen. Three kilometers away, the evacuation of the main camp had begun. Columns of prisoners weaved like a large black snake through the countryside. It was dreadful to think about the thousands of prisoners that now had to endure a cold winter made even more horrible because of hunger and sickness and wearing minimum clothing, shoes and belongings.

It was made clear that the march would be at least sixty-five kilometers, and each person would only have himself to depend on. Many of the sick police members had not recovered from the stomach typhoid, and others were fatigued, but they all wanted to be in the evacuation march. A rumor circulated that the Germans would shoot everyone left behind in the camp, and the Russians would shoot any prisoner they came across. After hearing of the ferry traffic across the Weichsel River towards the west, the police thought it would be impossible to evacuate the prisoners in that direction on account of the civilian evacuees' long lines. It seemed highly unlikely that the Germans would delay the civilian evacuation to accommodate concentration camp prisoners. The real possibility remained that the west's evacuation would be so slow the Russians would overtake them. The police thought that would be the best!

The evacuation would be on foot, with no possibility of sitting on a train as previously thought. The police asked themselves, "how can we evacuate our sick friends and what would happen to those who could not be evacuated?" Obviously, some of the police were too sick to be evacuated; the decision was made to transfer the seriously ill to the hospital in the main camp. In the hospital remained doctors and nurses, among them their own Heggenes and Eivind Luthen. Heggenes and Luthen were not to tell the sick of the evacuation, and there would be no farewells.

Many policemen still suffered from extreme diarrhea and would indeed insist on being part of the evacuation. But that would be dangerous, even if they were on a sleigh if it was possible to get one. It would prove impossible to pull all the sick on the sleighs. Each person would have enough to look after himself.

Pleni Norwegia

Meeting the Russians could present a big problem for the police. They feared being mistaken for Italian soldiers in their Badoglio uniforms or for Germans. They had secretly received small Norwegian flags in their packages from home, which were quickly sewn on to the uniforms. Hafstad made a large Norwegian flag that the police would wave if overtaken by the Russians. The police needed to do everything they could to be identified as Norwegians. They hoped some of the Russians spoke German or English, but if they didn't the police practiced the phrase *Pleni Norwegia* (Captive Norwegians). Hopefully, the Russians would identify them as Norwegians. They would ask the Russians to transfer them to Sweden.

Eckhoff instructed the police to pack two backpacks with sanitation products, medicine, bandages and a selection of tablets. In each of the packs, they included nourishing food supply, especially for the weak and sick among them. Olaf Takle was to pull one of the packages and professor Starkus the other. Those responsible for the distribution of food were told to bring spoons and other kitchenware. The shoemaker and tailor were to get their tools and raw materials.

That same afternoon, the police were ordered to send a thirty-man work detail with their packs to Danzig. There was no problem finding volunteers. Those in the work detail gave their sleighs away, then put their packs on their backs and headed out. Shortly after, another order followed to dispatch another work detail of 180 without packs to Nickelswalde. This particular work detail was to leave right away but would not be gone very long. The orders stipulated that all the police must be in this detail, including those who were mildly sick. Only the elderly and seriously sick were excused. It proved to be a difficult work detail to arrange. There were too many sick, and the rest were exhausted from the previous night work detail. It was a difficult assignment, but there was no other option for them but to go. In the end the work detail left with 140 Norwegians and 40 Finns.

Later that evening, orders came to gather at the Waldlager station by the next morning at 05:00.

CHAPTER 10 –
The Death March

The sky was clear and full of sparkling stars, but it was cold! On one hand the police had smiles on their faces, on the other they were apprehensive. They were to go into an unknown situation full of dangers, where anything could happen. The most likely scenarios were freezing to death or becoming sick on the way – meaning the Germans would shoot them. It certainly was no joke to be a prisoner evacuating in Germany during this period, with desperate and ruthless prison guards pushing them.

The evacuation column consisted of the oldest among the police prisoners and some of their sick who insisted on coming with them. The twelve men Werderhof commando, and some of the smaller commandos, came back during that night and joined the evacuation.

The Sonderlager column consisted of eighty-one Norwegian policemen and forty Finnish prisoners, including four women. The Lithuanian prisoner, Starkus (the professor), was among the evacuees, along with the much-detested *Teigenhof* Kapo, who a few days later deserted when he found himself in familiar territory.

The column marched to the Waldlager station at 05:00 and, when reaching the bridge beside Ziegelei, they cast a mournful glance towards Sonderlager, their home for the last twelve and a half months. At Sonderlager they had it fairly well, to some degree, compared to other prisoners. The police evacuees didn't say goodbye to their sick friends left behind in the camp, not knowing if they'd ever meet again. A few days earlier, Petersen had warned them that when the Russians come, all who were left behind would be gathered in one barrack and would either be burned to death or shot.

There were more than 10,000 prisoners left behind in the main camp. Most of them were sick. The police commandos to Nickelswalde and Danzig did not make it back to camp before the evacuation. The police were now separated into four groups: one group of 81 evacuated west along the Polish highways. A second group of 140, together with 40 Finns, was working at the Nickelswalde ferry terminal loading and unloading barges. The third, a work detail of 30 men, was working in Danzig. The last group of 13 men was left behind at Sonderlager and the main camp, being too sick to travel.

Column	Total	From Block	Date Evacuated	Description
1	1,600	1, 2, Hospital	January 25	Doctors, nurses, orderlies and four Norwegian patients
2	1,350	3 and 4	January 25	
3	1,400	5 and 7	January 25	Norwegian and Danish civilians
4	1,250	8 and 10	January 25	
5	1,100	9 and 13	January 25	
6	1,500	12 and 15	January 25	
7	900	Women's camp	January 25	Women, including twelve Norwegians
8	821	Hospital, Sonderlager	January 26	700 from main camp and 121 from Sonderlager

9	1,600	Jews	January 26	Mostly Jewish women
10	1,500		Mid February	Picked up 921 additional prisoners from Burggaben

Napoleon

Petersen met the police evacuation column at the control station at Danzig Strasse. He informed them that they were to wait for, and then follow, another prisoner column from the main camp. That was disappointing; they were hoping to march on their own. Petersen informed them that the transport leader was a former *Hauptmann* (Captain) in the Wehrmacht named Danesch. He was reported to be a fair man. The police later nicknamed him *Napoleon*.

As the police waited at the control station, a constant stream of Polish and German civilian evacuees driving cars, horse carriages and pulling sleighs passed by. While waiting, they were told that, if they wished, they could go back to the kitchen in the main camp and collect as many food provisions as they wanted. Several of their group left for the kitchen and came back with loaves of bread, packages of margarine and wieners. Arriving back, they reported a large fire at the edge of the forest northeast of the camp, close to the Jewish women's camp. Loud screams were heard coming from that area. The report left a deep impression on them.

There were about 12,000 prisoners from Stutthof that went on the death march between January 25 and 26, 1945. In addition, a column of 2,500 prisoners left in mid-February.

At 07:00, the column from the main camp arrived with transport leader Danesch, along with a dozen loud SS and several black uniformed guards. The guards were mostly Ukrainian, but also Russian and Baltic. They were criminals newly released from prison who had volunteered for service in the SS. They were terrorists and anxious to impresses their new masters. The transport leader, Danesch, arrived at KZ-Stutthof a few days earlier and was inexperienced in his new command. He seemed to be perplexed on how to deal with the Norwegian police prisoners. The police distinguished themselves from the other prisoners by their uniforms and appearance. They looked much better than most other prisoners and Danesch was obviously smitten by the 'Germanic complex'. He was easily fooled, and after a while the police convinced him that they should be treated like other prisoners.

The fact that the police were not driven and brutally treated in the days that followed caused envy among the other prisoners. It would not have improved other prisoners' situations if the police were treated the same way. As it turned out, the police were able to offer help to many during the march.

Column 8

Column 8 consisted of 700 male prisoners from the main camp, plus the Sonderlager group of 81 Norwegian police and 40 Finnish prisoners – including 4 women – for a total of 821 prisoners. Prisoners from the main camp in Column 8 consisted mostly of Polish, with some Russian and French prisoners. Several of these prisoners were recently released patients from the hospital in the main camp. They were a tragic sight in their light blue striped cotton prisoner uniforms. Many had jackets of the same material, but it did little to protect them from the cold and wind. Most had wooden shoes and several of them were without socks. The majority carried rolled up wool blankets under their arms or over their shoulders, while others carried them as sacks with their belongings in it. When they passed the police, they stretched out their hands and begged for bread. The police prisoners from Sonderlager had been invited to go back to the kitchen in the main camp, but these poor souls had nothing. There were also a few Jewish prisoners that had just arrived at the camp, none of them survived the first fourteen days.

The March Begins

As the evacuation column left the main camp, one of the sick prisoners fell just outside the gate and was left lying there. The *Death March* had begun.

Transport leader Danesch, riding on his horse, went twenty to thirty meters in front of Column 8 and determined the speed and the direction they would travel. The guards went in front and on both sides, and a row of forty guards went behind the first group in the column.

The Sonderlager group, now referred to by the Germans as the *Germanic Column*, followed fifty meters behind Column 8 with no guards around them. The Finns had made the police good sleighs. They glided easily, despite weighing between eighty and one hundred kilograms each when loaded. The weather had cleared and the sun came out by the time the convoy passed Steegen. When Column 8 passed Passewalk, and while nearing Nickelswalde, the police met a train traveling in the opposite direction and recognized some of their members. The members were part of the earlier 180 men Nickelswalde commando, now travelling back to Stutthof.

Death March Begins

Several of the Polish prisoners began to fall behind. They staggered for a while behind their section of Column 8 and began to edge themselves into the Germanic Column. The guards came screaming *"los-los!"* and chased the prisoners out. Predictably, several of them fell and were left lying on the ground. The guards noted the prisoner numbers and carried on. A German Kapo accompanying the Germanic Column said he had never seen the SS guards as considerate before, saying the SS used to be much worse.

When Column 8 arrived at the Weichsel River, they had to climb a steep dike on one side, then climb straight down the other side and continue towards the ferry terminal. At the ferry terminal, the police met several of their comrades from the earlier Nickelswalde commando. They were busy unloading railroad cars and loading it on to the ferry. They said that 100 of the group had left to go back to Sonderlager. Those were the ones the police saw earlier on the train.

The area surrounding the ferry terminal in Nickelswalde/Schiewenhorst looked like a barren wasteland blowing icy snow. The Nickelswalde commando had left Sonderlager thinly dressed, and the only available shelter was a non-insulated cargo hold in one of the barges. The temperature reached -25°C at night, and what saved them was a train that had stopped with a railroad car full of German military supplies, including jackets, gloves, insulated boots, scarves and a number of other useful items. During the night, they raided the wagon and took all the military goods they needed.

Column 8 was ordered to board the barge. A tugboat towed the barge to the other side. The trip only lasted a couple of minutes. Looking back across the river, the police could see their comrades following their column with their eyes and wondered if they would ever see each other again.

The road went along the dike high over the river for several kilometers. The wind and snow blew against them.

The snowy wind was extremely hard on the thinly clothed prisoners in front of Column 8. The prisoners hadn't gone many meters before one by one they began to sneak into the Germanic Column. The guards had become less tolerant now and used their rifle butts to drive the prisoners forward. In a matter of two to three kilometers, the Germanic Column passed ten to twelve dead prisoners.

Klein Zünder

A little Jewish boy of about twelve years of age, with a very handsome face, came staggering alongside the police. A black uniformed guard with a repulsive face hit the boy with the butt of his rifle so the boy fell and rolled end over end. In his anger, the guard hit the boy in the head again with all his might. The boy tried to get up, but the guard hit him again and again until his head was caved in. Then the guard kicked the body out of the way and continued. Only 100 meters in front of the police an adult prisoner fell, he looked like a skeleton. Right away a guard stood over him yelling *"Aufstehen weitergehen! Los-los!"* (Get up and go! Go-go!). The prisoner struggled to get up and only made it to a stooping position. The guard proceeded to kick him in the rib cage just as the police passed by, and they heard his ribs crack. They saw the grimace on his face as he fell and remained there, clutching his rib cage. The guard kicked him again and then took his rifle butt and hit him until the poor man was dead. The guard wore a green Wehrmacht uniform. The police looked at each other in disbelief. They were powerless to come to the prisoner's aid. If they would have interfered, they too would have been killed.

After a short distance, the Germanic Column passed another ten to twelve mutilated bodies. A truck followed behind the column and picked up the bodies. In the Germanic Column was four Finnish women from Sonderlager. The police directed them to move towards the center of the column so as not to witness what was going on.

A little Jewish boy of nine or ten was unable to keep up. His father walked beside him and tried to help him, but it was clear the boy could not continue. A couple of the police picked up the boy and put him on a sleigh, and they alternated pulling him. A guard noticed this and came running over to chase the boy out of the sleigh. *"Ich kann nicht mehr laufen"* (I can't walk anymore), complained the boy who understood what would happen to him. The column stopped and Danesch, who was in the vicinity, asked what the problem was. The police explained the situation to Danesch, and he gave permission for the boy to ride in the sleigh. The police were all happy to alternate pulling the boy. He was later delivered back to a very thankful father.

The sleighing weather was still good, but extremely cold.

When Column 8 passed the railroad station at Klein Zünder, they stopped. Danesch informed Eckhoff that the column was to overnight in a large hay barn that lay by the roadside. It was that barn the transport leader was looking for. After the prisoners stood and froze for a while, they turned around and headed back a short distance. The column had passed the barn. The temperature was now -25°C, in a snowstorm.

The Germanic Column was ushered into their own room in the barn, while other prisoners in Column 8 were ushered into a different room.

The next morning, Column 8 was gathered on the road at 06:00. Some of the police didn't have the insight to bring their sleighs inside the barn. During the night, several of the sleighs were stolen along with their belongings. They suspected the guards because the other prisoners were locked in.

It was a bitterly cold morning, and the wind blew briskly. The little Jewish boy from the day before came over in hopes that he could sit on a sleigh. After a discussion between the guards and the transport leader, it was decided that the boy, along with several sick prisoners, was to be left behind on the farm. One of the Finnish women was also left behind.

The column passed through an area called Grosse Zünder, where the women's column (Column 7) had stayed overnight. The women stood at attention along the roadside. Suddenly, a woman called out, "*Hei, Norge!*" (Hey Norway). It was Gerd Svanhild Håland from Sogn. The police called out a greeting to her. Unfortunately, she would go missing a short time later.

Praust

The convoy was heading towards Praust, a few kilometers directly south of Danzig. The conditions for pulling the sleighs and marching were ideal. On the outskirts of Praust, the convoy passed a military airport that was built by a woman's work detail. At around 14:30, the column stopped in the middle of a road and Danesch left to find lodgings. Several hours passed and a cold wind started to blow. Several prisoners sought refuge under staircases or behind gates, while others followed a road that led to an electrical station with an office building next door. Others sought refuge in several private residences and were served food.

A number of policemen strolled over to a Gasthaus (a small inn) and bought a cup of hot coffee. At the Gasthaus were several Germans, mostly Wehrmacht soldiers, also buying coffee. The Germans notice the police entering but said nothing. On the contrary, they offered the police cigarettes. It was clear that the Germans regarded the police as different from other prisoners. The soldiers made other prisoners stand outside in one spot.

A few prisoners from the column outside snuck away and came over to the police to beg for food. They said they hadn't eaten for several days, not even on the last day at Stutthof main camp. It deeply bothered the police to deny them, but they couldn't give the prisoners anything because the guards were watching. If they did, both the prisoner and the police would be punished. One policeman was overcome with pity for a prisoner and gave him some food. A guard noticed it and came rushing over, took the food and proceeded to kick the prisoner with his military boots while the prisoner lay on the floor until he rolled out the door.

The column continued to wait in the cold, but now the guards were angry and short tempered. After nearly four hours, Danesch returned with the news that they had to turn around and go back to the airport the column had passed earlier. There were now large snow drifts on the road, making marching and pulling the sleighs very tiresome. After about a kilometer, Column 8 came to a prison camp for Jews that was full. In the camp were also Norwegian civilians and Danish prisoners from Column 3.

Finally, the column arrived at the military airport and the prisoners were directed to a washroom that was incredibly dirty.

They were informed that each prisoner would get a cup of soup, though they doubted it. But after a short period, several police arrived with buckets of soup. It was hard to believe that prisoners were given soup meant only for the Germans. They learned later that several of the police had bartered with the chief cook to obtain the soup. During this period in Germany, nothing was done without bribery.

The women's column (Column 7) had been lodged in an empty warehouse without any facilities, not even hay or straw. The women were packed in so tightly they had to stand all night. They were blue from the cold when they came out. Police chief Guldbrand Nyhus and Dr. Gärthner acquired some coffee and gave it to the women prisoners. Nyhus and Gärthner had never seen so many humans in such a small place, and it was almost impossible for them to get past the door opening.

Several women had died right where they stood, and one woman gave birth. There were no toilets and the women relieved themselves where they stood. Just inside the door stood the Norwegian women. Nyhus and Gärthner passed them the coffee to distribute among the other women.

The other prisoners in Column 8 were lodged in a separate warehouse from the Germanic Column. By the warehouse entrance lay a Polish prisoner who had frozen to death, but no one seemed to care. The guards went through the warehouse and chased out several prisoners who, according to the guards, were trying to escape.

The weather was extremely cold and miserable, and the prisoners had to rub their faces regularly to prevent frost bite, though some did get frostbite and suffered for a long time afterwards. Immediately outside the gate lay a prisoner who had been shot. As the column passed the airport, they saw one body after another. Some were shot. Others were beaten to death.

Passing through Praust, the wind blew steadily, creating huge snow drifts making it harder and harder to pull the sleighs. From Praust the column proceeded north towards St. Albert, a suburb of Danzig. The road was well trodden and there was snow plowing, mainly from prisoners out on work details. The column entered a second suburb called Ora, where several police walked on the sidewalks. After a while all the Germanic Column did, while the other prisoners in Column 8 walked on the road. Pulling the sleighs on the sidewalks made it much easier. Neither the guards nor the civilians they met objected. The column passed English, French and Italian prisoners with snow shovels. The Italians especially looked at the police in surprise. After all, the police were dressed in Badoglio uniforms, and some of the Italians called out "*Banditos*". The police answered that they were "*Polizia Norvegese*". When they heard that, the prisoners changed their attitude towards the police.

After passing through Ora, the column encountered one steep hill after another, and several prisoners were unable to keep up. Those prisoners were picked out and sent off to a barn under the escort of several guards. The police knew what was going to happen to those prisoners, but they were unable to help them. Policeman Olaf Borgen, along with some Finnish prisoners, was sick and left behind in St. Albert.

Polish Prisoners

The Polish prisoners in Column 8 suffered much. One after another, they fell behind and ended up staggering around into the Germanic Column. There they would reach out with frostbitten hands to beg for bread, then fall over on the road. A guard would come and give the prisoner a kick or strike him with the butt of a rifle. This brought the poor prisoner to his feet until he fell once more a few meters further ahead, and there he remained. The guard would then kick him to the side of the road and put a bullet in him. On several occasions, relatives would come to the prisoners' aid to try to get them to continue. The relatives would go a short distance before a guard chased them away. Then the police would hear a shot.

Kalpole

Column 8 arrived at a location called Kalpole, where there was a military camp. There they were ushered into an area used as an assembly for prisoners, it even had a stage. The camp appeared to have been occupied recently because of beds in the guard quarters. It was determined that there should be two or three in each bed according to age and size. The rest were to lay on the stage or wherever there was room. The prisoners were greatly surprised when buckets of pea soup arrived. The soup was left over from the group that had recently left. At the military kitchen close by, they helped themselves to warm water. It was also where the *professor* set up his first aid station for prisoners who suffered from sore and aching feet.

The following morning, several police and a number of other prisoners in Column 8 were quite ill. If there was an ideal place to stay behind, this would be it. It was agreed that the sick in Column 8 would stay behind in Kalpole. However, none of the sick prisoners spoke German, Polish or English. Skjolden, who had problems with his feet, decided to stay behind as their leader. He was a good organizer and leader, and spoke German very well. In addition to Skjolden, ten policemen and several Finns, both men and women, stayed behind.

At 08:00 the column began marching on a narrow street named Radauenthal. A river ran beside the road with factories and power stations spread out along the river. It had snowed the previous night and the conditions were tough, with or without the sleighs. Prisoners started falling out of Column 8 right away. The guards no longer had patience with the prisoners and knocked them down and shot them. They didn't bother to kick the bodies off the road, and the bodies lay where they fell.

The column passed a prisoner who had just been shot in the chest and laid on the side of the road with blood streaming from his mouth and nose. A young German woman with a child came from one side of the road and passed by the dying prisoner. They stopped for a moment and then continued. It seemed they were accustomed to that kind of scene.

The brutal handling of the prisoners didn't impact the police as much as it had earlier. The consistent cruelty had become common place. The lack of compassion started to worry the police, and they feared developing an attitude of indifference to the suffering of their fellow human beings.

The column passed several bodies that had been there for some time, and in one place they passed a dead Jewish woman. That meant that the Jewish women in Column 9 had passed them, even though that column left Praust the day after them. It was now obvious transport leader Danesch had taken a wrong turn shortly after the column left Praust. Instead of marching directly to their current location, the column had made a circle north through St. Albert and Ora.

There was no traffic on the road the column was traveling, but it was hilly. The road went through large fields with huge snow drifts. The column struggled terribly. A fierce snowstorm began to blow.

After struggling for some time, the column changed to a road that was considerably better, there they stopped and waited for stragglers.

Nestempole

The column stopped for the day at around 15:00. The Germanic Column was sent into a barn on one side of the road, while the other prisoners in Column 8 were sent into a barn on the opposite side of the road. The place was called Nestempole.

A fierce snowstorm blew during the night. The storm was so severe that prisoners who needed to relieve themselves during the night couldn't open the door. It appeared to be a tough day for marching, so the column did not have to march.

On Tuesday, January 30, the column was ordered to get ready to march. By 08:00, the prisoners still had not received their marching orders. Several police prisoners began walking around the farm to stay warm. The farmer and his family were friendly, allowing as many prisoners into the kitchen as there was room, and offering them a hot drink.

At 10:00, the marching orders came, though the road condition was no better than the previous day. The wind had blown large drifts across the path, hindering their ability to march, not to mention to pull sleighs.

The column entered onto a wider road just outside Ellersdorf, heavy with traffic, cars and horse drawn wagons.

A Polish woman and her little boy had followed Column 8 for three days. Her husband was a prisoner at KZ-Stutthof and she thought he may be among the Polish prisoners in the column. Policeman Einar Nygaard pulled the boy on his sleigh for the next two days.

Maria Notwinski at Zukau

The column marched to a quaint little town called Zukau. In the middle of town, they came to a crossroad where traffic police stood directing Column 8 towards the town's east side. The column stopped near a railroad station as several people from the village gathered around the prisoners. The residents were friendly offered pieces of bread and water.

Column 8 was ushered into a large barn beside the railroad station. The barn had no straw or hay and was just one large room. That meant the Germanic Column had to spend the night with the other prisoners from the main camp, which they found disturbing. What that meant was they would forfeit their sleep to keep watch on their belongings. The Germanic Group would have rather slept outside.

The police learned that Hauptsturmführer Meyer was staying in Zukau. Some police went into town to try to locate him and to appeal for his help. The group returned without encountering Meyer but had learned there were no lodgings in town and the church was occupied with prisoners from Column 1. A few of the Germanic Column had disappeared and were able to find housing. They learned that if they went into smaller groups, there was a better chance to find a place to spend the night.

Magnus Kristensen went out to seek lodging for a small group. He returned and informed the rest of the police that Leif Horn and Claus Staurem had lodged at a small farm. The two were staying in a cow pen and there was room for several more. A few police set out and eventually found the barn. The doorway was low, and they had to crawl on their knees to enter, but they considered themselves fortunate to have found a place.

The men went to the house and knocked on the kitchen door, which was opened by a middle-aged woman. They asked if they could come in, wash and cook some canned food they had brought with them. At first, the woman looked at them suspiciously, but she let them in after a few minutes. She began right away to make stew from the prisoners' *Aladåb* (Swedish canned meat), with potatoes she provided. Simultaneously, the men were allowed to go into the living room to change their clothes and clean up. On the wall in the kitchen she had a heater that was heated from the kitchen stove. It had been a long time since the police had been in a real house; it was a great feeling to them. There were five police prisoners whom she served while she sat and talked with them.

It was unbelievable for the men to have a full stomach and feel warm in a comfortable room.

The men explained to the woman who they were and where they came from. She said her brother was a prisoner at KZ-Stutthof for a few months a few years ago, and that she was expecting him a little later that evening. Her husband, she explained, was in Slovakia. The woman's daughter, mother and sister lived with her in the house. Her daughter's name was Maria, a pretty and very bright little girl. The woman mended the policemen's socks while Maria proudly showed the men her schoolbooks. Maria told them all about herself and her family, and she became their favourite 'little darling'.

Maria begged the men to put her name in their diaries. The police explained that would not be wise, because if the journals fell into the Germans' hands with her name in them there could be a lot of trouble for her and her family. As a necessary precaution, the police gave her an imaginary family name: Maria Notwinski in Zukau.

After a while, Mrs. Notwinski's brother came. He was a Pole about forty-five years of age. He showed the police his *Entlassungsschein* (certificate of release) from KZ-Stutthof. It was signed by the infamous Max Pauli, who was the camp commandant at that time and a real devil. Their conversation was open and direct.

Zukau lay in an earlier Polish section established after World War I, and the population was overwhelmingly Polish. The Nazis used force to Germanize the area. The Polish language was forbidden and the Gestapo enforced the ban forcefully. The Gestapo would lurk behind walls and listen under windows to crackdown on people who spoke Polish. A large portion of the male population were prisoners in concentration camps, mostly at KZ-Stutthof. The remaining men were forced into work details, the same as the women. Mrs. Notwinski was recruited to shovel snow off the roads and had to be at work at 07:00 the next morning. The people were more than willing to take in evacuees, and the police found the population very knowledgeable about Norway. The prisoners explained to Mrs. Notwinski's brother that they were police officers from Norway, and he noted that they were different from other prisoners. The others nodded in agreement. The police explained they were arrested and sent to KZ-Stutthof because they refused to swear loyalty to the German occupying government in Norway.

In the morning, the police rushed over to the family Notwinski for breakfast and to say their farewell before they assembled at 08:00 to march. The order to march was delayed. The police went back to the Notwinski farm to help her. They shovelled the snow from the barn and walkway as a thank you for her kindness. Mrs. Notwinski informed the police the family had secretly listened to a BBC radio broadcast telling them that the Russian Army was quickly advancing westward. She said the Russians had captured several towns in the area, and she doubted the evacuation column would be able to get to Lauenburg or any other place.

Professor Starkus was called on to look at some sick people near the railroad station. He took his medical bag with him and disappeared. He was never heard from again.

Pommersdorf

From Zukau, Column 8 marched another nine kilometers to the small town of Seefeld, where the prisoners went to various houses to fill their water bottles. Some homes even gave them milk and pieces of bread, as much as half a loaf. The guards didn't say or do anything.

By 16:00, the column had arrived at the small town of Pommersdorf. The residents of Pommersdorf stood along the road and observed Column 8 in silence, but they didn't seem unfriendly. At Pommersdorf, the Polish prisoners were ushered into a church, then the doors were locked.

The Germanic Column was shown a large room in a school building close by, but it proved too small and several went out to find private lodgings.

The next day, Column 8 was ready to march by 09:00, but there were no orders to assemble and no marching orders.

The weather changed to rain during the night, and the conditions had turned wretched. There were several cars on the road going in front of the column, making the conditions better for marching.

Crucified Christ

At 11:00, the column received orders and marched the six kilometers from Pommersdorf to Lebno in just over two hours. In a churchyard on the outside of town, they saw people from the town throw bodies in a pile. There were close to one hundred bodies.

Occasionally, the prisoners heard shots in front of them. They speculated it was the partisans or their Polish friends that were shot. It proved to be the latter.

The column passed dead prisoners lying on the road;

they laid where they fell. One corpse made a particular impression on the prisoner column. For several days, the body had laid there with the flesh on his face torn away by birds and foxes. The corpse lay looking upwards at the crucified Christ statue, a statue familiar in a Catholic country like Poland. They passed several other crucified Christ figures and the Virgin Mary, where other corpses were laying. These prisoners could not carry on any further and went and bowed before the crucifix and the icons and prayed. The guards came from behind and shot them in the neck, but the prisoners knew this would happen to them.

At the entrance of Lebno was a large snowdrift, and several of the civilian evacuation wagons had become stuck. The town's people worked to dig them out. The workers took a few minutes to rest from shovelling snow and began to help carry dead bodies out of the churchyard as the Germanic Column stood and watched.

When the column began to march again, the rest of Column 8 was nowhere to be found. The group sauntered through town on their own. Some of the Finnish prisoners sneaked off to find provisions from the local houses. They were seen by members of the **Schutzpolizei**, who reported them to the transport leader. As the Germanic Column arrived at the end of town, Danesch came storming towards them, cursing and screaming for not staying with the rest of Column 8. If they didn't behave, he would treat them in a wholly different manner, he threatened.

From Lebno, Column 8 marched on a lonely road over a barren and dreary terrain. The Polish civilians stood fifty meters back from the road as the column passed. They watched in silence, though several civilians tried to give bread to the Polish prisoners as they passed but were brutally chased away. When the Germanic Column passed, they waved to them and moved forward to the roadside and gave them the bread. None of the guards said anything. Later, the column passed a dairy. A few policemen decided to pay the dairy a visit. The operator brought out one milk bucket after another and filled their cups.

Streep

Around 16:00, the column came to a town called Streep, approximately ten kilometers from Lebno. Here the column would stay overnight.

The other prisoners in Column 8 were sent into a school, and the Germanic Column was housed in a public hall a little further in town. There was a wood stove in a corner which they lit, but there was so much smoke they abandoned the idea.

The orders to march came at 11:00 the next morning. At first, it went reasonably well, until they came to the railroad station at Streep. There the road was blocked with rolls of barbed wire. The column was forced to continue on either side of the road. There was no indication of why the road was blocked by the wire.

The column passed Wahlendorf, the last town on Polish soil. That explained the barbed wire; it was the border between Germany and Poland. Rundown houses stood right up against the road, and the inhabitants were standing in their doorways and gardens to look at the prisoner column. One woman ran into her house and came out with a bucket of fresh milk.

Others came out with bread. The people gladly shared their meager supplies. Several guards came shouting and waving rifles. Soon the people scattered and went into their houses. The column was left standing while the guards scolded the prisoners.

Receiving food from the locals was always dangerous both for the giver and the receiver. A young Russian in Column 3 tried to take bread presented to him, but his hand was shot off as a punishment. An elderly lady threw a small basket of bread into the column when it passed by. A guard followed her and hit her in the face with the butt of his rifle.

CHAPTER 11 –
Evacuation Continues

The column continued its march over long fields and roads covered in snowdrifts. It became increasingly difficult, and several of the police abandoned their sleighs. At around 17:30, the column arrived at a town called Bukowin. It quickly became apparent that they were now in Germany. The streets and houses were cleaner, but inhabitants were more reserved and walked about with Nazi identification marks and the young people wore Hitler youth caps. Column 8 marched to a large estate on the other side of the town. There the Polish prisoners were lodged in the loft of a large barn. They were sent up a ladder with two guards stationed on top, and if they did not climb fast enough the guards would hit them with their rifles. There was a lot of yelling and shouting. The rest of Column 8 was lodged in a separate large barn. It was the most enormous barn the police had ever seen. It reminded them of the assembly hall at the University of Oslo. The middle of the barn was divided into pig pens with about thirty loud sows and their litter. At one end of the barn was hay and at the other, more stalls.

The prisoners were strewed everywhere, along the walls and in every available stall. It was too tight, with only a meter separating them.

The following morning, February 3, a strong but mild wind started to blow. At 08:00, the prisoners were ready to march, but as usual the orders were delayed. The prisoners took the opportunity to walk around the farm. The buildings were magnificent but had fallen into a need for repair. In the basement of the main house, the farmhands were busy cooking potatoes for the Polish prisoners. The workers said that the farm owner, who was German, was sitting in a concentration camp somewhere and his wife was the reason they were cooking for the prisoners. Two sacks of potatoes were cooked and delivered by cart to the Polish prisoners. All prisoners were given enough to eat, including hot potatoes to put in their pockets.

Torgeir Gjerde secured a wagon for the sick in the Germanic Column. Gjerde had made the arrangement with the mayor for two wagons and horses. One wagon was reserved for the sick, the second was to carry the baggage of those who were not well but could still walk.

Finally, at 10:00, the orders were given to march.

The column passed through Bukowin, and the road on the other side of the town was perfect at first. After the column turned off onto a country road, the conditions changed to wet snow and water puddles. After considerable struggle, the column came to a good road that led to the town Roslasin.

The column stopped at the outskirts of town and Danesch drove off to look for a place to spend the night. After approximately thirty minutes, he returned and informed the column there were no accommodations available. KZ-Stutthof Column 1 had arrived earlier and taken the only usable accommodation in the area. It happened to be the column which the police prisoner's friend Dr. Wojewski was part of.

There was no other option than to march to the next town where there was a RAD camp with lots of room, which the mayor of Roslasin had mentioned to Danesch.

The prisoners in Column 8 didn't understand why they were being driven so hard and had to march nearly every day. Other columns marched one day and rested the next. As a result, Column 8 caught up with Column 1, which left the day before Column 8. At 16:00, Column 8 left Roslasin and marched the six kilometers to Goddentow. It took about three hours.

Once the darkness set in, it became difficult to see. Several Polish prisoners took advantage of the darkness to make their escape. The guards shot indiscriminately into the forest, barely missing the prisoners, and forced them to dive into the ditch.

Eventually, they saw lights on the horizon from lanterns that were hung outside several houses.

On the road, cars were lined up behind emergency vehicles and the column was momentarily stopped. The wind started to blow snow into their faces, making them impatient to seek shelter at the RAD camp.

The prisoners moved closer to the center of the road, then a shot rang out. Policeman Lars Backer yelled out, *"Han ligger her!"* (He's laying here!) No one knew who was lying there. It proved to be one of the Polish escapees.

Goddentow

After a fifteen-minute march, the prisoners were relieved when they arrived at the RAD Camp, but it was full of prisoners. The column continued to march towards Goddentow. This was frustrating because the prisoners desperately needed to rest, and it meant another twenty kilometer march.

Column 8 came to a large barn just outside Goddentow where they would rest for the night.

The Polish prisoners were directed to the right. The rest were directed to the barn's left side, and the two were separated by guards between them. The Germanic Column grabbed their belongings from the freight wagon and burrowed themselves into the hay. The time was 22:00. The prisoners had marched for twelve hours.

The next day, February 5, the prisoners were awakened at 07:00 with the news that there would be no marching that day. Some police hadn't taken off their rubber boots from the night before, and their feet were swollen. They had difficulties in getting their shoes off because of the swelling. Thankfully, since there would be no marching that day, they could heal their swollen feet.

The police learned that Hauptsturmführer Theodore Meyer was in the town of Goddentow. Danesch had warned the prisoners not to seek accommodations in private residences. It obviously made a difference to Danesch that Meyer was in town.

Several had already secured private accommodations the night before, contrary to the transport leader's orders. Others also decided to go look for private accommodation. At one house, a police group headed by Finn Dahlin found that there were already three or four staying there, but still asked if the group could get a cup of coffee and some pieces of bread. The woman informed him that she had so many to feed that she couldn't spare anything more. However, the woman changed her mind and sat them down, insisting it would be the only time. The police finished quickly, thanked her and left immediately. All the Norwegian police prisoners agreed that they would always conduct themselves respectably. The police would never use pressure or tell lies. There was still the danger that a policeman may go too far, reflecting negatively on all of the police prisoners.

A few Finnish prisoners misbehaved, especially the one the police referred to as No.13. He had such a long name none of them could pronounce it. No.13, and a couple of his Finnish friends, was repeatedly the first to take off from the column when they stopped. They went from house to house and rudely conducted themselves. No.13 knew a little bit of German, just enough to get what he wanted.

Dahlin and his group knocked on the door at one house and asked the woman if they could come in and wash and cook some food for themselves. She hesitated at first but then agreed. After they had washed and shaved, the woman placed a large dish of steaming cooked potatoes and bacon with onions before them.

The woman then proceeded to tell the police that her husband was in Slovakia, much like Mrs. Notwinski had told them of her husband. The woman continued and talked about her brother. He was driven out of Finland by the Russians and evacuated into northern Norway, where he was now stationed.

The police gave her three children some candy they had received in a package from Sweden and gave her a Norwegian sardine box as a thank you. Both of these items were a rarity in Germany during this time.

A Close Encounter

The woman and her children went off to church, and the police went back to the barn. The woman invited them back at 14:00 for some cooked oatmeal, and they accepted. As Dahlin and his group sat and ate, two German soldiers asked if they could cook some food, and she said yes.

The soldiers believed that Dahlin and his group were part of a training detachment. The soldiers opened up and spoke quite candidly with the group. One soldier had fought on the Eastern front and said he had been in a battalion surrounded by Russians. Only a few managed to fight their way out, and he said the whole thing *"ging zur Hölle!"* (went to hell!). The police thought it was best to get out of there before the soldiers figured out who they were.

The following day the column began marching at 08:00, for once without having to wait. The column marched through the town of Lanz, where the road was excellent and frozen solid, with large fields on both sides of the road. At this point, Column 8 had significantly been reduced.

At each stop, the column spread out on both sides of the road to relieve themselves, men on one side and women on the other. It seemed bizarre as most prisoners had hardly any food to eat yet went to relieve themselves. *"Sie bekommen nichts zu essen, aber sie immer noch Mist Steine!"* (They don't get anything to eat, yet they still crap stones!) commented Danesch. It was something completely different than stones that came out; every one of them suffered from stomach ailments. Their stomachs must have been totally ruined from lack of nourishment and hygiene.

A road sign informed the column they were nearing Tauenzin. At 12:00, the column entered a RAD camp that lay on the outskirts of town. A few police were ordered into a barrack used as eating quarters and an assembly hall to make it presentable. The Polish prisoners were to be lodged there. The women were accommodated in a room in the administration barrack. The Germanic Column was given a barrack with four rooms and a total of sixty-one beds. The Finns were assigned one room, and the rest occupied the other three.

The Germans can be applauded for their road signage. There were signs everywhere, at crossroads and in large and small towns, which gave information about direction, distances and locations. Unlike with the signage in Poland, Column 8 never had any problems knowing where they were in Germany.

Below is a summary of the march so far, including the dates, places and distances.

Date	March From	Sleeping Arrangements	Distance Marched
January 26	Sonderlager	Barn by Klein Zünder	25km
January 27	Klein Zünder	Airport near Praust	17km

January 28	Praust	Barn near Kalpole	25km
January 29	Kalpole	Barn near Nestempole	6km
January 30	Nestempole	Dairy near Zukau	7km
January 31	Zukau	School in Pommersdorf	18km
February 1	Pommersdorf	Assembly hall in Streep	17km
February 2	Streep	Barn in Bukowin	16km
February 3	Bukowin	Barn in Goddentow	22km
February 4	Goddentow	Rest day	–
February 5	Goddentow	Tauenzin	12km
		Total Distance	**165km**

The RAD camp was located at the back of a large farm. Two rows of large elm trees ran from the farm and into the camp, which consisted of two large barracks side by side and a smaller third barrack that lay a little to the side of the other two. In front of one of the barracks was a grass lawn with a flag pole; fortunately, there was no Swastika flying, the prisoners said to themselves. The place was quite muddy with slush and full of water puddles. Members of the Volksturm, a national militia established by the German Army, were present. The Volksturm members consisted of males between the ages of sixteen and sixty who were not already serving in the German military. These particular Volksturm members were mostly older men with beards who wore strange clothing and were armed with old musket rifles. The mayor and members of the city council were occupied in a long and heated discussion with Danesch.

The Polish prisoners, with their usual shouting and screaming, were ushered into the first barrack. The rest of Column 8 was assigned the second barrack. The third barrack was for the camp administration and the transport leader. The guards were housed on a farm nearby.

Transport Leader Danesch

The transport leader, Danesch, was a Wehrmacht officer of fifty-five to sixty years of age. When the police left Sonderlager, Petersen advised them that the Wehrmacht had many scores to settle with the SS and SD. Danesch wasn't really the smartest of officers. His specialty was to go in the wrong direction, which the prisoners discovered on several occasions. However, to his credit, Danesch did not encourage mistreating the prisoners and put a restraint on the guards on several occasions. In that respect, he showed his humanitarian side.

Shortly after Column 8 arrived at the RAD camp, Danesch was stricken with influenza and became bedridden. Olav Takle and Gjerde nursed him back to health. The transport leader now trusted the Norwegian police totally and gave them much freedom. Danesch and Anders Eckhoff often talked while marching.

The Germanic Column had now been significantly reduced in numbers. During the morning roll call on February 6, a count was carried out of all prisoners in Column 8. Of the eighty-one Norwegian police who left Sonderlager, sixty-nine remained. Twelve of the police prisoners were left behind: Olaf Borgen and eleven others at Kalpole. Of the Finnish prisoners, forty remained, including four women. The Finns lost four prisoners underway.

Of the approximately 700 other prisoners who left the main camp in Column 8, 267 were missing. Many of the Polish prisoners would not make it much further. Several of the Germanic Columns were also in no condition to go much longer.

Column 8 had marched 165 kilometres in eleven days, less two days for rest. The pace was certainly not that impressive, but when one considers the conditions under which the prisoners had to march, it was a remarkable accomplishment.

The sick ones, and those not quite recovered from their stomach ailments when the column left KZ-Stutthof, suffered greatly under the march. Whatever they ate came back out like water. Several of the Germanic Columns were unable to eat at all. The police had witnessed brutal attacks on other human beings in Column 8. Sick and starving prisoners were driven forward with kicks and beatings. One guard in a green uniform bragged that he had broken two rifle butts on prisoners. The brutal treatment of prisoners began to weaken the police. The evacuation was an effective way for the Germans to rid themselves of the sick and weak prisoners. It also effectively demoralized the survivors and broke them psychologically and morally.

The police applauded when told by Eckhoff that they were to stay in Tauenzin for three to four days.

CHAPTER 12 –
Evacuation Eastward

The camp was a work camp for young girls, which was evident by pieces of paper with names and addresses on the side of the beds and on the cupboards. Over the following days, they came across schoolbooks, letters and postcards along with feminine items.

On the first day, the prisoners were occupied with personal hygiene. Due to the number of prisoners and the limited facilities, the first day was mainly spent brushing teeth and washing faces.

Next to the Germanic barrack lay a stack of coal, and the prisoners were permitted to get all they wanted. Even the Polish prisoners were allowed. Pieces of wire were strung for drying clothes, and the prisoners were extremely thankful to put on dry underwear.

The day after Column 8 arrived, most of the Germanic Column was required to go out on work details to the neighboring farms. At first, they were upset that they were made to work so quickly after such a challenging march, but it would prove to benefit them.

The oven was always warm, and the only trouble they had was finding wood for kindling. The prisoners gathered what they could find but occasionally had to take wood from the barrack walls. There was much cooking and frying over the oven, and boiling water for washing – not only for themselves personally, but also their clothes.

The prisoners received a ration of 200 grams of bread each, which was the first ration of bread the Germans had given them since they left KZ-Stutthof. The only problem was that the 200 grams was their total ration. Each prisoner also received a bowl of soup made by women from the town. The prisoners were warned that such provisions wouldn't continue. As a result, the police devised ways to secure food for themselves and the other prisoners. At first, the police would use potatoes and carrots left behind in the camp. The prisoners lived more or less on those potatoes and carrots. This quickly became boring. Worse, they were running out. The bland food and the lack of activity contributed to stomach problems. The daily activity consisted of sitting around a large tub peeling potatoes. The kitchen happened to be in the Polish barracks close to where Hauptsturmführer Meyer was staying. During the march, Meyer would appear now and then. When Column 8 was in Tauenzin, Meyer resided in Lauenburg, a town of 26,000 residents that had swelled to nearly 60,000 during the evacuation.

On one occasion, Hauptsturmführer Meyer threatened Danesch with arrest because he was unable to control the prisoners. The Finnish prisoner, No.13, was the main problem. No.13 had gone around in his usual manner and looked and acted like a criminal, causing local residents to fear him. The residents complained to the city mayor, who complained to Meyer, who had ordered the work commandos. Meyer ordered that No.13 was not to be part of the work details and not to go near the town. Despite the order, No.13 and one other Finn continued to go to town. They were both arrested by the **Feltgendarmeriets** folks and released after a strong discipline. No.13 and the other Finnish prisoner were ordered to appear before Eckhoff, but they refused. The Finns were then brought by force. After being interrogated, they were brought before Hauptsturmführer Meyer, who dealt with them.

The Police Cooks

Small work commandos were sent out regularly, and the workers were well taken care of. For payment, they were served three meals. The main issue was securing food for those back at the camp who were too sick and other prisoners who could not get out of the camp. It was important for the sick to receive nourishment to restore their health because the order to march could come at any time.

Magnus Kristensen found a butcher on the other side of town that was relatively modern for a small country town like Tauenzin. The police cooks were given permission to cook soup at the butcher shop. At first, they were given permission to only cook every other day, but eventually they were allowed every day. The butcher and his wife were compassionate people, but were cautious at first. After a short time, the cooks were accepted, primarily because they handled themselves in an honorable manner. Although there were pieces of meat lying around, the cooks never once helped themselves to anything. The cooks were then trusted and given much freedom. Occasionally the prisoners would find a generous portion of meat in their soup. The three police cooks were extremely good at making soup. A number of the old horses in the area found themselves in the soup.

On occasion, a hind quarter was cut up and put in a grinder to be made into meatballs. Supper at 16:00 included sixteen meatballs each. The prisoners were glad the Germans didn't eat horse meat. The local residents had nothing to eat but soup, although it must be said that the soup was delicious. Thankfully, the food helped bring the prisoners through this period. After fourteen days, the portions to be divided increased, and there were no restrictions on food rations. Even the civil defense members were given rations brought back by the work commandos.

A local farmer had to butcher a pig with a broken foot. The farmer invited the cooks to take the pig on one condition: only prisoners could eat it and none of the guards were to have any part of it or know anything about it.

Eckhoff spoke to Danesch about it, and they formed a plan. Danesch sent the guards on a mission at a different location. Simultaneously, Gjerde and several others left with a bedsheet. The group returned shortly, carrying between them a forty- to fifty-kilogram pig. The pig was placed in one of the rooms. That evening, John Ljosland, along with several other police prisoners, prepared and cut up the pig. The following day the prisoners had pork roast for supper. There were pork chops and pork stew and soup for many days afterwards.

The cooks gave Danesch a good portion for his cooperation.

Danesch was relatively good towards the police and the Polish prisoners. He went around to the various farms to secure horses ready to be slaughtered. He tried to do whatever he could for the prisoners. Quite often, farmers came with old horses they hoped could be of value to the prisoners. The horses ended up in the stew. Occasionally, the prisoners were given horse livers; the livers were fried in the oven in the prisoners' rooms.

A Time for Reflection

Some police took the opportunity to catch up on writing in their diaries. The diaries became a sort of therapy to relive the events and a chance to get out their frustration and aggression in a nonviolent way. They could close their eyes and ears to the earlier horrible events. It was clear that the police became more and more accustomed to the cruelty they witnessed that they thought unbelievable just a few days earlier. Sadly, the gravest cruelties did not have the same impact on them as before. Perhaps it was their conscience's way of adapting to their circumstances, enabling them to continue to survive.

To this point, the march had left the prisoners famished; they would consume a large amount of food and sleep all day. They hoped they could stay at their present location for the rest of the war. The police often thought and talked about their colleagues in other parts of Poland and wondered how they survived. The Russian army was advancing rapidly from the east. Many regions of Poland had already fallen to the Russians. Several thousand KZ-Stutthof prisoners should have been freed by the Russians by now, they thought. How would the Russians treat their colleagues?

If the Russians were that close, why could the prisoners not hear shots or explosions? The only evidence of Russian advancement was the large columns of refugees fleeing from the east.

Mainly women and old men were left to do the work in the district. Therefore, the demand for laborers was high. The mayor of Tauenzin asked Hauptsturmführer Meyer to leave one hundred Norwegian prisoners to work around the district when the colony left, saying the town would feed and house them. "*Kommt gar niche in Frage!*" (It is out of the question!), answered Meyer. He informed Danesch that the work details were to bring back food for the rest of the prisoners. The police had already practiced this for quite some time. It had always been the police's goal to work for food for all the prisoners, especially the sick.

Mrs. Tarnowsky

It didn't take long for the German civilian community to distinguish between the Norwegians and the other prisoners. On one occasion, a small group of police prisoners were chopping wood for Mrs. Tarnowsky on "Main Street", as it was called. The woodshed was attached to the kitchen with a narrow walkway between. There were a couple of large maple trees estimated to be at least several hundred years old that laid before them. The timbers, it seemed, must have laid there for six to seven years. While the police were busy chopping, an elderly blind woman put her head out the window and explained that she was a refugee from East Prussia and had no one to chop wood for her since she lived alone. She said, "*und die Norwegen sind so angeneheme Leute!*" (the Norwegians are such nice people!)

Mrs. Tarnowsky provided the police with breakfast, veal cutlets and a glass of wine for supper, together with cake and coffee for an evening snack. She asked the police how much she should pay them, but the police declined and said they had been paid through her generosity. It was pleasant for the police to be in a private home and eating in a clean and finely decorated kitchen. While the police were eating, Mrs. Tarnowsky joined them and began chatting. She was curious as to who they were and thought they might be officers. The police didn't deny it. She cautiously asked what their opinion was regarding the German civilian evacuation ahead of the Russians. "*War es wahr, dass die Russen die Kinder in den von ihnen besetzten Gebieten getötet haben?*" (Was it true that the Russians killed the children in the territories they occupy?) she asked. The police answered that they didn't believe so, and she agreed.

Work details continued as long as Column 8 remained in Tauenzin. The civilians the commandos worked for were always kind and generous towards them, except for one!

The Stingy Widow

The Bonschwitz Estate was owned by a young widow whose husband had been killed at the Eastern Front. The work detail to the Bonschwitz Estate became known as the *den gjerrige grevinnes arbeidsdetaljen* (the stingy widow work detail). The widow ordered a work commando of twenty-five men, and the first detail was deployed on February 13. When the workers returned, they complained that they were only served thin oatmeal soup for breakfast and worked all day in the forest without food. When they returned at 17:00, they were served the same light oatmeal soup. The workers complained to the widow, and she promised better food the next day. However, she didn't keep her promise, and the workers returned as hungry as when they left in the morning. Instead of bringing food back to the camp, the workers ended up eating in the camp. Eckhoff told Danesch that it served no purpose to send work details to Bonschwitz as the workers came back as hungry as when they left. He argued the workers could be used at other work details that would benefit the camp. Danesch explained that Hauptsturmführer Meyer had given the widow his promise of the work detail.

The following day, when the names for the work detail to Bonschwitz were read out, several refused to go. After some heated discussion, Eckhoff laid down the 'law' that if anyone refuses to go on a work detail, they will not be allowed to go on any work details. That became the standard. The Bonschwitz work detail was reduced to twenty men.

The work detail left camp at 06:00 and marched for fifteen minutes over a field to the Bonschwitz Estate. On this particular day, the commando was directed to a dark room in the basement. The room proved to be the servants' kitchen, which was small. The workers crowded around a small table, where they were served a hearty oatmeal breakfast by a cheerful Polish woman. The woman told them, *"Gut Essen, gut Arbeit"* (Eat well, work well). They were also given a glass of milk.

After breakfast, the commando mounted a large hay wagon and travelled for two hours. The wagon drove through Tauenzin eastward, among the shifting landscape of open fields and small country communities. The destination was a wooded area on a small town's outskirts, where the commando felled, cut and split wood all day. Before they left for the day's work, the widow came to the kitchen and told the workers they had to cut one cubic meter for each worker, plus one for the cook and one for the Kapo; twenty-two cubic meters in all.

While they were working, a cold wind started to blow and the workers had to labor in all their clothes to stay warm. At noon the Kapo gave each worker two pieces of bread; one was dry and the other had *pultost* (a soft, spreadable sour milk cheese flavored with caraway seeds) without butter. There was nothing hot to drink. They all felt it was a lousy work detail. The workers returned to the estate at 16:00, where they were served stew containing a couple pieces of meat. They were told they could eat as much as they wanted. Afterwards, the workers were each given a stack of straw to take home.

The work commandos often saw other war prisoners and wondered how free they actually were. In most cases, the other prisoners seemed to freely go about between farms, from one landowner to another. The prisoners seemed to be trusted, especially the French and English, who often had positions of responsibility. Several had been prisoners since June 1940, nearly five years after the tragedy at Dunkirk.

Secret Organization

Column 8 workers were told by the farmers that earlier, Russian prisoners served in the district as farmhands until it was discovered they had a secret organization. The Russians held secret meetings in the forest and their tools were to be used as weapons. The plan was to take over as leaders in the community when the time was right. The Germans discovered their plan and executed most of them. There remained very few Russian prisoners in the region at this point. One Russian prisoner confided to the police that there was still a small underground movement.

By mid-February, the Column 8 prisoners had become quite comfortable. Considering the circumstances, they were well off.

The power to the camp blacked out continuously, at times remaining off for days. As a result, the police decided to build their own lamps out of bottles with *solarolje* (sunflower oil) and wool threads as wicks.

The Germans were very concerned about transmitted diseases, especially lice and the possible spread of typhus. The prisoners were ordered to hand in their underwear for disinfection. Three German soldiers were travelling around with this new *Abwehr von Läusen* (defence against lice) that would guarantee their clothes to be free of lice for three months. The process consisted of a powder mixed in water to rinse the clothes. The clothes were then hung outside to dry because of the strong hydrochloric acid smell. The process was not as simple as one may think because there was a snowstorm outside. The prisoners had to put on their underwear before they were dry, and they all smelled of acid from afar.

The prisoners' underwear was so worn that it would hardly stay together. In fact, the holes were more extensive than the material.

Farmer Patsowsky

A farmer just outside Tauenzin named Fritz Patsowsky hired a wood cutting work commando. Herbert, the farmer's fourteen-year-old son, came out of the house with a small bag of tobacco that the workers divided. There was enough tobacco to last them for two days. They asked Herbert if he smoked. Herbert looked at them confused and explained that, in Germany, it was a punishable offence to smoke before age eighteen.

The other prisoners in Column 8 had it markedly better than before, especially the Polish prisoners. The Poles were left more or less alone by their tormentors and had a bearable living condition, but there was a lot of sickness among them. Every twenty-four hours, three or four Polish prisoners died. There were now only 250 Poles left.

Wagon from Kalpole

On the evening of Saturday, February 24, the supply wagon arrived with Skjolden strolling behind. Skjolden was initially left behind at Kalpole with eleven others from the Germanic Column. The group remained in Kalpole for three days before being driven the same route as Column 8 to Zukau, where Skjolden had a chance to speak with Hauptsturmführer Meyer. Meyer gave the group permission to take the train the rest of the way. Each member of the group was left on his own to try to get a place on the train, but the train was full. Skjolden was the only one able to board the train. Later, Skjolden ended up in a school at Lauenburg until he was ordered to follow the provision wagon to Tauenzin.

Skjolden explained that the Germans intended to evacuate the KZ-Stutthof prisoners in Lauenburg's direction and continue on to KZ-Sachsenhausen. This, however, was prevented by the Russian advance.

The next day, a small platoon of police prisoners came marching into camp, along with one Finn and six Lithuanians.

On the morning of February 25, a column of Jewish women prisoners marched into the camp, followed by two sick prisoners' wagons. They were a smaller group of Column 10 from KZ-Stutthof/Burggraben. Early in February 1945, two columns left KZ-Stutthof consisting of 1,500 Jewish men and women prisoners. They were joined by a column of 991 Jewish men and women prisoners from Burggraben sometime after the middle of February, making it a column of about 2,500 prisoners. Column 10 was later split into several smaller columns, and one of the columns ended up in the camp at Tauenzin. The women had nothing with them. The Germanic Group gave the women straw to sleep on, which they brought back from the widow's estate. They looked after these women with supplies and support for as long as the women were in the camp.

Red Cross Packages

The police learned from a guard that there were rumors Red Cross packages had arrived for them in Lauenburg. Danesch gave permission to send a small detail to Lauenburg and arranged for a horse and wagon from farmer Mede. The wagon returned with 115 packages distributed among the Norwegian, Finnish and Lithuanian prisoners.

Each package contained one-kilo oatmeal, a box of pork, fruit marmalade, crispbread, vitamins and malt drink.

One day forty private wagons arrived with civilian evacuees from the town of Königsberg. The evacuees looked tired and worn and said they had been travelling for five weeks and were now to spend three to five days resting in Tauenzin. The town was to look after them.

As usual, the evacuees were mostly women and children, together with several older people, with prisoners as drivers.

The refugees were fleeing from the Russians to the East, hoping to land under Allied forces' protection in the west. What lay before them were profound hardships.

Several events indicated the end of Column 8's stay at Tauenzin was near. All the road signs had disappeared, and different contingents of prisoners marched past with all their belongings. All the SS guards, the civil defence and the communication soldiers working on laying the telephone cables disappeared. Only prisoners, Wehrmacht soldiers, guards in black uniforms and local residents were left.

The police followed the movement of the German and Russian troops with detailed interest. Each evening they overheard the German communication with the high command in Germany. The police plotted the troop movement on a map Skjolden had brought with him. While out on work details, they would read the newspaper *Lauenburger Zeitung* and occasionally hear the news over the radio while eating at the farmhouses.

August Walth

During the early days in March, three police prisoners were on work detail at farmer August Walth's in Karlkow about two kilometers from Tauenzin. It was a fun work detail because there was very little work to do. Along with his wife and two daughters-in-law, August Walth had earlier evacuated, fearing the Russian advancement. They eventually returned and found their home had been used to house evacuees from East Prussia. The police were hired to help put the house in order, but the job didn't take long, and afterwards they sat in the living room and chatted. After that, Walth took them into the forest to cut firewood, which also didn't take long.

Walth treated the police well. He fed them fried bacon, lots of potatoes with gravy and pea soup. They were also able to fill their pipes with Walth's tobacco. The police were convinced that farmer Walth was mostly interested in gaining some good references if, or when, the Russians came.

They heard, on the evening news, that a Russian tank division had reached Köslin. Walth's farm was eighty kilometers from Köslin and fifteen kilometers from the Baltic Sea.

Russian Advancement

The prisoners learned that the Russian army had reached Kolberg west of Köslin and the Baltic Sea. Column 8 was now cut off from the east, west and south. To the north was the Baltic Sea. On the morning of March 7, they heard bombs from the direction of Stolp, which lay fifty kilometers west of Lauenburg.

The prisoners in Column 8 all wondered what the Germans' plans were. Would they evacuate via Leba, march to Gdynia and out from there or would the Germans leave the prisoners in the camp? They couldn't imagine being evacuated towards Leba, seeing as the town was most likely full of refugees, sick and wounded. Skjolden had mentioned earlier that the road from Lauenburg was full of ditches where the Germans were dug in with artillery, undoubtedly fighting the advancing Red Army. The latest rumour was that a Russian tank division approached Lauenburg and the town was in chaos. Der Kreitsleiter (the district manager) was hanged, apparently because he was unable to carry out his duty. The town had obviously become lawless.

On a roll call on March 7, there were only 120 Polish male prisoners; 80 were sick. Five to six Poles died every night. Most of the Germanic Column survived well in Tauenzin, although a few had become ill. On the morning of March 9, Danesch gave word that Column 8 must march as soon as possible. The word was the column was marching to Gdynia. The prisoners were also told they would be evacuated by boat if they were evacuated at all. A rumor circulated that several ships with refugees had been sunk in the Baltic Sea.

Eckhoff and Gjerde drove to the widow and were promised a wagon and two horses. Nothing was of value anymore with the Russians so close. The cooks prepared many potatoes and opened a Danish pork box to give the prisoners a substantial meal, not knowing what the future would hold. The meal was just finished when Danesch called for them to assemble outside. *"Antreten zum abmarschieren!"* (Line up to march!)

CHAPTER 13 –
Germanic Column

At 18:30, the prisoners had just rushed out of their barracks when a good-sized hay wagon pulled by two horses arrived. The wagon was provided by the widow Bonschwitz, as she had promised.

The sick were to ride in the wagon and the half-sick would put their packs in the wagon. It appeared there were quite a few who all of a sudden felt too sick to carry their packs. This was not the intention, and it took quite a while to sort out the packs. In the meantime, no one noticed that Danesch, the guards, Polish prisoners and Jewish women had left before the Germanic Column. When the column was ready to march, they discovered they had been left behind. No one had seen which direction Column 8 went. The Germanic Column marched to the intersection by the railroad station they passed before entering Tauenzin a month ago. There were no guards to be seen and no Column 8 or road signs to follow. They found themselves in a very peculiar situation. Being left behind provided them with a golden opportunity to escape. They discussed whether they should go back to the RAD camp and let fate take them where it will or try to catch up with Column 8.

The discussion was lively, and one could say their circumstances were bizarre as they found themselves in the middle of a country road intersection on a dark night in war-torn Germany. The entire horizon, except to the north and east, was lit up from explosions and fires. Occasionally it was so bright that it lit up around the prisoners. The group agreed that they could not remain behind, as it would look too much like they were trying to escape. They risked the guards coming back to shoot them as escapees, which they had witnessed on many occasions.

Wagon with Packs

A civilian worker came riding his bike out from the nearby forest and informed them that he had passed Column 8 on a narrow road that led to Saulin. This was the same road that the wood cutting commando had travelled several times through the woods. They now knew which direction to travel. The roads were laden with heavy snow, making it difficult for the wagon. Besides sick police and several sick Lithuanians, many of their packs had found their way on to the wagon. Eckhoff and those who were half-sick followed the wagon and were confident they were on the right road.

The Germanic Column came across an elderly woman who laid on the side of the road with her eyes closed; she didn't have much time left. Continuing further, an elderly woman keeled over. As the column passed her, a young woman came crying and threw herself over the woman. Several bodies lay by the roadside as the column passed. Darkness had set in, but the light from explosions lit the road. Explosions and loud thuds were heard all around them, also from the southeast. They learned later that evening that Danzig had been extensively bombed. Now and then, they heard shots in front of them and would march towards the shots.

The Wagon Became Separated

The wagon became bogged down, and several in the Germanic Column were needed to push it. Magnus Kristensen and Ivar Homnes, among several others, went back to help push the wagon. The rest debated if they should stop and wait for them, but decided against it. They reasoned that it wouldn't be long before the rest would catch up.

Eventually, the Germanic Column caught up to Column 8 and took their place at the rear of the main column. On March 10, Column 8 passed the small country town Saulin, the earlier wood chopping work location. The prisoners were told there was an estate close by. Danesch went to investigate. A shot was heard in the forest, and Danesch came rushing back with orders to turn around quickly. The column turned around and headed eastward, putting the Germanic Column in the front of Column 8. The weather had become windy with snow flurries making the conditions horrifying. Military vehicle convoys passed the column regularly, making it difficult to walk on the narrow road. When the Germanic Column left Tauenzin, they only had the opportunity to pack a little oatmeal and some sugar. The oatmeal was so dry it clung to the roofs of their mouths, and all their other provisions were on the wagon.

In front of Column 8 lay a large open field. It was very quickly filled with men and women prisoners that squatted to relieve themselves.

The civilian evacuees stopped to frantically look for overnight accommodations before it got too dark. If the evacuees didn't find a place, they would stay in their wagons. As soon as it became light, the evacuees filled the roads in a futile effort to fight their way westward. Sadly, the prisoners regularly saw dead horses along the roadside.

Danesch Panics

Column 8 continued to Rieben railroad station, then turned off onto a smaller road that would lead the column to a RAD camp where they would spend the night. Once in the camp, Danesch had the guards take roll call. It turned out that several Norsemen were missing, and it was rumored they had escaped. The police advised Danesch that the missing Norsemen had turned back to help with the wagon. Danesch asked for Eckhoff, and he was told that he was with the wagon. *"Ja, das überrascht mich nicht, der Schlaue!"* (Yes, that doesn't surprise me, the shrewd guy!), answered Danesch.

At the RAD camp, other KZ-Stutthof prisoners were lodging. The police recognized several of the prisoners and Kapos that were part of Column 6 from Barracks 12 and 15. Danesch learned that there was typhus in the camp and ordered Column 8 to march back to the Rieben railroad station. The Polish and other prisoners were called into a large machine shop at the station, while the rest of Column 8 was taken to a barn. There was a strong protest from some of the farm women, but the SS guards chased them away. It was now 22:30, and the prisoners had been marching continually since 18:30 the night before. Danesch told the police they would be there till the following day, and they were ecstatic!

The police had a good view of the machine shop, when suddenly they saw prisoners come streaming out and a man come running towards them waving his arms. They recognized it was Danesch, who was screaming, "Gleich fertigmachen Antreten!" (Get ready right away. Line up!). Danesch was completely beside himself; he was cursing while ushering the Germanic Column out. Standing in the barn door, he yelled, "los – los!" (go – go!) while waving his pistol. The prisoners were somewhat confused, as earlier they were told they would be there till the next day, but it didn't take them long to figure it out.

Quickly, the Germanic Column was ready to go. The other prisoners in Column 8 were lined up in front of the machine shop and were also ready to go. The police discovered that Jacob Jacobsen was missing from the column, and when the marching orders were given they saw Jacobsen lift his arms but then drop them again. He showed signs of having hepatitis.

The Germans were panicking at this point! Danesch continued waving his pistol, and the guards drove the prisoners forward using their rifle butts, yelling *"los – los!"* (go – go!). The police didn't have a chance to follow up with Jacobsen before they were underway, but they saw Jacobsen standing and leaning against the cement wall as they were leaving. It looked like he had given up. The police comforted each other with the thought that maybe Jacobsen regained his willpower, and he would be ok.

That did not happen. Jacob Jacobsen died that night.

When Column 8 approached the RAD camp, they noticed that those prisoners were also being evacuated. Everyone in the camp was to be evacuated, except for the sick. The column passed a supply wagon at the camp's outskirts, where a man stood with open crates throwing margarine packages to those passing by. The police grabbed several half-kilo packages.

There had to be something dire happening for the Germans to be in such a panic. It was learned that the Russians were within a couple of kilometers of Column 8. Fear of the Russians had panicked Danesch earlier, and that explained why the column did a U-turn.

At 15:00, the column entered the main highway where the traffic was at a standstill. As far as the eye could see, ahead and behind was one continuous column consisting of all types of vehicles. The stop 'n go traffic moved less than one hundred meters at a time.

Travelling on foot, the prisoners could move faster by maneuvering around the vehicles. The column passed vehicles where they heard children crying and saw many desperate faces staring back at them.

Most were evacuating westward, though a few were heading eastward. The situation was chaotic, and with no control the civilians were in a difficult situation. With the speed they were travelling, the Russians would no doubt overtake them very soon. The civilians would then be forced to travel back to ransacked and burning farms.

An earlier group of KZ-Stutthof prisoners, including some Danish prisoners, came marching from a field and joined Column 8. The prisoners explained they had been at the RAD camp for several weeks while working for the Germans and digging ditches for German tanks. It was clear that the Germans intended to take a stand, but the Russian army had advanced too quickly. Column 8 turned off the main highway and onto a farm road. A few hundred meters down the road lay a farm where many prisoners had gathered. As the column got closer, they saw that bread had been thrown out and some of the prisoners were fighting. Others were yelling and screaming while chasing each other out in the field. Here, it appeared, the strongest would survive. The scene was uncomfortable for the police. It was chaotic and lawless, with no guards to be seen anywhere. The police were shocked at the prisoners fighting all around them and couldn't understand how they could carry on in such a way. They then realized that they, too, would have acted the same way if they had been as hungry and desperate as those prisoners were.

Mingling with Other Prisoners

At this point, Column 8 had broken up and many mingled with the other prisoners. Several guards had turned back to take care of the stragglers. The same cruelty and brutality the police had witnessed before would be applied to the dawdlers. The chaotic scene before them was in stark contrast to their beautiful surroundings in the forest. The prisoners were exhausted and entirely spent after marching around the clock. The column passed a twelve-year-old boy who was so tired that he could hardly stand on his feet. His father tried desperately to take him with him but decided to stay with his son. A guard came with a pistol in his hand. Shortly afterwards the prisoners heard two shots.

Two young Jewish girls were crying and trying to convince their elderly mother to keep moving. They fell behind, and the police never did find out what happened to them. But they could imagine the worst.

A Polish prisoner sneaked in among the Germanic Column. After looking around for the guards, he dashed into the forest and gave the police a wink. A few moments later, from a hill to the left of the column, Russian artillery was heard. The road continued over the hill, and at the top of the hill Danesch came riding on his horse. He clearly looked exhausted. The police asked him where they were marching to, but Danesch just shook his head and said he didn't know.

The column marched for another two hours before they came to the main highway. The side trail through the forest had obviously been a short cut. The traffic going west was larger than the prisoner column travelling east. Going east, Column 8 could only cross over the road in small groups.

The prisoners were continually bumping into horses and wagons, and the whole thing seemed hopeless. Several times the police attempted to join the prisoners in Column 8, but they were again separated. The police were of a particular group of Norsemen that tended to cling together. At 20:00, the police turned into an open field and were directed into an area by a couple of men passing by. There the police were united with the Germanic Column.

Close by was the local police station, and Skjolden proceeded over to inquire about lodging for the night. He was directed to a Wehrmacht staff office on the other side of the highway. The Wehrmacht officer just shrugged his shoulders and told Skjolden to take a place wherever he could find one.

Seeking Accommodations

The Germanic Column sought accommodations in private houses, but every place was occupied with Wehrmacht soldiers. Four guards came up to the column and told them to accompany them to Putzig. It was an uncomfortable night of marching and the conditions were terrible, with wet slushy roads coupled with a strong wind. Thankfully, the traffic had slowed down and soon the column had the road to themselves. Only an occasional military vehicle convoy passed them. The column marched half asleep. Even the guards were exhausted, occasionally one would stoop over.

Finally, after an hour, they rested. Dahlin found a wood stump to sit on, and a Polish prisoner came and sat beside him. The Pole fell asleep while leaning against Dahlin. A car came by and shone its light on them for a split second. To Dahlin's horror, the Pole had part of his chin and mouth missing, and he could see right into the man's gums.

There were no signs to indicate how close the column was to Putzig. Again and again, the prisoners complained to the guards that it was too far to march at night. Finally, the guards agreed that they could lodge in a barn as soon as they found an unoccupied one. In reality, the guards were themselves too exhausted to continue. The guards checked each barn they saw, but the barns were all full. After some time, the guards finally found one that was not occupied, and they all dove into the hay. It was around 01:30. The place was called Darslub.

The prisoners awoke at 06:00 on Sunday, March 6, with orders to start marching in thirty minutes.

When the orders came to line up, Dahlin went into the barn to check that no one was left behind. Beside a wall, there was a cap sticking up out of the hay. When he lifted the cap, he looked right into the face of the Polish prisoner he met on the wood stump the night before. It took quite an effort to wake him. The prisoner looked terrible. What was left of his lips was bloody and swollen and dangled loosely. He was obviously shot at close range. The whole right side of his chin was torn away.

After an hour's march, the prisoners saw the ocean. It was Danzig Bay on the Baltic Sea. They could see the long peninsula shaped like an appendix and the popular town of Hela at the end of the peninsula at a distance. The guards had become quite accommodating, so when the prisoners suggested they needed a break, the guards agreed. After a short break, they continued and met a Hauptscharführer riding on a horse. A tall, lanky person, he was the prisoner column's transport leader stationed at Rieben.

He directed the column towards a farm alongside the road and instructed them to wait there. As the column continued, their old friend and transport leader Danesch came strolling down the street. They greeted each other wholeheartedly.

Danesch never brought up the fact that they were late in joining the march. He told them that if they didn't hear from him, they should march to a park in Putzig and be there by 11:00.

Putzig

Putzig was not far away, and they arrived there in short order. The park in Putzig was to be an assembling place for all stray evacuation columns. When the Germanic Column arrived, a significant number of prisoners had gathered and more kept coming. The park had a low fence around it, and the local residents would walk around the fence and look at the prisoners. They had now come back to the Polish section under the march, and the residents were openly friendly. They were now in the former Kashubian region of Poland. For many years, the region had a strong anti-German population that had been bounced between Poland and Germany. It was easy to contact the residents, and they sneaked several food packages to the prisoners. They even took letters through the fence to mail for some of them, indicating that some prisoners had a real knack at finding ways to make contact with sympathetic guards, fellow prisoners and civilians.

In the park were the remainder of three KZ-Stutthof columns. The rest of the three columns were cut off by the Russians. There were 100 left in the Germanic Column, divided between Norsemen, Finns and Lithuanians. The police accepted that the wagon containing their sick friends, along with their belongings, was now in the hands of the Russians.

Twenty-two men were left behind, among them Anders Eckhoff and Magnus Kristensen. Eight policemen had escaped into the forest. The police also wondered what had happened to Jacob Jacobsen. Of the 700 male prisoners that marched out of the main camp in Column 8, only 60 were left. Of the 200 Jewish women in the column that followed Column 8 from Tauenzin, only 50 survived. Approximately 600 prisoners were assembled in the park, but more kept coming.

After an hour of waiting, the prisoners were ordered to assemble by none other than Hauptsturmführer Theodore Meyer, who came strolling into the park. Meyer conducted a short inspection and then ordered Danesch to take a roll call. They surmised that Meyer was now the leader of the KZ-Stutthof evacuees.

Orders were then given to march. The prisoners went out of the park and onto a crooked and narrow road. Then they marched through the large gate of a local brewery. As they marched in, Meyer stood on a platform and gazed down on the prisoners. The guards lined up inside the gate, followed by male prisoners in Column 8. Those prisoners were rushed into the basement of the brewery. Taking up the rear of Column 8 was the Russian bath guard from Tauenzin. He was drunk and tried to protest, but was given a kick and fell headfirst down the basement stairs.

Following the male prisoners came the women prisoners through the gate. They were directed to a warehouse a little further on.

The police estimated there were about 100 women that passed through the gate. The Germanic Column was the last group, and they remained standing for a time. The group was ordered to pick ten men to arrange lodging for the rest of the column. Skjolden took command of them and followed Meyer down towards an outbuilding that the men cleared for the column. The building was used as a stable and along one side stood horses. The other side was unoccupied but had straw spread on the floor as an under cushion. The column settled in and got as comfortable as they could.

The Jewish Women

The Jewish women were lodged just outside the building. Whenever the police went in or out, the women surrounded them and begged for some straw and hay. The women were afraid they had to overnight outside and worried they would freeze.

The Germanic Column had been asleep only a few hours when they were awakened by terrible screams and shouts. There was such commotion they thought the Germans were massacring the women. It proved to be that the women had been given bales of hay and were fighting over them. It was a clear and cold night, and the women were afraid they'd freeze to death in their thin prisoner uniforms.

At about 19:00, everyone had quieted for the night. The Germanic Column lay close together along the wall and outward to the middle of the floor. If one had to go to relieve himself, he would have to climb over bodies and legs. There was a little light from some lanterns hanging in the stalls where the horses lay. The SS guarded the entrance and prevented the women from trying to get in from their hell hole outside. Several women made it into the building despite the guards.

The prisoners were awakened at 21:00 by what sounded like brakes squealing from a locomotive. It squealed several times and sounded like a signal. They also heard artillery fire at a distance. Shortly after, a guard came in and spoke with the stableman regarding *Die zwei Braune* (the two brown horses). The stableman went in and loosened the two innermost horses. The horses were used to having lots of room around them. One of the horses jumped out into the hay where people were sleeping. The people jumped up or rolled around and pulled their legs towards themselves for fear of being trampled. Luckily, none of them were trampled on. There came, however, a loud scream from a woman who had sneaked into the building. The horse had stepped on her stomach, and she lay there screaming in pain. The worst always seemed to happen to the women.

It became quite apparent something was happening, and the prisoners began to pack up. It was too much to expect a full night of peace. Then someone yelled through the door, *"Nordmänner und Finnen und Ehrenhaflinge machen sich bereit, bald mit dem Marsch zu beginnen*" (Norsemen and Finns and political prisoners get ready to start marching soon).

The Germanic Column pulled themselves outside and assembled. As they did, the women rushed inside. On their way out, the police saw the old Lithuanian that roomed with them in Tauenzin. He was lying just inside the door and did not indicate that he wanted to go with them. He just shook his head and sadly said that he was sick and unable to march any further. He wanted to stay behind and face whatever would happen. The police knew what the cost would be for this decision. Political prisoners could count on being shot or hanged by the Russians. There had been too much collaboration with the Germans in their homeland. There was nothing left for the police but to wish him well and say goodbye.

Tjiremesin

At 21:30, the Sonderlager group marched out of the brewery gate and continued through the streets of Putzig. Several large explosions, along with gunfire, could be heard close by. A large contingent of guards surrounded them, and they overheard the Germans had received orders to withdraw from Putzig. There were no prisoners with the guards. That led to the speculation that the prisoners were probably killed by the Germans. It was not until sometime later that they learned the prisoners' fates. Dr. Gärthner informed them that 1,500 men and women prisoners were locked in the brewery basement in Putzig – the same brewery the Germanic Column stayed in. The Germans had locked the door and nailed the windows shut. After this, everything was quiet. Unusually quiet! A Russian prisoner, Tjeremesin, pried the door lock and sneaked out while most of the other prisoners slept. A short time later, Dr. Gärthner also went out. In the courtyard, he found Tjeremesin lying dead over a strangled SS guard. Beside the SS lay several boxes of Zyklon-B poison. Apparently, the prisoners were meant to be gassed, but Tjeremesin prevented the execution. To this very day, a plaque on the outside wall of the brewery reads, '*tutaj armia rosyjska uwolniła 1,500 jeńców z KZ-Stutthof 12 marca 1945 roku*' (here the Russian army freed 1,500 prisoners from KZ-Stutthof on March 12, 1945). The police prisoners also learned that the

Germans selected 243 prisoners to be marched away and shot that night, burying them in the churchyard.

Column 8 left Putzig on March 11 at 21:30 – just ahead of the Russians entering the city – and marched towards Gdynia. The occupation of Putzig actually began at 03:00 on March 12. The road was wide, and the column made good time. The column came to a large intersection beside a dairy and was commanded to rest just past midnight. Several police prisoners said they had seen Danesch sitting by the roadside looking sick and despondent. He seemed to have lost his drive to continue.

There was a lot of traffic on the road now; Column 8 was forced to take a side street. The street was steep and slippery, making it difficult to walk in the dark. The prisoners struggled for several hours until they came to the main road again. On the main road was an endless parade of wagons and sleighs. After a while, there was an opening in the traffic and they could continue on. Column after column of trucks drove past the prisoners with their loads sticking out, occasionally knocking down those walking.

Dahlin was among the last in the column. He had developed sores on his feet and sat down on the roadside to change into his rubber boots. After he had finished changing, he discovered he was alone. The others had disappeared. A couple of guards stood with their rifles by a tree nearby and looked at him. *"Können Sie nicht weiter marschieren?"* (Can't you march on?), asked one of the guards. Dahlin figured out they were an after patrol that was ordered to shoot stragglers. *"Ja, gewiss!"* (Yes, certainly!), Dahlin answered as he slung his backpack on his back.

CHAPTER 14 –
Back To KZ-Stutthof

At dawn, the column came to a crossroads. The road to the left was the faster way to Gdynia, but it was blocked; to the right was groves of trees. Coming towards them was a detachment of about thirty to thirty-five men carrying artillery, with a lieutenant in the lead. Most of the squad was young boys. Their appearance was not particularly military, and they looked tired and wasted as they marched towards Putzig. It suddenly occurred to the prisoners why there was no traffic coming from behind; they were the last to leave Putzig. The detachment they met was to engage the Russians advancing from behind the prisoners.

Column 8 came to the little country town of Kasimir. Just inside the forest lay a camp only thirteen kilometers from Gdynia. They saw several wagons, horsemen and a captured Russian soldier laying against a stone fence. The Russian was clearly not dead, as the prisoners passed they could see he had color in his cheeks and was breathing. He had most likely been captured recently, indicating the Russians were not far away.

The column passed several houses on their left and open terrain with rolling hills and no buildings to their right. Around them they saw camouflaged artillery that had previously shot over the prisoners' heads and towards the advancing Russian army. While marching, the prisoners saw a continual barrage of explosions from Russian grenades. The shots went over the prisoners' heads, aimed at the German artillery locations. They were concerned about being caught in the middle of the artillery barrage.

Column 8 kept bumping into German artillery divisions scrambling to re-establish their positions in front of the advancing Russian army.

The traffic had increased significantly with a variety of different vehicles parked overnight.

The column came to Gutenberg, a suburb of Gdynia. There were now only six kilometers left. At Gutenberg, the column stopped to assemble themselves, as it had spread out. After marching a little further, it was discovered the column was on the wrong road. It was too far to go back. The column then turned and marched through several fields in the direction of Gdynia. The areas had fences to climb and ditches to cross, making the journey difficult. A sudden air alarm and anti-aircraft fire drew their attention to a Russian plane swerving through the clouds. The scene ended as quickly as it started. The column came to a large railroad work yard, where rows of trains were neatly lined up. This was Gdynia! So began the long march towards the center of the city. The prisoners had now arrived in the area of a *Kriegsmarinenlager* (Naval War camp) in the harbor.

The prisoners were made to camp at a cinema. Skjolden took command of a work commando to gather sacks of sawdust to spread along the walls and floor. The sawdust was spread relatively thin, but it was a good insulator against the cold and hard cement floor. The prisoners were each given a scoop of kohlrabi soup. The best part was it was warm. The soup was the only provisions they had received since leaving Tauenzin three days earlier. They were able to use the washroom to clean themselves in a nearby Red Cross barrack.

After getting oriented, the prisoners realized the cinema was actually a prison camp. It was in the middle of the harbor. Approximately 400 meters from the camp lay two German cruisers. This made them feel very uncomfortable. On the other side of the cinema wall came a terrific explosion intended for the cruisers. While still at the Sonderlager camp, the police remembered hearing of a bomb that hit a prison camp in Gdynia, killing and wounding many prisoners and soldiers. Among the fatalities was the former Barrack 19 Wing B cabin chief, Gutlob Kübler. The police also recalled that Dr. Wojewski had to travel to Gdynia and help with the wounded.

There was no electricity in the cinema; therefore, things had to be done during daylight hours. By 18:00, it was dark. There was nothing to do then except lay down and sleep.

At 20:00, they were awakened by a deafening sound. For a brief moment, they sat on the floor stunned, unable to think. They were quickly informed that the area was under attack, putting the prisoners in a panic mode.

Someone was whispering the same thing repeatedly, and it proved to be a Lithuanian who had been outside during the first explosion and was in shock. He kept repeating, *"Wir werden bombardiert; wir sollten besprechen, was wir tun werden"* (We are going to be bombed; we should discuss what we are going to do). His voice became louder and louder, when all of a sudden a Norwegian voice called out, *"Hold kjeft og legg dere til å sove!"* The words were aptly spoken by Kristian Østensvig, (Shut up and lay down and go to sleep!).

After breakfast on March 13, the prisoners were ordered to march toward Danzig. They were happy to comply. The cinema was not a safe place for them. Six policemen remained in Gdynia; they were recruited at the spur-of-the-moment by Organization Todt, a state organization for building and road construction. Skjolden put it upon himself to get the police work detail with him on the march and gained permission to go down to Organization Todt and negotiate. He came back with the promise that the men would be given back when the column marched through the city. However, that promise was not kept.

At 10:00, the column marched out from the Kriegsmarinenlager, over a tall bridge in the center of town and continued through the picturesque city of Gdynia. It was a lovely city and the damages were slight, but the destruction was great in the suburbs on the outskirts. Several places were cratered from bombs, and houses were levelled. Roofs and walls were missing from many homes, enabling them to see different floors with people crying and gathering their belongings. Parts of horse flesh lay spread all over the streets. The smell from artillery was everywhere. The road bore the great name of Adolf Hitler Strasse and connected Gdynia and Danzig with all of their suburbs.

There was great confusion on the road, with a continuous evacuation stream towards Danzig and military columns travelling in both directions. In several places just inside the street curb lay scaffolding of large timbers. The timbers could easily be tipped over to block the road from the advancing Russian army. The column marched through the beautiful Zoppot beach and came to a Red Cross food station in a park beside the road. The prisoners were told to take a twenty-minute rest and that the food station was set up for others, not them.

The kitchen help drove around giving food to the military, but ignored the prisoners.

Danzig

The march continued between Oliva and Langfuhr, both suburbs of Danzig. In Langfuhr, the prisoners were pleased to see several damaged German planes. Approaching Danzig, the prisoners saw more and more of the German defence measures. The Germans dug trenches, landmined the road junctions and built barricades of large timbers. In the alleys were trees cut in half that could easily be overturned to block the road. Explosive charges were also tied above and below the trees. In Danzig, the Germans had dug trenches in parks and gardens.

The column continued marching partly on the road and partly on the sidewalk. The column came upon an evacuation wagon in the middle of the road. The prisoners saw the grizzly scene of the horse's body still in the harness while its head lay further down the road. The column marched for another hour and came to the older part of town towards the harbor. This was an area that Gisle Ianke was well acquainted with. It was one of the work commandos he was on earlier while still at Sonderlager. He was an excellent guide as they marched through the area. The column came to a stop and then waited. The guards drove off to a food station while the transport leader flirted with a female SS guard nearby.

When the column started again, they were told they had an hour march in front of them. After marching for quite a distance down to the harbor, the guards realized they had been traveling in the wrong direction, and the column did an about-face.

Troyl Labour Camp

Finally, around 17:00, the column arrived at Troyl work camp. It was a central work camp under KZ-Stutthof, the main camp.

Troyl lay on the outskirts of Danzig on an upward slope southwest of the city. It was at this camp that prisoners from KZ-Stutthof stayed during the work detail in Danzig. The column went into the camp single file. The Danish director Andersen appeared and told them several Norwegians were in the camp.

The police were reunited with eighteen of their mates. The prisoners were provided with a good portion of warm soup and a piece of bread, the first real food they had received since leaving Tauenzin. The prisoners were distributed between rooms 21 and 22.

The rooms were poorly equipped with bedding, and most of the prisoners lay on the floor. Martin Presthus, on the other hand, hijacked a bed that even had a mattress.

The only food the prisoners had as they marched was the scoop of kohlrabi soup in Gdynia. The distance between Tauenzin and Danzig was 109 kilometers.

The Russian army was on the heels of Column 8 the whole time they were marching. Watching the Germans' conduct, the prisoners assumed the column could have been overrun at any time during the march. The Russians captured Gdynia a short time after Column 8 had left. The prisoners found themselves in no-man's-land, caught between two evils.

On the morning of March 14, a roll call was taken where 61 Norwegian police, 1 Dane, 33 Finns and 9 Balts were tallied for a total of 104 men. Of the 61 Norwegians, 43 were from the original Germanic Column and 18 from the Nickelswalde work detail. Of the 76 policemen that started on the second leg of the evacuation from Tauenzin on March 9, only 43 entered Troyl. Of the Germanic Column of 121 Norwegian and Finnish men and women, only 86 had survived the death march thus far.

The Finnish prisoners were immediately transferred to a different camp upon their arrival at Troyl. Einar Hjellemo was selected as the police leader in the absence of Eckhoff. Hjellemo had served as the foreman on the Nickelswalde work commando and had proved to be a skillful leader.

The police were assigned two rooms, and another two rooms were occupied by women. The women were members of a Jehovah's Witness sect and had arrived directly from KZ-Stutthof. The male Jehovah's Witness members were conscientious objectors, which is almost unheard of in Germany. The male members were given an ultimatum to join the war or be detained in a concentration camp. They chose the latter. The female members were somewhat at peace with the Nazis, even though they interpreted the Bible differently and were against Hitler. The women had it relatively good in KZ-Stutthof main camp; one member had even served as a nanny to Hauptsturmführer Meyer.

The Germanic Column arrived at the Troyl camp with tattered clothing. Their pants had gashes on the knees, and the backside was torn in several places. This was no problem as long as there were only men around, but now there were young women. Kristoffer Hval was a master tailor, and their clothes were repaired in no time.

After arriving at the camp, the police were asked to provide twenty volunteers to be transferred to the Kahn work detail at Neufahrwasser. The commando was promised better food, but it also meant working on the docks. Several volunteered and were sent off. The food was much better, but the danger was greater in Neufahrwasser. A grenade had exploded in the camp of the Finns, who were transferred there earlier. The constant barrage of Russian rockets that flew over the city exploded in the region of Neufahrwasser.

New Transport Leader

Unfortunately, on March 17 Column 8 got a new transport leader who decided the police should be treated as ordinary prisoners and did everything possible to make their lives miserable. Hjellemo sought to leave the camp and go to the post office in Danzig. There he intended to ask about the police's mail for KZ-Stutthof. The mail for KZ-Stutthof arrived from the main post office in Danzig and was then forwarded from there. The haughty transport leader denied his request to leave the camp without a certificate. Further, the transport leader ordered a lineup and picked out another twenty-five men to pack their belongings and go to the Kahn work detail at Neufahrwasser.

To everyone's surprise, several of the older policemen had to leave, among them were John Trøen (50) and Martin Presthus (57). Sometime later, the Finns arrived back in Troyl camp. During evening roll call, there were thirty-seven Norsemen, forty-one Finns, and nine Balts.

On March 18, several prisoners arrived in the French camp adjacent to the Germanic Column. The French prisoners were better off than the Germanic Column and had their own camp director and camp officers. Every day they were out on work commandos in the Danzig vicinity, and every evening they returned with a variety of goods they had *orge*. The Germans knew about it but did nothing to stop them.

Column 8 was trapped on both sides. On the one side was the French prisoners, and on the other was the Jehovah's Witness women.

Sanitation became a big issue. There were two holes cut in a small shed, one for the men and the other for the women, with a thin wall separating the two. The walls had large cracks in them so each could sit and wave to the other. On several occasions, the toilets overflowed. Occasionally, prisoners from the French camp came and dumped their toilet buckets in front of the Germanic Column's windows. There were long lineups in front of the toilet, and if one really had to go, he would relieve himself somewhere outside. This lack of sanitation could become a serious health issue if the prisoners remained there for a long time and the weather warmed up. In order to not get sick under such conditions, the police exercised cleanliness whenever possible.

Watching the Fireworks

Troyl camp lay on a ridge that afforded a good view of the waterfront, the city and the innermost part of Danzig Bay. It was like being seated in an Amphitheater.

They could see the city come under attack from four Russian planes. Smoke rose from anti-aircraft shells exploding all around them, but the aircraft swerved and the planes were unaffected.

A continuous stream of planes appeared over the city, and when darkness fell the spectators experienced a rare spectacle of spotlights catching the aircraft in the light cones and holding the planes captive while the anti-aircraft artillery kept shooting. Thousands of projectiles rose and exploded all around the planes. The aircrafts soared around in circles like ghosts, without being hit. Shrapnel from the German anti-aircraft shells exploded over the prisoners' heads and fell inside the camp. The spectacle lasted until evening, and strangely enough the air raid sirens didn't go off until several hours after the attack.

There wasn't a single German aircraft during the attack, which led them to believe the German Air Force was destroyed.

Early the following day, explosions that lasted for several hours were heard from the direction of Zoppot. This time the air raid siren sounded for thirteen minutes, though nothing happened.

Around 18:00, the roar of many aircrafts flying into the city was heard. The planes were Russian, easily recognized by their stumpy form. The German aircrafts were much sleeker. The curtains went up for a repeat performance of the day before, but this time the Russian planes dropped bombs continually. The bombs lit up the city as one squadron after the other released their bombs. The sound was deafening.

Each squadron disappeared from view then reappeared to inflict more havoc. The bombers initially appeared to be targeting a location south of the camp. It now seemed the bombs were getting closer. The prisoners found it unnerving to be outside and rushed back into the barracks. At least the barracks gave them a certain sense of protection. Then there was a deafening explosion that shook the barracks and knocked out the lights. Several prisoners jumped out of their beds and crawled under them while others rushed outside, reasoning it was better to be outside than to have the barracks fall over them! A piercing cry came from the camp, where half of the sanitation barrack fell over. The bomb that narrowly missed the barrack left a vast crater. Several prisoners had fallen into the toilet, and one guard was wounded. The crater was only one hundred meters from the Germanic Column barrack. Outside, the action continued, and some preferred to stay out. The Jehovah's Witness women did what they usually do under such situations; they gathered in their rooms and sang hymns.

A Russian plane was hit and swirled towards the ground, the pilot parachuted out. The spectators watched as the Germans fired at the parachute. A second and third Russian plane was hit, and the explosion lit up the sky.

The bomb attack lasted for nearly two hours. The last two days' attacks had rattled the prisoners, and they assumed the attacks would only worsen. The camp offered little protection for the prisoners, and they felt like rats in a trap.

The Russians were now thought to be only ten kilometers from Danzig and had advanced into the suburb of Langfuhr.

Explosions continued the next morning and were getting closer. The big event that morning, March 20, was the transport leader ordering the Germanic Column to pack and evacuate for KZ-Stutthof. The evacuation would happen early the next morning. The news was received with great joy.

What concerned the prisoners most was if the Russians carried out new attacks it could prevent their evacuation. The Finnish prisoners did not receive the same order to evacuate. The least popular Finnish prisoner, No.13, came on his own to Troyl that afternoon. No.13 had an adventurous journey from Rieben, but no one had missed him!

Troyl to Stutthof

The Germanic Column was awakened at 03:30 the following morning. They were given coffee along with a large piece of boiled meat from the camp's chef. The chef and the police cooks had become good friends. The column was also given a loaf of bread and butter for their marching ration. It worked out to six men per loaf of bread.

The column marched out of the Troyl camp at 05:00, under a **Scharführer** (squad leader) and surrounded by several guards. They traveled through the old part of Gdansk, which now showed a lot more war damage than when they arrived eight days earlier. As usual, the column took a wrong turn heading in the Reichsbahnhof station's direction, but the train going east was at the Kleinbahnhof station. The column proceeded full speed to the Kleinbahnhof train but was too late. The train had left!

An SS guard informed them the train left at 05:30 with several Norwegians aboard. The guard proved friendly and accommodating, stating the police would only be in KZ-Stutthof for eight days before being evacuated to Pillau. He also mentioned there were thirty police prisoners working at Weichselbahnhof reloading trains. Without being asked, the guard stated the war was "kaput", and it wasn't long before it was over.

The police boarded a couple of open rail cars and started their journey eastward at 07:30. It was sunny but cold, and a strong wind blew, making the trip miserable. The train was exceptionally noisy, but they were pleased not to be marching on foot. Russian bombers were seen flying overhead and heading towards Gdansk's old town; the column had just evacuated.

The train had stopped at Gotteswalde when five Russian fighters swept low over the train. Everyone on the train jumped off and hid wherever they could find shelter. Fortunately, the fighter planes didn't fire. Russian fighters frequently flew near the train but didn't open fire.

The road along the railroad tracks was full of what looked like bottomless mud, where vehicles were stuck and cadavers of cows and horses lay.

When they stopped at Klein Zünder, they saw the same barn where they stayed the first night of the "Death March". The wind had now picked up considerably as the prisoners were ferried across the Weichsel River. They now sat on a real train and away from the wind. The train had several cars with large timbers that proved too heavy for the locomotive. When going up the slope to the dikes, the locomotive would take a run and barely make the incline. At the top of the dike stood several rail cars, allowing the police to be reunited with some of their group. The commando had been working in Danzig and took the train the original police group missed. The reunion was jubilant as they hadn't seen each other for nearly two months. When the train started again, Russian fighters appeared. The train stopped and everyone rushed into the fields for safety. German anti-aircraft artillery opened fire, and it became apparent that the anti-aircraft battery was what the planes were looking for. No one on the train was hurt.

Once again, the police saw the old, familiar places and had a strange sense of coming home! They marched into KZ-Stutthof main camp at 13:00 on March 21, 1945.

Looking back showed that the entire evacuation march, including stay-overs in Tauenzin and Troyl, lasted for fifty-five days – from January 26 until March 21. Of those fifty-five days, fifteen were marching days. During the first part of the march to Tauenzin, the column travelled 163 kilometers in eleven days.

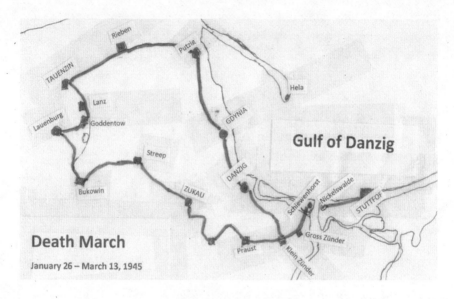

The Death March Route

From Tauenzin to Troyl they marched 109 kilometers in four days, for a total of 272 kilometers in fifteen marching days. Because of poor navigation by the transport leaders, the column marched several times in the wrong direction, so the actual distance was more like 300 kilometers: approximately twenty kilometers per day of marching.

A few days after the police evacuated the Troyl camp, Russian aircrafts dropped leaflets over Danzig and gave the city an ultimatum to surrender. If the city refused, it would be eradicated. The deadline was March 26. Gauleiter Albert Forster was determined not to surrender and stated that Danzig would fight to the last man. Russian bombing then began in earnest, dropping bombs weighing up to 500 kilograms on the city. Russian bombers dropped load after load of bombs on Danzig, and the damage was extensive. The prisoners sat on the roofs of their KZ-Stutthof barracks and, with amazement, watched the bombs explode and the anti-aircraft fire exploding like little cotton balls around the aircraft. The concern was the police work commando in the Danzig area. Without the Danzig work detail of thirty men, and the five men work detail at Werderhof, the police members were now 193 in the camp, from the original 271 Norwegian police prisoners.

CHAPTER 15 –
Main Camp Stutthof

The reunion among the police members at KZ-Stutthof was earnest and heartfelt. The police who evacuated had lost almost everything they had, and what they carried with them was practically nothing. For what they had experienced during the Death March, they considered themselves fortunate. All food provisions provided upon leaving the Troyl camp were gone. The reunion was celebrated with bread and pieces of horse meat.

The police members who did not evacuate now lived in Barrack 5 in the main camp. With the return of the evacuees, they were all transferred to one half of Barrack 12. There were already Danish, Finnish and Baltic prisoners in the barrack. The section of the barracks allocated to the police was 175 beds. This was not enough! Therefore, the police rigged up fifty new beds in the dining room, with a very narrow path between the beds. The person going through would need to go sideways, but there was also no place to eat.

Meals had to be eaten on the bedsides or on top of beds. There were no lights, and water was available for one hour each day. There were only two basins between 220 men! The toilet proved useless without water. With so many men under such circumstances, the conditions became quite appalling. In short, their accommodations were cramped, dark and dirty.

Nothing noble could be said about the German leadership either. At the morning assembly on March 21, the disgusting little Lagerältester Otto Selonka was wearing his riding pants and boots, with a long whip in one hand. Selonka gave a speech, in which he sneeringly mentioned the police were in the same class as other prisoners and must greet superiors with *Mützen ab* (Hats off). Their barrack leader, an old German, was not a criminal – an exception to the rule. During a discussion once, he had said something unfavorable about Hitler. Though his punishment had long since expired, he was forgotten and was still in the camp. He was somewhat cranky and took little interest in what was happening in the barrack. The chief executioner at KZ-Stutthof was now SS Oberscharfürer Ewald Foth.

There were now 3,000 male prisoners, and a corresponding number of female prisoners, in the KZ-Stutthof camp. Another 1,200 prisoners returned to KZ-Stutthof a few days after the police arrived. There were between 7,000–8,000 prisoners in the camp at this time.

Returning Evacuees

When the Germanic Column returned to KZ-Stutthof, they suffered from mental stress. After their two-month ordeal, several developed depression. The constant reminder of marching day and night, witnessing human tragedy, starvation and pain took its toll on the police. But one thing they took pride in was that they conducted themselves tolerantly and respectfully. Now it had come to this! Being harassed and abused as *Häftlinge* (Prisoners) and *Svinehunder* (Pig dogs), and by such low lives!

Barrack 12 was dirty and disorganized. Not even during the Death March was their accommodations that cramped and dirty. The prisoners had no place to eat, no room to move, no tobacco, no water and no electricity.

Andreas Irgens served as the leader of the police left behind in the camp. During a general meeting of all the police, they unanimously agreed that Irgens should continue. He was well known and well respected by the camp authorities. The police also unanimously decided that Julius (Julla) Hordnes should continue as the 'Germanic-kitchen' chef. Hordnes had shown excellent skills as a cook and was very popular among the Germans.

Commandant Werner Hoppe had left the camp. Hauptscharführer Paul Ehle took his place as the camp commandant.

The police all agreed that Irgens should try to convince Ehle to accept their wishes to move from Barrack 12. Irgens brought their request before Ehle, and he agreed. Ehle said the police should move to *Altes Lager* (Old Camp – also known as the women's camp), into a building called *Tischlerei* (Carpentry shop). Irgens, along with a few men, went to inspect the conditions of *Tischlerei*. It didn't look good. However, the bright spot was that the police could leave their cramped conditions and have more space. They would also have their own camp management, and this lifted their spirits. Petersen arranged for other Germanic prisoners to move with them.

Another result from the meeting with Hauptscharführer Ehle was that Irgens received permission for the *Mützen ab* to cease immediately. At evening roll call that same day, when the old grumpy block leader commanded *Mützen ab*, not one policeman obeyed the order. The block leader looked utterly astonished. He sprang forward and shouted: *"Warum?"* (Why?). Selonka, who was standing behind him, was made aware of the situation and amused himself. Selonka explained that the greeting was not in effect for the police prisoners. To the police's delight, the old block leader had to stand and deliver his report to Selonka with his hat in hand.

The fierce bombing and artillery fire over Danzig continued each night. The police watched the performance. Though they were relieved not to be in Danzig anymore, they were deeply concerned for their members still in the town.

As they watched, they could see fighting in the easterly direction, which was in the region around Königsberg and Elbing. The explosions sent shockwaves through the barrack, causing the walls to vibrate.

At night, Barack 12 stood unguarded. This meant that anyone could sneak in and steal the police's possessions under the cover of darkness. Their packs were stored outside for lack of space inside the barrack. For those not out on work commando, arrangements were made to stand guard over the belongings while the rest slept.

Other Prisoners Return

The Finns from Troyl arrived at KZ-Stutthof camp the following day. They said they were transferred to the same labor camp the police vacated. During the morning roll call, the camp was hit by a bomb killing the *Lagerältester* (senior camp elder) and the *Blockschreiber* (camp clerk) standing in front of the assembly. The same fate came to a Finnish boy. If the police hadn't left the camp when they did, the tragedy could have happened to them.

The female Jehovah's Witnesses arrived at KZ-Stutthof the following day and were housed in the women barracks at Altes Lager (Old Camp).

The SS guards lost more and more interest in bullying the prisoners. The guards were now more concerned about their own fates, as they realized that the war would soon be over. The police took advantage of the situation to gain more freedom.

Tischlerei

On the Saturday morning of March 24, the police moved to *Tischlerei* in *Altes Lager* and proceeded to wash and disinfect the floors, ceilings and walls. *Tischlerei* was a 55-meter-long barrack without any rooms. The first thing they did was divide the building into separate rooms.

The Norwegian civilians, Danes and Balts got five rooms between them while the Finns got one. The forty-five oldest Norwegian police were awarded the westernmost room, referred to as the *Gamle hjemmet* (Old Home). The other three rooms were each divided into fifty, fifty and forty-five police in them. Irgens got a private room in the middle of the barrack. There was also a large laundry room beside the Old Home. After sectioning off the rooms, they collected materials to make beds.

Next to *Tischlerei* was a pharmacy, a hospital and an isolation unit. Just outside the barbed wire was the hideous gas chamber and crematorium.

Directly in front of *Tischlerei* ran a wide street that the prisoners walked on in the evening; it served as a courtyard. During the morning roll call on Palm Sunday, March 25, a total of 187 Norwegian police, 72 Finns, 1 Dane and 7 Balts were tallied. Among the missing were twenty-six policemen at the work detail in Danzig. That work detail arrived the next day and was among the last to leave the town, although Kristoffer Søbø and Trygve Thomasgaard were left behind. They came back to KZ-Stutthof a week later.

In early April, several Poles came wandering into the street in front of *Tischlerei*. The Poles were themselves crammed into a barrack across from *Tischlerei*. Irgens received permission to put up a fence to divide the yard between them. But it proved hard to keep the Poles away; they would climb over or creep under the fence. Initially, the Poles came begging for food, but soon they came to use the *Tischlerei* outhouse. The police made every effort to keep the Poles away from the outhouse for fear of lice and typhus. Unlike the police, the Poles had not gone through the lice debugging process.

When the police first arrived at *Altes Lager*, there was no bathroom in the barrack. A policeman came up with a brilliant solution by cutting a hole in the bottom of the empty two-compartment rabbit hutches and mounting them at the appropriate height. Then the police could sit comfortably and be sheltered on three sides. An old bucket was put at the bottom. The toilet hutches were then placed one after the other in the yard. It was these toilets the Poles wanted to use. This forced the police to move the toilets further into their area and assign two guards from 21:00 till 05:00. The Poles would regularly defecate throughout their site, and their site looked and smelled terrible. The Poles would dig small holes in the field and line the holes with bricks. They would then use the feces in the fireplace and cook their food.

The Polish prisoners kept inching into the police area, especially at noon when they knew that many police prisoners didn't want the soup made in the prisoner kitchen. They would gather in small clusters in front of the doors, forcing the police to chase them away. Turning away the Poles may seem inhuman in retrospect, but in reality it proved lifesaving to keep the Poles from both their rooms and outhouse. The police prisoners' hygienic standards were very much different from the Poles. That reality would become necessary as the police would find out later.

Bombs and Grenades

Before March 21, there had been little aircraft activity over the KZ-Stutthof camp. The brief activity was mostly Russian planes flying overhead. Only in late April did the prisoners observe a few German planes. They were surprised by the aircraft circling the camp and then quickly disappeared when the Russian planes appeared. The airspace was controlled by the Russians. There had been some Russian aircraft activity around the camp, and on several occasions prisoners dove for cover from low flying Russian fighters. Several times the fighters would shoot at the prisoners in the camp, and other times they could see the pilot waving at them. In late March, Øivind Lunde and Eivind Luthen found flyers outside the camp. They were written in German and dropped from a Russian aircraft. On the flyers was the following text:

Die russischen Piloten wissen, dass sich im Lager Stutthof Häftlinge befinden und haben den Befehl, es nicht zu bombardieren. Wenn jedoch eine Bombe in das Lagergelände fällt, war dies keine Absicht. Sie können sicher sein, dass Ihre Befreiung nahe ist.

(The Russian pilots are aware that there are present prisoners in Stutthof camp and have orders not to bomb it. However, if a bomb falls within the camp area, it was not on purpose. You can feel confident that your deliverance is near.)

Lunde and Luthen buried the flyers so the Germans wouldn't find them. The police often observed Russian planes flying low over the camp and only firing after they had passed the camp. They now began to feel safer behind the barbed wire.

On one occasion, Arne Sundvor found himself under attack near the crematorium when a Russian aircraft struck. Sundvor sought cover in a two-to-three-meter-long tube of metal.

Crawling out of the tube after the air attack, he discovered that the pipe was the old crematory oven, discarded after the crematorium burned in October 1944.

The Germans mounted anti-aircraft artillery in several parts of the camp. It was apparent the Germans built military installations near prison camps and hospitals and the like. When a Russian aircraft came close, it was attacked from all sides by the anti-aircraft artillery. This, of course, drew the attention of Russian bombers and fighter planes. That meant the prisoners were once again at risk.

Air activity began to increase, and the prisoners saw several large squadrons of Russian bombers fly over the camp and towards the west. Explosions were seen and heard on all sides except the north. Several explosions were so powerful that the barrack walls vibrated. Smoke began to arise from the village of Steegen, including the farms the police had worked on earlier. An outbuilding at Werderhof was also hit.

Russian Attacks

Shortly after the Germanic Column relocated to *Tischlerei*, a bomb hit Blocks 5, 12, 16 and 18. It became apparent the Russian pilots were looking for the administration building. That fact added to their tension, as *Tischlerei* was no more than 100 meters from the administration building.

Several other barracks were also hit. The Jewish women barrack received a direct hit. In her book, Trudi Birger said it was her room that was hit, and she was in the room when the bomb hit.

During the same attack, Odd Fjælberg was on his way to a work commando in the main camp with nine other policemen and a German guard. They were marching along on one of the main streets in the camp when three Russian planes appeared. The commando dove for the ditch as the aircrafts dropped their bombs. The bombs exploded all around them, twirling shrapnel and splinters everywhere, but the ditches saved them! Sadly, fifty women were killed merely fifty meters away.

On Monday, March 26, the police were on a work detail in *Altes Lager*'s barrack, close to the administration building. They observed two Russian bombers flying overhead, dropping bombs on the village of Stutthof a mere five hundred meters from the camp. While watching the flames and smoke rise from the village, they spotted three fighters flying low towards them and coming from the south. One of the planes dropped a bomb while the work detail dove to the floor.

In the explosion, the walls curved. They waited for the barrack to collapse around them. Luckily, the walls remained standing, and the bomb had fallen in the street between the barracks only fifteen meters from them. Walls and windows in the women's barrack exploded, and two women were killed.

Marie Altona, a Finnish woman who had given birth to a little girl on February 1, was severely wounded.

Time and again, fighters came flying overhead without any advanced warning. The pilots would turn off their engines at high altitude and come gliding down before turning the engines on directly above the camp. It felt as though the final act had been reached in the drama. The warning in the camp was to not go outdoors when the Russian aircraft flew overhead.

Later that same evening, another bomb was dropped in the camp. The bomb struck the kitchen in the main camp, and eighteen people were killed or wounded. Holy Week had not been so holy after all. In fact, it was the most troublesome week the police endured during their entire imprisonment thus far. Over three days, nearly eighty prisoners were killed and many more wounded.

After a week of bombing, the SS guards fled into the woods and ordered the prisoners to dig bunkers for themselves.

One day, a work detail of ten police prisoners who happened to be considerably taller than the ordinary German or Pole encountered a guard. The guard stood and looked at them with wide eyes as they marched past. *"Eine Kompanie von Riesen"* (A company of giants), he said.

The Russians were not fooled by the German guards hiding and followed up with bombing into the woods. Working on the bunker commando, Finn Dahlin observed a crater near the bunker where they worked. It was not deep, but the explosive impact had been significant, with about twenty to twenty-five trees severed at varying heights depending on the distance from the crater.

On April 1, around 13:00, a fighter plane switched off its engine and came, like a shot, out of the clouds. The pilot then switched on the engine just above the camp, flew across to the courtyard and dropped bombs. This came as a surprise, and prisoners jumped from their bunks onto the floor and took cover. The bombing missions continued until 15:00 when there appeared to be a break. The prisoners assumed the bombing was finished for the day, but the planes returned and dropped more bombs, mostly in the new camp. One bomb fell in the flower pond just north of the administration building. The intended target was obviously the administration building. However, the bomb ended up in the duck pond on the west side of the building. The attacks continued over the next few days. During the evenings, the glorious moonlight and mild temperatures were similar to what the police would experience in Norway's May evenings. Walking down the street in the moonlight helped create a fairytale atmosphere, but reality set in when they looked towards Danzig, where massive pillars of smoke rose into the air.

The bombing of Danzig continued throughout the night. For the first time since leaving Troyl, they heard the sound of Russian rockets flying over the camp towards the west.

On April 9, while walking in the evening, the prisoners saw fierce bombing in the northwesterly direction towards Hela. The attack lasted an hour with explosions so powerful it shook the barrack walls. That night they also heard explosions coming from the village of Stutthof.

Until now, it was a miracle that none of the police, other than Ulf Engh, had been hit. At *Tischlerei*, they discussed among themselves what they needed to do to protect themselves inside the camp. Several suggested moving to the forest, but the overwhelming majority wanted to stay in *Tischlerei* and secure the camp as much as possible. The large empty rabbit hutches standing outside were then filled with sand and placed against their barrack wall. This provided excellent protection from the side.

The prisoners found themselves in a precarious situation. They were locked in with SS people who were under strict orders to fight to the last man. Russian troops would soon be standing outside the barbed wire fence. Each day that passed was one day closer to them travelling home!

The back wall of *Tischlerei* was completely unprotected. A work detail sent to *Baulager* (Storage Building) helped themselves to large boards, using them to create a double wall around the barrack. The sand was put between the boards and the wall. It was so effective that it also gave protection to the beds on the second and third floors.

The Mole Holes

It was no longer a criminal offence to steal German public property. Under the floorboards, they dug rooms and passages in the sand. Some passages were long and ended up reaching the courtyard. When the alarm went off, they would all head for their holes. The 'mole holes' wouldn't help in a direct bomb hit, but it was hoped they'd be effective against shrapnel and bullet ricochets. The measure could mean life or death for them. After the first few days of panic, it became a standard procedure. Each man had his own shelter where he could take refuge. When they saw or heard aircrafts coming, they would escape into their safe house. In *Tischlerei*, they would also hastily run into the laundry, where several laundry tubs were made of cement. The tubs offered adequate protection, even if the rest of the barrack would collapse.

When the task was completed, the prisoners felt the barracks were well protected. Most of them took the situation with poise.

On the whole, it was a miracle that none of the police were injured during this time. There were 219 Norwegian police members who were shot at multiple times, and more than once they were forced to dive for cover. Other prisoners in both the old and new camp had been wounded and killed.

Water, Hygiene and Disease

Water was a big problem. The water came from a tap in the main laundry room in the Old Camp, for only one hour each day. When the time came, all prisoners would line up outside the laundry room for their turn. The police would gather anything that could hold water and then transport the water to *Tischlerei*. They *orge* a small hand cart that was formerly used to carry the heavy water vessels from the laundry room to the barracks for this job.

One day the water line broke. Despite their diligent attempt to repair it, they didn't succeed. The police were then told to fetch water from a pump in the main camp. The pump was in the middle of the camp, where prisoners from other barracks also got their water. The pump was overwhelmed every day during the hours water was available. When the water finally came, there was constant strife and fighting among the prisoners.

Skjolden took the responsibility upon himself to divide the water between the Germans, English and French prisoners, the Kapos and whoever else was in the lineup. The water they were fighting over was yellow and dirty and chock full of bacteria, not fit for anything other than washing floors!

In the village of Stutthof was a well of usable water. The police water detail went to the village well to fetch water specifically for cooking. There were long lineups at the well. Bringing water back to *Tischlerei* would have been difficult if not for the handcart.

Surprisingly, one day usable water flowed from the taps in the laundry room. The quality of the water was so good that it could even be used for cooking. There was great joy in the camp, and the water detail distributed the water among other prisoners. Later they learned the machines at Ziegelei were in operation again. However, this lasted only a day, then things were as before.

The days of rain were most welcome. When it rained, the prisoners gathered every item to collect the rain, including bowls, cups and whatever else they had in their hands. Water running down the dirty tar paper on the roof was collected in buckets and placed in the washbasin. The rain helped clean the air for a short period; it got rid of the disgusting nauseous smell from the crematorium, at least for a while. At no time during their imprisonment had the water situation been as dire as this period. Personal hygiene and general cleanliness had become a severe issue, and cleanliness was the best defense against disease. They would only brush their teeth with rainwater or water from the well in the village.

At *Tischlerei*, they carried out constant lice inspection and delousing. A few remaining bottles of the Danish delousing solution were left in the barrack. The police would shower and put the solution on their hair, neck and a bit down the chest. The delousing solution smelled a lot like liquor. In fact, several Kapos, thinking they had alcohol, offered two to three pieces of bread if they would trade.

Despite all their precautions, several came down with an abdominal infection and *Scheisserei* (diarrhea), vomiting and sluggish periods. One case of typhus after another arose, including the Lithuanian Dr. Germantos who suffered from shell shock in Gdynia and who did the whispering that unnerved the Germanic Column.

By late March, there were three Norwegians and three Finns down with typhus. The number of cases increased to ten in the following days. Fortunately, their sickness was temporary, mainly due to the excellent care provided by Heggenes and his helpers.

On April 24, Heggenes reported that he was looking after twenty-seven Germans in the hospital, and six of them were too sick to march if they needed to.

None of the police members died while staying in the Old Camp. This was indeed a miracle, but the blessing was, in part, due to the excellent care the patients received.

Catering and *orge*

There was no organized food preparation at the camp during this period, and there was a continual shortage of supplies. When supplies arrived in the camp, it was so little that it could only be divided among a few and into small portions. If a prisoner didn't get anything, he had to wait for the next time supplies arrived. When that would happen was anybody's guess! The Russians had cut off the supply lines from the rest of the country, making it necessary to seek supplies from the surrounding region.

With the constant influx of refugees from the east ahead of the Russian advances, the area became overcrowded and the demand for food supply kept increasing.

Farms with herds and crops in the region were bombed, and most farms were on fire.

Potatoes played a large part in the prisoners' diets, and thankfully there was an adequate supply in the camp. The food that was distributed relatively regularly was the camp soup made from red beets, but it was basically inedible! Prisoners would end up with severe stomach ailments. After many police were exposed to the soup and became sick, they stopped eating it.

The Werderhof work commando came back each day with bottles of milk for the sick in the hospital. Every morning during milking, the Norwegian civilian prisoners would have a representative in the barn helping the Danish manager, Ingo. For this they received milk in two liquor bottles, which they then smuggled into a warehouse. Karl Strand and Karl Petersen smuggled the milk into the camp when they returned from picking up the mail at the Stutthof village post office. This was a risky undertaking, for theft and smuggling of milk would have had severe consequences if the Germans discovered it. The milk, on the other hand, was a vital diet for the sick. The police ended up smuggling fifteen to twenty liters per day.

Over time, the Nickelswalde work commando police managed to *orge* many military effects such as winter fur coats, boots, underwear and socks. The German commander of the Nickelswalde commando had asked them to get the soldiers some winter clothing. The commander asked for furs. Incredible as it seemed, the police provided the Germans with their own fur coats and received bread as payment.

On occasion, their *orge* almost went wrong.

The police *orge* coats and felt boots when it was cold. When the weather turned warmer and it began to rain, they *orge* raincoats. An SS officer saw the prisoners wearing military raincoats and gave orders that they should immediately put them back. Einar Hjellemo responded firmly that prisoners were under his command and that none of them would take off their raincoats. The SS officer drew his pistol and aimed at Hjellemo, who casually replied: *"Schießen Sie einfach! Die Männer werden nur meinem Befehl gehorchen!"* (Just shoot! The men will only obey my command!). The officer just stared at Hjellemo, his mouth wide open. He then put the gun in his bag, turned and walked away. They all breathed a sigh of relief! A Wehrmacht *wachtmeister*, who was close by, smiled happily that the SS officer was put in his place. The wachtmeister waved at Hjellemo and brought him a glass of liquor and divided some cigarettes between the other police members.

At KZ-Stutthof, the SS had carried on an extensive breeding program of Angora rabbits.

After the SS evacuated the camp in April, four policemen were ordered to kill all the rabbits that were left. As a reward for their work, 360 rabbits were divided among the Germanic community, including the male and female prisoners in the Old Camp.

With Julla's (Julius Hordnes) culinary skills, the Old Camp enjoyed several delicious rabbit dinners. The Julla-soup was the primary source of nutrition during this period. There were not many days Julla failed to conjure up a soup that was both tasty and nourishing.

All the *orge* goodies were used as ingredients in the Julla soup. Irgens had managed to put aside a supply of Danish packages that also made it into the Julla-soup. The soup was always made from water drawn from the village well, and the produce was still thoroughly washed. Julla's soup was quite different from the beet soup made with dirty water that had sand in the bottom. Later, horse meat and potatoes were the main ingredients in the soup. Julla was not only an accomplished chef, he also had a distinct talent for *orge*. Cunningly, he succeeded in obtaining fifty kilograms of salt and fifty kilograms of coffee substitute. He put the salt in buckets and buried them in the sand outside the barrack.

Julla often went on his own *orge* tours. Once, he had gotten ahold of a horse harness and a wagon. He found a "stray" horse and hitched it to the wagon. Julla then drove into the camp, gathered four 50 liter buckets, and drove out of the gate again. When the German guard asked him what he was doing, he answered, *"Wasser holen"* (Fetch water). Julla drove straight to the potato cellar and, with help from Norwegian civilian prisoners, filled the buckets with potatoes. He then filled the buckets with water over the potatoes and returned to the camp where the potatoes, water and the horse ended up in the soup.

The work details outside the camp were particularly effective in securing supplies. They even brought back women's finery such as scarves, shawls and lace undergarments.

The work detail also brought back other highly sought after commodities such as toothpaste, soap and the like. Among the police members were those outstanding at *orge*. Others were less talented, and others still had no talent for *orge* at all. Most of the police members belonged to the latter group. When it arose, they all took the opportunity, but not everyone was equally adept at seeing where the options lay. Towards the end of their stay, all bartering centered on food such as bread, butter, eggs, meat and such. One could trade a Waterman fountain pen for several loaves of bread from the baker in town.

In *Tischlerei* was an elongated flat furnace with several holes, ideal for frying. All day there was a fire in the furnace. At around 20:00, the fire was put out; otherwise, those lying closest to the furnace would overheat. The police had *orge* some wheat grain and wondered if there was a simple way of making flour out of it. One resourceful policeman came up with a way by using the coffee grinder in the hospital! They would grind all day and into the night, and finally they had flour. Together with potatoes, they made stacks of potato cakes.

Old and moldy pieces of bread were also bearable when toasted in the oven. Prisoners from other barracks lined up when the police were frying or cooking food. They would line up in several rows to wait for their toast. Prisoners also waited their turn to boil and fry eggs. A question had plagued the police; if they had to live on canned food alone, would they have survived? The prisoners were thankful for Julla and his helpers' culinary skills.

Two Norwegians and a Cow

Lars Solli and a colleague made the boldest *orge* while left behind during the earlier evacuation. There were rumors about a particular company that was bringing in cows. As the cows roamed along Danzig Strasse, they tried to *orge* one. But when a couple of guards intervened, they abandoned the idea. Afterwards, they had a chance to *orge* another cow. They found a piece of rope and brought it with them to the guard hut, where they reported: *"Zwei Norweger und eine Kuh!"* (Two Norwegians and a cow!). Luckily it was Petersen sitting in the guard hut, who just shook his head. Solli interpreted this as a sign that everything was in order and led the cow into the camp, which ended up in Julla's pot. Solli and his associate doubted it would have worked if someone other than Petersen was in the guard hut.

Orge Horses

Irgens had taken the food situation to the camp commander SS Hauptscharführer Paul Ehle. Ehle told them frankly to start eating horse meat. Thus began the *orge* of horses. Large herds of horses roamed the area, horses that the evacuees couldn't take with them and were therefore set loose. The horses even came voluntarily towards the prisoners. Then they had to select the best.

The police didn't have butchering equipment or large enough pots to cook the meat. William Jensen took a trip to the main camp kitchen, where the chief chef let himself be bribed with some cans of sardines and the promise of several kilos of horse meat. Jensen got axes and knives, as well as a 300-liter cooking pot. Petter Dalen was the chief butcher and had many helpers. When the Poles later moved into *Altes Lager*, the police already had three horses waiting to be butchered. They had to move the horses before they would be *orge* by the Poles. They transferred the horses to the spacious laundry room. By April 11, there were three horses and a pig in the laundry room. Thorleif Lie's German Shepherds served as guard dogs. The laundry room was also Irgen's secret warehouse; therefore, the guard dogs were really needed.

The horse meat was portioned out raw or cooked based on preference. Some meat was also smuggled into the women's barrack.

Horse meat wasn't bad tasting, but there was no fat on the poor animals. Horse meat, therefore, had limited nutritional value and was dry and tough. But it filled their stomachs.

Butchering Horse

When the camp was evacuated on April 25, the police set seven horses free from the laundry room. In one month, they slaughtered and consumed nine horses.

Those among the police who had taken up smoking had a hard time securing tobacco. Olaf Bjelland gained permission from the camp management to purchase twenty kilograms of leaf tobacco from the Germans. The payment was made in Reichsmark, and the tobacco was divided into twenty-gram portions. The procedure took place in the pharmacy, where there was a weigh scale, and each person was checked off the checklist. The druggist and his assistant were Poles and also received tobacco for their service.

The prisoners also *orge* a large quantity of potatoes from the main potato cellar near Danziger Strasse. A few policemen carried two potato sacks to the womens' barracks every day.

The *orge* of potatoes from the cellar was well organized. Two policemen stood as guards to warn when danger was near. None of the police were ever caught in the act.

Inventory of the main potato cellar began to noticeably dwindle. It was estimated the cellar would store a month's supply at a time, but unforeseen circumstances could play a role. This was often the case when, during the evacuation, military units would come and requisition larger quantities of potatoes; this couldn't be avoided. The potato cellar also held a large inventory of mineral water. There were not just bottles, but crates of bottles, much of which made its way to *Tischlerei*.

The mineral water was a huge blessing; it allowed them to drink liquids without the risk of getting sick.

On one work detail carrying cement bags, Odd Fjælberg and his group noticed Polish prisoners under German guards' supervision a short distance from them. They were carrying flour sacks from an open railroad car. The flour was of considerable interest to Fjælberg and his group. They observed that the Germans and Poles stayed on the same side of the railway car and then walked to the car's back. When the opportunity presented itself, Fjælberg took a sack of flour and hid it among the cement sacks. Later, when the wood commando came by to retrieve it, they hid the flour sack among the wood they were bringing to the police barrack.

In late April, on a similar work commando, Fjælberg and his group found a German truck that had gotten stuck in the mud at Ziegelei, close to the former police home, Sonderlager. They scrutinized the truck to see if there were any items they could *orge*. The truck contained several cartons of artificial honey, and the German guard had fallen asleep in the front seat. The group helped themselves to two cartons of twelve kilograms each and carried them off. As Fjælberg and his group left, they mused at how the guard would explain the missing two cartons of honey.

While working at Werderhof, Karl Haugan *orge* a piglet and brought it back to the camp. It was decided that the pig would be shared among the camp prisoners, and it was placed in a separate room in the laundry. The plan was to feed it a few days and then take it back to Werderhof and replace it with a bigger pig. The police knew the Polish pig attendant, who was more than willing to help for a little remuneration.

After three weeks, a grown pig went into the Julla pot during one of the camp's last days. This was the best dinner the prisoners had during their entire stay at KZ-Stutthof.

CHAPTER 16 –
Daily Life at *Tischlerei*

Tischlerei was a fifty-five-meter-long barrack where the Germanic prisoners lived. The barrack was cramped with 300 men living in the tight quarters without room to spread out. The prisoners would either lay or sit on their beds to read, play cards or play chess. It was a welcome distraction when Øivind Lunde would occasionally lead out with a Norwegian song, or when a particular musical Polish prisoner would walk into the barrack and play his violin.

An alarming distraction was the overhead sounds of the Russian shelling of targets to the east of the camp.

During the day, most prisoners were out on different work details. Those working in the potato fields were particularly at risk from air attack, with little opportunity to hide or go for cover if being shot at. There was no choice other than to throw themselves down and make themselves as horizontal as possible.

The prisoners remaining in the camp couldn't fail to see the daily ritual of corpses being transported to the crematorium. Between twenty and twenty-five prisoners died from typhus every day. The corpses were all skin and bones. On one occasion they saw a corpse move.

Dahlin observed Oberscharführer Ewald Foth come walking on the road just behind the police barrack with a Russian prisoner, and they both looked relaxed and calm. Dahlin naively thought they were out for a walk to get some air. It proved to be the prisoner's last walk. Foth shot the prisoner in the back of the neck and then dragged him to the crematorium. Executions were a daily occurrence during the last days of Stutthof. From the hospital window,

Haugan and Kristiansen watched Foth shoot nine Russian prisoners in the neck. They learned that Foth had shot nineteen other Russian prisoners the same way. Foth was a cold-blooded murderer. The number of prisoners Foth killed is unknown, but some had said Foth wouldn't feel well unless he killed at least five people every day.

Spring was coming, and the days were getting longer. During a morning roll call in early April, the prisoners saw a flock of swans flying eastward. Others saw storks. They thought there would be many homeless storks that year, for many of the area's farms were bombed and burned down.

On April 9, the Danish and Norwegian prisoners held a small memorial service marking the German invasion of Norway and Denmark. The prisoners gathered inside the barrack at noon. First, there was a two-minute silence, followed by a short talk from the Danish prisoner Thøgersen.

The morning roll calls were at precisely 06:15, with a guard doing the counting. The guards doing the tally now started to show up less frequently. The roll calls were very unpopular to begin with, and some prisoners pretended to be sick. Others simply didn't bother to get up, and attendance kept dwindling. Around the middle of April, the roll calls were cancelled altogether. The cancellation met with general approval, and luckily there were no consequences.

Visiting Werderhof

During one of the last mornings of their stay at *Tischlerei*, some police visited the work detail at Werderhof. They intended to visit their old home, the Sonderlager camp. It wasn't hard for the police to get out of the main camp, as Germanics they only had to report to the guard when leaving the camp and again when they returned.

The road to Werderhof was partially flooded before they reached Ziegelei. In desperation, the Germans had flooded the fields. The machine shop at Ziegelei had received a direct hit, and the wall facing the road was blown out. There were prisoners doing repairs, and they managed to get a few of the machines working. Those generators provided the camp with electricity for lights and its water pump.

It was distressing for the police to walk past Sonderlager, where they had many good times. Sonderlager didn't look much different, except the phrase *Kampf, Sieg, Freiheit* (Fight, Win, Freedom) was painted on the walls. There were also trenches dug around the camp. There was a constant roar from the direction of Pillau, and it seemed to be getting closer when suddenly four Russian fighter planes came over Ziegelei from the east heading straight towards them. They leaped for cover as the aircraft circled over Steegen and then disappeared.

The stable at Werderhof had burnt down after a direct hit, and the other buildings were riddled with holes from bullets and shrapnel. The whole area was riddled with craters from bombing. The Werderhof work detail of five Norwegians and five Danes lived in a little house with an abandoned stork nest on the roof.

The work detail had renovated the house and built three bedrooms and a kitchen. The group alternated the cooking details while the others worked on the farm. The farm had most of the old Sonderlager library. After the evacuation of Sonderlager in January, the library was moved to Werderhof.

At dinner, the Werderhof detail told of significant changes at Sonderlager; the walls were dismantled and used by the first prisoners who lived at the camp after the police. Now there were only a small number of sick, French prisoners living there.

They also explained that when the Russian planes attacked the anti-aircraft artilleries in the region, they would see that the pilots attempted not to strike the camp. It was a pure accident that two Frenchmen were killed by bullets.

On their way back, the police saw civilian refugees had settled down below the Ziegelei director's residence, where Hauptsturmführer Meyer had lived previously. There were a lot of people there washing their laundry and cooking food.

Andreas Irgens was a skilled leader of the Germanic prisoners during this period. He had the full support of all the police, including the Danes, Finns and Balts. Irgens had many unpleasant tasks to perform, but only as a last resort would he step in. There was constant nagging among the various nationalities, but Irgens remained remarkably calm.

He was also respected by Hauptsturmführer Theodore Meyer and later SS Hauptscharführer Paul Ehle. The good treatment the Germanic prisoners received was mostly thanks to Irgens.

Fall of Danzig

Danzig fell on March 30, 1945. Danzig's fall left the Nazis only a narrow beachhead from the easternmost portion of the Vistula River (longest river in Poland) west of Elbing to Königsberg in the east. Immediately east of Stutthof lay Frische Nehrung, or just 'Nehrung' as the police called it. Nehrung was a long, flat sandy spit stretching in a north-easterly direction, ending at Pillau. A narrow strait led into an inlet called Frische Haff. Pillau was the shipping port for Königsberg. After Danzig fell, there were no other evacuation options other than from the Vistula River's mouth or from Pillau.

The advantage of Pillau as an evacuation point was that the evacuees would escape directly over the open sea. Evacuation over the Visula River meant the evacuees would end up in Danzig Bay, which was now controlled by the Russians. Sitting on the roof of their barrack, the police saw the evidence of the Russian army advancing on Königsberg. The skies lit up like Christmas lights.

Shortly after Danzig fell, the bombing intensified over Königsberg and then over Pillau. The bombing was so intense that the barrack walls vibrated.

One squadron after another flew westward carrying bombs towards Hela. Each squadron consisted of thirty large bombers. The fortress town of Hela was the last to surrender when Germany invaded Poland in September 1939. Now Hela would be the last fortress to surrender to the Russians in 1945.

Skies Litup like Christmas Lights

The battlefronts were now forty kilometers to the south and fifty kilometers to the west of KZ-Stutthof.

Rumors circulated that The German Foreign Minister Joachim von Ribbentrop and Franz von Papen would be travelling to England to negotiate for peace. In the meantime, it was rumored there would be a ninety-day truce. If the rumors were true, it would undoubtedly have been historical, but the optimism was quickly turned into disappointment.

Irgens, along with the Danish representative, was summoned to appear before the camp commander SS Hauptsturmführer Paul Ehle. They were informed that Ehle had telegraphed Berlin to request that the Norwegian and Danish governments send ships for the prisoners. The commander said he had spoken further with the Danish Consulate General in Danzig about the arrangements and was waiting for a Berlin response. If he did not hear something soon, he would push for a reply. There had also been a radio-telephone call from Germany to the Danish government to send a ship to Hela to pick up Scandinavian refugees, Ehle said. A reply was expected shortly.

The expected departure would be in five to six days! The discussion among the prisoners was lively.

From previous experience with the Germans, the police doubted the report.

What surprised the police was that the Germans had managed to keep Nickelswalde as long as they had, five to six days. The rumors kept coming. Rumors now circulated that Berlin had made direct inquiries to the Norwegian and Danish governments.

The prisoners remained skeptical. Which Norwegian government would the Germans have contacted? Certainly not the Norwegian NS government of Vidkun Quisling! It would be doubtful the NS would care about a group of troublesome Norwegian police members in Germany. It had to be the Danish Government the Germans had contacted. Even that seemed unlikely.

In Hela, the ships would risk being bombed or torpedoed by Russian submarines. No ship captain in his right mind would put his boat or crew in such danger.

The Swedish Red Cross had received permission from Reichsführer Heinrich Himmler to bring the Scandinavian KZ camp prisoners to KZ-Neuengamme near Hamburg, transported by the White Buses. The camp administration was advised of this via teletype. The fact was that the White Buses couldn't reach Stutthof because the area was cordoned off by the Russians, but they could send a Red Cross ship to Hela to bring the police home. In that case, maybe the rumors were not so unrealistic after all!

The prisoners heard that the English had taken Hannover, and the Allies stood at Osnabrück, 300 kilometers north of Berlin. Rumors also circulated that the Russians had taken Dresden. It seemed clear to everyone that the war was in its final phase.

Eastern Front Moving West

On April 12, a Wehrmacht report confirmed that Königsberg had fallen. It happened on April 11. With these events, the German-controlled area was squeezed considerably. Now only Pillau was holding out, but it would not last long. In the following days, the police spoke with wounded German soldiers who had returned from the east. They said it was pure hell in the city and could only hold out a few more days. They were right! On April 22, German radio reported that the German army had retreated from Pillau. In the following broadcast, General Otto Lash, the German general, said that because he voluntarily surrendered in direct defiance of Hitler, his family was arrested and punished. Hitler sentenced Lash in absentia to death by hanging. General Lash had fallen out of favor because he had surrendered the town, which was necessary for the Germans as an evacuation port and support for the **Courland Peninsula**. Pillau fell between April 18–20. There were no longer any German defenses between the Russians and KZ-Stutthof. The Commander of the SD in Weichsel district said that, though the rest of Germany may surrender, he would certainly not surrender.

Air attacks subsided, and from April 12, it seemed as if the planes no longer had any interest in that area. The evacuation was in full swing in the districts around KZ-Stutthof. The prisoners could see the railway line one hundred meters away from their window, laden with military transports from Nehrung towards Nickelswalde. There were many wounded among them. This was the evacuation of troops from Pillau and Königsberg. Often the police would see trains with both military and civilian evacuees. These trains were crowded, with passengers both on the platform and on the steps.

German soldiers came lumbering in droves. It was not a particularly pleasing march to watch. The soldiers were all dead tired, and most of them had a sense of hopelessness on their faces. There came the occasional cluster of prisoners of war or civilians evacuating by wagon and wounded soldiers lying inside the wagon. It did not seem like anyone was worried in the least about what others were doing; they appeared apathetic to the needs of others.

The police had, for some time, kept their clothes on at night. It would be damning if the barracks collapsed on them, and they had to work their way out without clothes. Being fully clothed made them feel safer.

Again, there were rumors about evacuation. A higher SS soldier on a work command said that the Norwegians would soon be evacuated westward. They had heard such false statements before. Skjolden mentioned that he had seen a notice posted in the village from the SS commander in Weichsel district that all civilians were to evacuate in small boats from Schiewenhorst and out into the open sea. The civilians would be picked up by larger ships and taken to Denmark and Norway. Rumors circulated that a floating dock into the sea was to be built north of the camp; everyone could be evacuated from there. This would most likely be the last resort if the escape route over Nickelswalde was attacked and blocked by the Russians. In the communiqué, many ignored the evacuation order and hid in the woods. Rumors had circulated about the sinking of vessels full of refugees. The authorities assured the prisoners that, so far, no boats were sunk. It was underscored that it would be dangerous to remain in the district, everything would be bombed and the area was declared a war zone.

German law enforcers chased civilians who had defied the evacuation orders and had escaped into the woods. They caught some, but not all.

One German soldier was shot as a deserter and hung on a tree in the Stutthof village main street. The placard read: *Ich werde wegen Desertion und Plünderung erschossen* (I'm shot because of desertion and looting). It appeared to be imperative for the Germans to give dramatic warnings!

Otto Kristiansen was stopped by a German law enforcer during an 'acquiring' tour in the village of Stutthof. He was to be shot as a German deserter and for looting. Kristiansen managed, however, to convince the German that he was only a Norwegian KZ prisoner. The German was apparently not entirely convinced, for he drove with Kristiansen to confirm he spoke the truth.

If civilians remained much longer in the region, it could prove totally unbearable for them due to the bombing attacks, disease, and hunger. However, it would be better than to be evacuated by sea, which would be considered a death sentence. To the police, all exits were equally insane.

Looking Back

In retrospect of the time the police were imprisoned in Germany and Poland, they had to admit that they had it relatively good while at Sonderlager, especially compared with the other prisoners in the main camp.

The police believed that the main camp KZ-Stutthof was among the worst concentration camps in Europe. In size, KZ-Stutthof can undoubtedly be compared to KZ-Ravensbrück, and it had three times as many Norwegian women and men as other KZ-camps.

Of the thirty-two days the police stayed in *Tischlerei*, they were attacked by Russian planes for over twenty. Fifteen of those attacks were directed at the camp or targets just outside. The attacks often happened several times per day. It was eerie and nerve wracking to experience direct or indirect targeted bombing and shelling while being incarcerated behind electric barbed wire.

The prisoners kept wondering about the Russian attacks. The Russians surely understood this was a prison camp, and there was no doubt it was the SS soldiers the Russians were targeting. Later, the Russians took aim at the troop transports beyond the Nehrung, and thankfully the Russians used small scatter bombs. Regular bombs would have caused more significant injuries. They wondered why the Russians failed to hit the administration building despite so many attempts. The bombs fell throughout the area of the camp. They thought of no other explanation other than the pilots were young and without experience.

Remembering the SD commander that said, "*Wenn alle Deutschland kapituliert, gäbe es hier keine Kapitulation sein*" (if all of Germany surrendered, there would be no surrender here) made the prisoners feel uneasy.

At this point, the homesickness felt much more potent than before. The prisoners discussed the situation among themselves daily. Could they manage to stay alive for the time that was left in the camp? Constant depression and despondency fell upon them. The hope for a speedy resolution to this 'hellish' situation lay like a pale morning twilight before them. But the thought that the war was soon coming to an end gave them new hope; the only question was would they be able to make it through? The news that Field Marshal Walter Model had capitulated in the Ruhr area after being nearly annihilated by the Allies, and that he committed suicide on April 21, encouraged them that the war would soon be over. According to the Wehrmacht report on April 22, the Red Army had entered the northeastern districts of Berlin. On April 23, the Russians were a few kilometers from Unter den Linden, a boulevard in the central **Mitte** district of Berlin, and three kilometers from the **Alexanderplatz**, a large public square and transport hub in the central Mitte district of Berlin. Now the end was indeed near!

On April 24, the Germanic representatives were summoned for a conference with the camp commander, SS Hauptsturmführer Paul Ehle. The commander stated that it was now pertinent to evacuate the Germanic prisoners, and he would give those orders the next day. Ehle emphasized that they had to be prepared, for the orders could come at any time with as little as fifteen minutes' notice. The camp was to be evacuated! Germanic prisoners were to go first, followed by Eastern European and Jewish prisoners. The police gathered what they were forced to leave behind in an unlocked room, in case they had to return. It was possible that there were so many evacuees to Nickelswalde there would be no boats available. If so, the police would be forced to return to camp.

None of the Danish and Norse prisoners wanted to join the evacuation. They didn't want to embark on what they were ninety percent sure was a suicide sailing on the Baltic Sea. They had set their minds to remain and be freed by the Russians. But that did not prove to be the case.

CHAPTER 17 –
Second Evacuation

The order to evacuate came in the morning on Wednesday, April 25, 1945. The camp was to be cleared by 21:00. The evacuation orders were carried out by the Wehrmacht, with only soldiers to remain behind. Six sick policemen who could not march were transported by train at 10:00, the rest of the Germanic prisoners would evacuate at 15:00. The evacuees were going to Nickelswalde. From there, it was rumored they would journey to Sjælland and Copenhagen. Some food rations were provided. While this was going on, a squadron of thirty Russian aircraft flew above, heading west.

The Germanic prisoners were given orders to assemble at 15:00 and be ready to evacuate. Olav Skjerven and several others were in the hospital, ill with stomach typhus. It would be entirely irresponsible to evacuate under normal circumstances, but now was not normal! It was assumed that all who remained would be shot by the Russians. Faced with that option, the police insisted that their sick be evacuated along with the rest. The sick police were assisted by one man on each side. There were four Norwegian police who were too weak to join the evacuation: Per Norddal, Reidar Kvammen, Mikael Pettersen and Karsten Lütken.

Herman Heggenes and Eivind Luthen volunteered to remain and look after the sick policemen. This was the second time that Heggenes and Luthen remained with the sick when the rest evacuated. There was a tremendous amount of admiration for their selfless and loyal acts. The evacuees went to the window of the hospital to say goodbye. Each Norwegian police prisoner was aware of the gravity of the situation, but they reminded each other of the good times they had together. While they said their goodbyes, they didn't know if they would ever see each other again. As they thought about the evacuation, they wondered about their comrades who were away from the camp, and about whether the sick would be able to survive. Would they ever see them again?

Assembly on Wednesday, April 25 was at 05:00. The weather was clear, but a few Russian scout planes circled over the camp. The Germanic prisoners were each given half a loaf of bread, a pound of butter, and a piece of dried horse meat, all from Irgens' secret stash that was now depleted. They also managed to get one package of flatbread each and a can of fish *balla* to be shared among three men. The previous day's dinner was an excellent soup prepared by Julla, made from the pig that 'grew so fast'.

Evacuation Begins

The Germanic evacuation began at 15:00. They reached Danziger Strasse train station after an hour and a half march. When they passed Werderhof, the Werderhof work detail joined the evacuation. At the train station, the prisoners sat for three hours while a Russian reconnaissance plane circled overhead. More columns joined the evacuees, among them women from the Old Camp. While they were waiting, Martin Fossen took the opportunity to get Scheissevann (mineral water) cases from the potato cellar. The bottles were divided among the Germanic prisoners.

Russian bombers kept flying overhead. Every time they did, the prisoners sought refuge in the woods. The bombers proceeded towards Steegen, which was being bombed extensively. After several trains carrying soldiers had passed, the prisoners were ordered to *"Abmarschierren!"* (Move on!). They boarded a train with flat deck wagons and cast their last glance at the main camp as the train continued towards Steegen.

Herds of stray horses roamed along the railroad tracks. Just past the Nickelswalde station, the prisoners disembarked at 21:00. They marched northward along the banks of the Vistula River and came to a sandy area named Stralun-Weichsel. The fog had settled in, and the moonlight cast an eerie glare over the surface of the river. Marching forward, they discovered that the area was full of prisoners. It was as if the entire strip along the riverbed was alive with people sitting or lying on the ground with blankets around them.

The Germanic prisoners were ordered to sit. Their main question was how long before they would cross the river? It seemed an ideal day for an evacuation, with dense fog over the river. They could travel effortlessly over to Hela without being spotted by Russian aircraft. The transport leader, a *Schupowachtmeister* (Schutzpolizei guard) who spoke Danish, told them there was a steamer from the United Danish A / S flying the Red Cross flag waiting for them in Hela. It sounded promising, but from previous experiences, they doubted it. The police who were sick and evacuated had arrived at the riverbank earlier in the day. They were transported by rail and then motor vehicles, but still lay in the vehicles a short distance from the rest of the Germanic prisoners. The police members went over and greeted them.

Later that night, the police received the joyful news that Heggenes and Luthen would be arriving with the last of the sick.

Boats Arrive

The prisoners were awakened by the sound of a boat coming up the river through the fog. They all jumped up and got ready to depart, but there were no orders to board after the boat had unloaded. There would be no evacuation that night! When the prisoners awoke the next morning, April 26, there was light fog and frost. As they gathered wood to light a fire and cook breakfast, they saw hundreds of little fires all around them with people doing the same. They realized they were on a large, undeveloped sandy bed that stretched along the river, but there was also a dock. Everywhere lay columns of prisoners. Most were prisoners from the main camp. Word spread that the Wehrmacht had demanded all prisoners be evacuated from the main camp so it could be cleared and prepared for a military offensive. The camp had simply moved to the riverbed! Camped beside the police was a column of 1,500 Jewish women that had arrived a day before them.

Guards informed the police that a ship had not been arranged for them at Hela. They had to wait until one was available – after all Germans were evacuated from the city.

Many German civilians gathered by the dock. On the road from Nickelswalde, they could see a continuous column of vehicles of all types. The police questioned the Germans' priorities in allowing prisoners to evacuate while German civilians were standing in endless queues waiting. It made more sense for the Germans to evacuate their own citizens first and leave the prisoners to the Russians. The prisoners were certainly not more important than the German civilians.

Suddenly they heard the shout, *"Aufstehen und fertigmachen!"* (Get Up and Get Ready!). As they got ready, they noticed four Jewish women had died in their sleep overnight.

The prisoners were moved to a sparse forest nearby to avoid being detected by Russian planes. As the prisoners dispersed, several police members ended up on a high slope.

The fog had cleared, and the sun began to shine. They faced northwest from the slope, which gave them a panoramic view over the river and across to the other side. They could see the Bay of Danzig's outer part and the spit beyond Hela on the bay's other side. Behind that, they saw the open sea.

It was strange to think that the Russians controlled the inner, western part of the bay and that the Russian Army was only eight or ten kilometers from them. A steady barrage of anti-aircraft fire and the stutter of machine guns from aircraft flying overhead was heard. The police observed several motorboats chugging on the river as well as several smaller steamboats sailing along the banks. They also saw several wrecks in the river.

The Germanic prisoners consisted of Norwegian police and Norwegian, Danish, Finnish, Polish, Baltic and German civilian prisoners, both men and women. In addition to the Germanic prisoners, were Jewish women.

A Pitiful Sight

Even though the police found themselves hopeless, they could not avoid being moved by the many broken lives all around them.

Next to the police sat a small group of Finnish women. One of them had a baby of barely three months, born in KZ-Stutthof. The mother, Marie, had been badly wounded in a bomb attack but survived. Further down the riverbank was a nursery for small children, with their mothers tending to them the best they could. There were continual sounds of screaming children and the sight of children's diapers hanging to dry on the trees. The police observed several groups of Jewish women, and it was a pitiful sight. The women were just skin and bones, wearing nothing but rags. In one place lay a few women closely entwined on a blanket and looking into each other's eyes. Toilets of various kinds were set up evenly among the various groups, and they were used unashamedly. Everything the police saw made a lasting impression! Out of nowhere, the tune *Solveig's Song* streamed over the area. It was their violin-playing Polish friend wandering around and playing. The song was their Polish friend's tribute to the Norwegian police.

Later that morning, the prisoners moved down to the riverbank. Many took the opportunity to wash in the murky Weichsel water. The prisoners were served soup for lunch. It consisted of unpeeled potatoes, but was still edible.

Across from the prisoners lay a forest road with two-meter-tall pine trees, separating a small plantation. The Poles and Jews, who seemed to defecate wherever they found themselves, were warned that the field was off-limits. Once, the police heard terrible scolding coming from the plantation as a guard objected to the field being used for sanitation purposes, most likely because the trenches served as execution trenches. The prisoners were driven away by the guards, but a young Jewish girl did not obey fast enough. She was first reprimanded, then shot through the head. The guard immediately ordered some prisoners in the proximity to bury her. In the same vicinity, a Jewish girl was gathering firewood and crossed over an imaginary border that restricts the movement of the Jews. An earlier guard had not set such boundaries, and neither were the police aware of such a border. A guard fired point-blank past the polices' heads and hit the girl in the temple. She plunged to the ground and rolled down the incline. A little further on was another Jewish girl on the hillside close to the imaginary border. The same guard aimed his rifle at her. Several policemen shouted at her and told her to hurry down the hill again. *"Halt den Mund!"* (Shut up!) brawled the guard. *"Lass sie kommen! Ich kann mehr schießen"* (Let them come! I can shoot more). The girl understood the danger and disappeared. *"Scheisse!"* (Shit!) said the guard when he saw that she had disappeared.

The police avoided seeing the two hundred Jewish women murdered on the riverbank south of the Nickelswalde ferry near the terminus for Kleinbahn, but they heard the shooting. The killings were carried out by Untersturmführer Schmidt and Oberscharfürer Ewald Foth.

There had been no air raids throughout the day, almost as if the Russians were finished in the area. But at 16:30, there came another heavy attack. Anti-aircraft artillery thundered around the prisoners on all sides. Towards the east was intense bombing, and they saw fire and smoke rising; it was from KZ-Stutthof main camp. The police hoped Heggenes, Luthen and the four sick policemen came out of there in time!

Rumors Persisted

Various rumors circulated about where the prisoners were to be evacuated. It depended on which guard repeated the rumor. One rumor had the police going to Kiel, Lubeck and KZ-Neuengamme concentration camp. Denmark was no longer mentioned! They couldn't understand why, other than it might have been impossible to travel to Denmark. They thought it would inevitably lead to new evacuation orders, depending on how the war was developing.

Orders came that all civilians were to gather by the riverside at 18:00 and be evacuated. An hour later, the prisoners received orders to finish packing and be ready to move at a moment's notice. Half an hour later, the order to evacuate came. Poles and the Jewish women went first. The Germanic were lined up in four columns facing the river. They were now referred to by the Germans as *Norweger*. Earlier, they were collectively referred to as Germanic and Aryan; now, they were referred to as *Norweger*, including the Danes, Finns and some Balts. They were now a group of 359 *Norweger*. There was the impression that the designation *Norweger* garnered respect. When the police were on the earlier Death March, it was often asked what kind of people they were. *"Es ist die Norweger"* (It's the Norwegians), replied the guard, "Ah – die Norweger," (Ah – the Norwegians) was the response.

Torpedoed

Three medium-size landing crafts carried off the civilians, and six large landing crafts came up the riverbank at 21:00 to board the prisoners. There was a stillness in the air, an eerie silence. The explosions seemed quieter than usual. But to the north of the isthmus, towards Hela, they could see the light from bombs exploding. It appeared as if the sky was on fire.

A Lieutenant, who spoke Danish and proved to be a rather good fellow, promised to do what he could for the Norweger and put them all together in the same boat. After roll call, the Norweger received orders to take off their packs and sit down. This was a strong indication that evacuation was near. Civilian evacuees were gathered on the riverbed as more of them kept streaming in.

Women from the Old Camp were sent on board first, the Norweger followed. They were crammed together with barely any room to sit. There were approximately 300 on the roof and just as many down below.

A guard asked the prisoners sarcastically if they were good swimmers. The question coincided with the rumors they had heard that ships in the area were sunk with evacuees aboard.

Below is a list of ships torpedoed by Russian submarines.

Date	Ship's Name	Passengers	Fatalities
January 31, 1945	Wilhelm Gustloff	5,000	4,100
February 10, 1945	General von Steuben	3,000	2,700
March 12, 1945	Andross	2,500	200
April 4, 1945	Albert Jensen	Unknown	Unknown
April 11, 1945	Moltkefels	Unknown	Unknown
April 11, 1945	Posen	4,500	1,000
April 13, 1945	Karlsruhe	1,000	850
April 17, 1945	Goya	5,383	5,220
April 25, 1945	Emily Sauber	2,000	50

It was ideal evacuation weather: fog over the river, partly cloudy and the moon shining. It was a good evening to be under way. It was dark, but good light came from the spotlights. There was singing and even violin music on the landing craft. The landing craft was called the Wilhelm Lang and the sailing took three hours. There were 3,310 prisoners on board as the craft crossed Danzig Bay where they knew there were Russian submarines. The crossing was the most suspenseful and perilous part of their journey thus far. Most prisoners saw this as a pure suicide mission and waited expectantly for it to happen at any time. Constantly, someone needed to go to the bathroom, which was right behind where the Norweger were sitting. Every time someone used the bathroom, everyone in the way had to be woken to move. Upon his return, the sequence was repeated.

At 06:00 on Friday, April 27, the landing craft arrived at Hela. The prisoners had dreaded this portion of the journey for a long time. Now that it was over, they were in much better humor.

The Norweger were informed that KZ-Stutthof had been bombed the day after they evacuated. The question was, did Heggenes and the others get out?

After waiting for half an hour aboard the landing barge, the prisoners disembarked. They marched through a big harbor where different types of vessels were anchored. Evidence of bombing was all around and the streets they marched on had sustained substantial damage.

The Corral

The prisoners marched straight out of town and into a manicured pine forest where the air was nice and warm. At 08:30 they arrived at a large clearing in the forest, surrounded by high barbed wire fences resembling a corral. The facility looked improvised.

At 09:00, several Russian planes appeared. The anti-aircraft artillery was located everywhere, even in the woods near the prisoners. There was a large coastal artillery installation close by, and it was obvious this was the Russian target. Several bombs fell nearby, and it seemed as if they fell inside the fence. The attack was quickly over, but it was the worst bombing the prisoners had experienced during their entire capture. The encampment contained no water, nor any buildings and no washrooms. It seemed as if the place was meant for short stays while waiting to board the ships.

The Norweger gathered themselves together in a corner of the encampment as more prisoners continually arrived. They reclined in the sun but were required to be at least twenty meters from the fence. The anti-aircraft artillery once again let loose, and the sky was now filled with one bomber squadron after another heading towards Hela. The noise was deafening over the area, they saw exploding shells covering the entire sky. Then the bombs fell! The bombs must have been big, because the earth shook after the explosion and the shock wave could be felt by the prisoners more than three kilometers away. The prisoners had only tree stumps to hide behind. This attack was worse than the last. Just as suddenly as they appeared, the planes disappeared. The attack was concentrated on the fortress city of Hela. The planes returned later, and the scenario was repeated. This went on for some time.

At 14:00, when the attacks had paused for a while, a loud voice commanding *"Fertigmachen und Antreten"* (Get ready and fall in) was heard. The Norweger were positioned up front. The prisoners proceeded back the way they came. Ten prisoners were left behind inside the barbed wire. The Norweger didn't know whether it was because of being hit by shrapnel from bombs, abuse by guards or another reason.

After half an hour's walk through the woods, they stopped and were ordered to sit down. The prisoners were told they were not ready to be received on the docks yet. The guards told them there was a well with good water somewhere behind them. Many Norweger, equipped with buckets, cups and bottles, headed for the well. The other prisoners were forced to stay where they were. It was a hot day and people were thirsty. When the Norweger returned with their buckets full of water, there were many pleading eyes that gratefully accepted the water as it was being offered to them.

Entering Hela

At 17:00 the march continued. The prisoners entered Hela and then turned eastward following the main street down to Kriegshafen (war harbor). Now the prisoners understood why they had to wait a couple of hours in the woods, there were many places the Germans hadn't managed to clean up after the last bombing. A house was hit directly, and the residents lay strewn all around. Half of a horse lay on top of a roof, and further down the street lay two buses overturned with several dead. They passed a hospital with *Rote Kreutz* (Red Cross) painted in large letters on the roof. The hospital was badly damaged from a bomb exploding a few meters from the wall. The open doors allowed the prisoners to see people busily carrying the dead and wounded into ambulances. A few hundred meters further on, they saw a well-camouflaged artillery position that had been directly hit and turned upside down. It was most likely the artillery position that was the target, not the hospital. More bodies lay along the wayside, as well as people weeping hysterically while holding their faces in their hands.

Leif Tackle and several policemen found a door from a bombed out house and laid Henry Ulfsrud on it, carrying him down to the harbor. Ulfsrud was extremely weakened by his illness and weighed a mere 38 kilograms (84 pounds). When the prisoners reached the innermost part of Kriegshafen, they passed the commander's residence that was full of craters. Part of the building was gone, but it avoided a direct hit. It was this inner area that the planes targeted. It looked like they had entered hell! There was hardly a house left standing. People stood silently in the streets perplexed; they seemed paralyzed.

The prisoners followed a steep sandy slope down to the beach, where there lay long narrow stones as breakwaters. Behind the breakwaters lay several large barges, patrol boats and vessels of various sizes. From the beach, the prisoners had a good view of the entire harbor with many large ships scattered around. Not far from where the prisoners stood was a large steamer. The steamer looked very attractive to them, and they hoped to board it and evacuate further. They hoped the barges would be used to take the prisoners out to the ship.

Rumors circulated that all 359 Norweger, including guards and German civilians – a total of 900 people – would be sent to Denmark and Lübeck. The Poles and Jewish women were ordered to sit down on the sandbank, but the Norweger were sent beyond the breakwater where four barges were moored. When the Norweger were about to board the first barge, they were ordered to stop. They were informed that they would be boarding the barge but needed to wait.

Unexpectedly, four planes came from land, flying at a high altitude in the direction of the harbor. Anti-aircraft fire let loose all around them. A small patrol boat, moored at the pier a few meters from where they were standing, began shooting at the planes. The aircrafts dove at the big steamboats further out in the bay, dropping bombs on them. One vessel was struck; fire and black smoke rose heavenward. The aircrafts took a big turn and headed back as the prisoners breathed a sigh of relief.

Then a cry rang out that more planes were coming. Over the peninsula, heading straight towards the prisoners, were two planes flying at a higher altitude. Like lightning, the Norweger jumped down between the pier and the barge. John Ruud and several others jumped into the ocean, while others threw themselves down where they stood. Some headed full speed towards the land. The four that were carrying Ulfsrud put the door down on the pier and jumped for cover. Ulfsrud remained there until the attack was over. He just lay there on his back and looked at the planes. They heard the ominous whistling of bombs, watching two fall into a cluster of houses on the beach nearly three hundred meters away. In less than a second, two houses disappeared, followed by billows of black smoke rising towards the sky. It whistled again, and two bombs fell into the sea a few hundred meters from the small patrol boat. Pieces of cement and bricks from the buildings splashed into the sea while dust and ashes sprinkled down on the prisoners. The planes then turned and disappeared northward towards the open sea.

On shore lay 2,000 to 3,000 people prostrate on the ground, without any cover, while stones and cement blocks rained down around them. Two Jewish girls were grazed; no one else received a scratch. The police often mentioned that incident as being one of many miracles they experienced during their imprisonment.

The guards came rushing and screaming that the Norweger should hurry on board the barge. They were informed that the back room was reserved for the guards.

The rooms at the bottom of the barge were so far down they needed to use the ladder. No sooner had the Norweger descended to the bottom of the barge when they were ordered to come back up. The bottom rooms were reserved for the Jewish women.

The Poles and the Jewish women had arrived at the pier and were ready to board. The Norweger decided to take the second last room, which turned out to be where the sick policemen from the beach at Nickelswalde were. The inner part of the room was reserved for the sick and their nurses. The room filled up gradually and became so cramped that the prisoners could barely move, and still there were more prisoners clamoring to board. Something had to be done! Dahlin took command and suggested all packages be stowed and stacked along the walls. While that was happening, a cry came from the deck that several planes were circling the harbor again. The rest of the prisoners waiting to get in were dragged down. The prisoners heard the planes, but no bombs were dropped.

None of the Norweger were hurt on that hectic day, but it was close! Had they marched through the city when the bombardment struck, it might have been different. Had they been half an hour later arriving at the breakwater in Hela or left half an hour later from the camp in the woods, they would have ended up in the middle of the Russian air attacks. Similarly, before embarking, had the bombs from the two planes had a slightly different direction, it would have been disastrous. The bombs were undoubtedly intended for the patrol boat that was docked where they were. In the police's mind, this was yet another example of a miracle.

A powerful tugboat with the name *Adler* came up alongside the barge. A long tow rope was attached to the barge, and at 20:45 it was pulled away. After their experiences on the docks, the prisoners were relieved to be away from there.

Wolfgang

The barge had not gone far when Nils Kjærnet spoke up and shouted that he had something important to tell them. He said they should be prepared for a long stay on board the barge, at least twenty-four hours but maybe more. The prisoners were not to go aboard any ship, but might later switch barges. The police all stared at him. Some angrily argued that he shouldn't make up such a lie, even as a joke. It seemed incredible that he said the prisoners should endure the barge for twenty-four hours. Kjærnet assured them that his source was reliable, but the Norweger just laughed at him. It seemed so unthinkable. It turned out he was right.

The police proceeded to settle in, and their packs were stacked along the walls on top of each other. Not everyone was able to sit. After a quarrelsome few hours, all had their say. Three Poles came down to sit among them. The Poles were quickly chased back over to their own side, and eventually the tension sub-

Wolfgang

sided. A quick count let them know that there were ninety policemen in the room, in addition to the fifteen men and their attendants in the infirmary. The chief in the infirmary was Øivind Lunde. The sick had to lay down, therefore the police built a small barrier of packs between the sick and the rest of the room so the sick could rest in peace.

Wilhelm Lange measured the room, finding that it was three meters wide and eight meters long, a total of twenty-four square meters. With ninety men in the room, each had only 0.27 square meters. It was a full three meters up to the edge of the hatch, and the ladder had to be used when they were going up or down. Two diagonally laying shutters formed the ceiling.

The barge bore the proud name of *Wolfgang* and was used in the canals. The Germans called the barge *Kahn*. *Wolfgang* was a large, flat-bottomed, thirty-meter barge with a wheelhouse in the back, where the skipper stayed with his wife and daughter. The barge had seven large rooms across. In addition, there were two smaller rooms, one at the front of the barge and one just in front of the wheelhouse. In the rear were the SS guards, while the Schutzpolizei stayed in the front. The Schutzpolizei were, for the most part, elderly, quiet men, while the SS guards were younger and looked like bandits.

There was a total of thirty guards on board. A Schutzpolizei **Oberleutnant** was in command on board the barge. On several occasions, he was shown to be a reasonable person, at least towards the Norweger. Of all the large rooms, the Norweger were allocated the three rooms beside each other, closest to the SS room.

There were 359 Norweger on board as follows:

Nationality	Prisoner Status	Male	Female
Norwegian	Police Officers	223	–
Norwegian	Civilians	9	5
Danes	Civilians	25	6
Finnish	Civilians	72	7
Lithuanians	Civilians	10	2
Total		**339**	**20**

Poles and Jewish women had the two rooms nearest the Schutzpolizei. Overall, there were 1,000 on board, the oldest was eighty-seven years old while the youngest was three months.

Another barge named *Vaterland* was pulled by the tugboat *Bussard*. The commanding officer on the *Adler* tugboat was Rudolf Struecker, a very reasonable man.

The Oberleutnant gave the Norweger permission to go up on top and to stay on the sloping shutters at their own risk. The other prisoners were not allowed. Several Norweger went on deck and took their wool blankets with them to spend the night, laying on their stomachs for safety's sake. It was quiet and mild, with a slightly hazy moonlight. They found it a refreshing contrast to the confined space and poorly ventilated rooms below.

The transports out of KZ-Stutthof were as follows:

Date	From	Vessel	Prisoners	Survivors	Destination
Mar 25	Gotenhafen	*Elbing*	Unknown	Unknown	Hamburg
Mar 25	Gotenhafen	*Zephyr*	719	300	Hamburg
Apr 27	Nickelswalde/ Hela	*Wolfgang*	1,000	Unknown	Neustadt

Apr 27	Nickelswalde/ Hela	*Vaterland*	2,000	1,237	Neustadt
Apr 27	Nickelswalde/ Hela	*Anne Marie T* New tugboat	610	473 351	(ran aground and sank) Klintholm
Apr 27	Nickelswalde/ Hela	Barge no. 4	500	234	Kiel/ Eckernførde
Apr 28	Nickelswalde	*Olga Siemerse*	1,060	630	Flensburg
		Total	**5,889**	**3,225**	

CHAPTER 18 –
Voyage Begins

The voyage began dramatically, but now it was quiet. At 23:00 the vessels were on the open sea. Although the prisoners were safe from the planes, they were now in greater danger from submarines and mines. The *Adler*, with *Wolfgang* in tow, sailed at a good pace towards the northeast, but suddenly slowed down and eventually stopped, laying quite still. The prisoners could see some dark dots in the distance that proved to be two other tugboats towing barges. They wondered if there were other tugboats they couldn't see and if they were part of a larger convoy. Patrol boats cruised the area, and after a flare was spotted all tows began to move in a north easterly direction. After some distance, the convoy turned northward, and then northwesterly.

The first evacuation took place on March 25, 1945, from a work camp in Gotenhafen with 719 prisoners. They were evacuated by two small passenger boats, *Elbing* and *Zephyr*. On board the *Zephyr* were six Norwegian civilians. *Zephyr* developed engine problems and fell behind. When *Zephyr* arrived at Kiel, *Elbing* had already gone through the Kiel Canal and onward to Hamburg. From Hamburg the prisoners were transferred to KZ-Neuengamme. Prisoners from *Zephyr* landed in Kiel and remained there for some time. They were made to work at the Kiel harbor and were constantly in danger from air raids. The prisoners were eventually taken by train to KZ-Neuengamme. In April, they were taken on White Buses from KZ-Neuengamme.

The Jewish Women

The Jewish women on board *Wolfgang* and *Vaterland* had a terrible time. There were 300 women in a room similar to the Norweger rooms, making it 7.5 women per square meter. The police asked themselves if this could be possible. The women had to stand on top of each other.

From the time the prisoners arose, they heard piercing screams from the Jewish women's room. It wasn't only a single scream, but rather screams from hundreds of voices in unison. The women kept screaming and crying hour after hour. Sometimes there was a hard knock on the wall by the Schutzpolizei and it was quiet for a moment, but then the screaming started again. This went on for nearly two days. The Norweger tried not to think about the women's conditions, for there was nothing they could do about it.

In their own room, very few Norweger had space to sit. They realized this couldn't go on much longer and decided they should sit on the floor straddling each other's legs. One would sit between one's legs with his back towards the person, and as close as possible, across the room. In this way, they could all sit. It wasn't long before one after the other began to moan and twist. It eventually got so bad that one by one they had to stand and stretch. It proved that it was better to stand than to sit straddled. The Norweger held out till 03:00, when many of them crawled up to the deck again. It was a little scary to sit on the deck, but it was a much better atmosphere. Lights from a patrol boat ran across the barge now and then, everything was silent and still. Even the Jewish women were silent for the moment.

The Norweger laid there for several hours until sunrise. They discovered that two Jewish women fell overboard that night, when they were up on the deck to relieve themselves. A third woman had thrown herself off in a fit of desperation. Both Ole Bakke and Otto Kristiansen saw several Poles deliberately fall overboard. One can be pretty sure that no one would be picked up if one fell overboard!

Man Overboard

Then it happened. A policeman fell overboard, but Olav Brudvik was standing in the stern and saw him fall. He quickly reached over the side to grab him and held on while help came. Leif Tackle and one other came to help get Berg on board. Finn Mortensen found a place on the deck but was afraid of falling into the sea. He found a large iron hook fastened to the deck and threaded his jacket onto it to secure himself to the deck. Kristiansen did the same, threading his belt strap onto a similar hook.

While walking on the deck in his sleep one night, Ole Bakke was tackled by the policemens' "favorite" Finn friend, No.13, to prevent him from walking off the deck. Bakke said he dreamed that there was a large German tank after him and he was trying to run for cover. After this incident, Bakke took a rope and tied himself to a hook.

The weather turned to rain, and most of the Norweger packed up and headed down to their room. Those who had raingear and proper equipment stayed. There had been so many on the deck that those below could lay down and sleep, but now the sleeping prisoners were awakened. Arousing "dead tired" men to make them stand up was not pleasant for either party. Everyone was, to a large extent, testy. Angry words were spoken. They decided on a different approach. They divided the men into smaller groups. One group would sit for two hours while the other stood. After two hours they would switch. However, this proved to be very unpopular. Those standing couldn't move their feet, making the conditions even more intolerable. Some became seasick and vomited right on the floor. The stench was appalling. Several of the sick fell to the floor, which further complicated the situation. There was no sleep to be had that night.

The continuous screaming from the Jewish women's room had died down for a while, but it soon started again. Eventually there were longer pauses between the screams. Every day a dead body was thrown overboard. One morning, eight corpses were recovered from the Jewish women's room, with another six at noon. The reason for this was typhus, along with hunger and thirst. On several occasions, the Germans also threw near dead prisoners into the sea. *"Sie würden sowieso bald sterben, und das ist eine praktische Lösung"* (They would soon die anyway, and it's a practical solution), they said.

Early on Sunday, April 29, light spring rain fell, and the prisoners set about collecting the rainwater. They laid pots and pans out on the deck, but it yielded very little. A resourceful policeman, Anton Aaby, made a larger catchment area by rigging up a piece of canvas from the wheelhouse, getting some of the police to hold the ends. It worked well. They were able to fill a saucepan of water for the infirmary. The sick suffered most from thirst. In an unguarded moment a thirsty soul drank all the water in the saucepan.

Several prisoners decided to drink sea water. They were strongly advised not to, but drank it anyway. Of those prisoners, some went insane and jumped into the sea.

Several of the police had brought barley and wheat flour with them. They mixed this with the sea water and made a porridge mix with a little salt; it proved good both as food and drink.

The night passed, and it turned into a nice morning. The vessel was now heading into the open sea. The guards were on constant lookout for Russian boats controlling the coast. Skjolden, a former marine expert, took compass readings and various samples to determine how fast the vessel was travelling. He did this by throwing wood chips at the bow and figuring out the time it would take to reach the stern of the barge. He determined that the barge was travelling between six to seven knots.

The convoy had not met any vessels except two steamers and four warships entering the bay to Hela the morning before.

Hvor skal vi? (Where are we going?) was the main question on everybody's mind. Rumors suggested Lübeck, Swinemünde and Copenhagen. The Norweger inquired of the skipper, who said he had been ordered to sail to Lübeck.

Skjolden kept careful track of the convoy's course. The day before, the course was north, and later it changed to the northwest. The vessel went far out to sea, which made the police hopeful they were heading for Bornholm in Denmark. A Danish prisoner from Bornholm had said the prisoners would be warmly welcomed there. Hopes faded when the course was changed to westward. The vessel passed Bornholm on April 29 at about 00:30.

Odd Fjælberg and Walther Tvedt had agreed among themselves they would try to escape as soon as an opportunity presented itself, and Bornholm looked like an ideal option. They considered whether they would unhook the dinghy hanging in tow from *Wolfgang* and try to paddle to Bornholm but found it too risky. First, they would have to get a good rest, as it was a long way to Bornholm. When it was dark the patrol boats constantly moved up and down the convoy, but Bornholm was still occupied by the Germans.

Tore Jørgensen

Danish Islands

Since leaving Hela, the prisoners had not seen land, but at 09:00 that morning land appeared in the west. It was a dark strip of land with white spots on it. One policeman, who had previously sailed on the Baltic Sea, determined it to be Rügen.

The convoy passed two hundred meters off the coast and arrived near the northern tip of Kapp Arkona, when the direction was suddenly changed to northwest. The new course excited the Norweger, for that indicated the vessel was en route to the Danish islands.

The wind picked up and nearly became a gale. The police watched as the tugboats maneuvered the barges that were now completely helpless on the sea. Several policemen had noticed that there were a lot of iron bars serving as counterweights in one of the rooms. If the bars shifted, they could easily go right through the bottom of the hull. The barges took a tremendous beating. They were not designed for the open sea and could simply break apart in the turbulence.

The convoy did an about-face, and the Norweger waved goodbye to the Danish islands, sailing to the east of Rügen to seek more shelter. The high sea caused the convoy to turn north towards the northern tip of Rügen. This move separated the vessels, and three other barges could not be seen anymore.

There lay several wrecks along the beaches around Rügen, among them was a German warship. The convoy entered a sheltered harbor behind a protruding breakwater; this was Sassnitz. The city lay in terraces up from the harbor, with hillsides full of spring flowers in the background. However, it clearly bore signs of being hit by bombs. After a masterful docking by the skipper of the tugboat *Adler*, the *Wolfgang* tied up at Pier 13. The barge *Vaterland* came up beside.

What was primarily on the minds of the prisoners was provisions, especially water. Since leaving Hela on April 27, the prisoners had received neither wet nor dry provisions. The police thought with horror of the Poles and Jewish women, who must be desperate by now. The Oberleutnant went to shore, and shortly after gave orders for a water detail of twenty Norweger. It wasn't hard to get volunteers. Fjælberg and several others went away with tubs, buckets and anything else that could be used. They got water from a water main that was cemented into the breakwater. There was much rejoicing when they returned. While the Norweger were distributing the water, the order came to *einsteigen* (board), and at 18:00 the convoy was off again. Rumor was that the convoy was sailing to Stralsund to receive further orders.

When the prisoners woke the next morning, it was Monday, April 30.

The *Anna Marie*

That morning, the Norweger learned that the barge *Anne Marie T527*, with 610 prisoners aboard, had arrived at Sassnitz the day before. It ran aground in the strait between the mainland and Rügen, on a reef named Greifswalder Oie. They learned that 473 prisoners were rescued on board an ammunition barge and brought to the small port town of Lauterbach on the island of Rügen.

The weak and the sick had to remain on board the grounded barge. It later broke apart. All of those prisoners drowned.

In Lauterbach, provisions were arranged for the *Anne Marie* prisoners. In the confusion, 120 prisoners fled into the woods. Many of them were caught and shot where they stood. The other prisoners were loaded on board a new barge pulled by the tugboat *Danzig*. For fear of the Russians in the narrow strait near Stralsund, one barge and an escort vessel headed along the east side and later headed north, setting course for Flensburg. The barge later developed problems with leaks, and it was considered too dangerous to continue. The head of the escort vessel chose to head for Klintholm on Møen in Denmark. The escort vessel left the harbor while the barge was tied to the wharf. This happened early in the morning of Saturday, May 5 – the day peace was declared in Denmark. A total of 372 prisoners were taken care of by the Danish population. Of these, 22 died in the next few days while 350 survived. On board were Jehovah's Witnesses, among them was Hermione Schmidt.

The Norweger also learned what had happened to Barge No.4. There were 500 prisoners on board, mostly Jewish women. The barge was pulled by a tugboat that flew a yellow epidemic flag. For this reason, they were not granted entry to any port along the way. The barge arrived in Lübeck Bay on May 1. SS men onboard the tugboat tried to ditch the prisoners, but no one would accept them. The barge arrived at Kiel on May 4, where

190 prisoners were taken ashore and hospitalized. Some Germans drove off with the barge, even though there were sixty-six weakened and sick prisoners still on board. On May 5, the barge ran aground sixty meters from shore at Bookniseck in Waabs. British naval forces were involved in the rescue operation. Of the sixty-six prisoners who were still on board, twenty-two died of drowning, exhaustion or illness before or after landing. The other forty-four were brought ashore and hospitalized. The twenty-two dead prisoners were buried in a church yard in Eckernførde. Trudi Birger and her mother were on board the barge.

A convoy of eight ships passed in front of *Wolfgang* and *Vaterland* into the strait between Rügen and the coast. One of the ships was a training ship, which a Danish prisoner assumed was the vessel *Horst Wessel*. The wind had picked up greatly as the convoy travelled along the south side of Rügen. They heard bombs exploding and saw smoke from large fires; it was from Greifswald. Russian armored vehicles had penetrated northwest from Stettin and surrounded the city. From *Wolfgang*, the prisoners heard and saw exploding grenades as well as smoke columns rising into the air.

The convoy continued into the narrow fairway leading to Stralsund. After passing through a drawbridge, they entered the harbor at 10:00 and anchored some distance from the dock. The Oberleutnant went to land while the prisoners waited for further orders. The docks had been damaged from bombing but the harbor was full of activity, with vessels moored along the quays wherever they found space. Outside lay hundreds of barges waiting their turn while tugboats darted back and forth. Once a barge was finished, it was towed out and another took its place. Clothes, boots and different needs for the evacuation were handed out from an extremely large, moored barge. *Wolfgang* was constantly cut off by both large and small vessels sailing toward the west and fully loaded with people, animals and household goods. Two Red Cross ships also sailed out towards the west. The Oberleutnant returned and ordered twenty Norweger to go fetch supplies and water.

Odd Fjælberg was put in charge of the provisioning command, while the Oberleutnant escorted them.

At 15:00 there was a very loud bang and a massive fire and smoke column rose into the air at the tip of the isthmus to the west. It was the Ernst **Heinkel Flugzeugwerke** (Airplane Factory) in Rostock that was bombed. Rumors spread that the Russians were just outside the city of Stralsund. A panic came over the docks. Moorings were cut, and vessels rushed to get out. The rumors were true. Greifswald fell on April 30, and Russian armored divisions were moving rapidly towards Stralsund. In reality, the Russians were at the outskirts of the city while *Wolfgang* was in the harbor. It appeared to be well into the twelfth hour.

The Oberleutnant came back with *Adler* and the supply detail. He frantically ordered to cast off while leaving the skipper and members of the Schutzpolizei on land. *Wolfgang* was being towed out towards the strait that was now full of fleeing vessels. A little way out, the Oberleutnant was advised that the *Wolfgang* skipper and the other Schutzpolizei were not aboard. *Adler* pulled the *Wolfgang* aside and moored it to a buoy, then went back to retrieve those left behind. They saw the captain and a few men come rowing, then boarding *Adler*. They sat on the hatch and looking gloatingly on the evacuation as the master race was fleeing. They thought it was too bad it would affect so many innocent civilians.

What the commando brought back was outstanding: liver, butter and good drinking water. The Norweger had eaten the last remnants of their provisions from KZ-Stutthof that morning.

Behind the convoy, the constant roar of explosions and machine guns was heard. Eleven heavy bombers thundered overhead while rockets from the anti-aircraft battery on the western tip of the isthmus fired at them. The planes paid no attention and flew undisturbed in the direction of Greifswald.

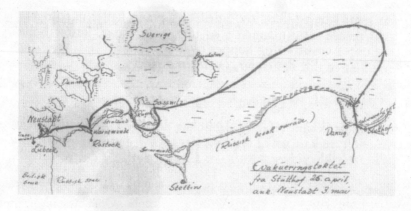

Second Evacuation Route

The convoy approached the shipping route between Denmark and Warnemünde. The Norweger were anxious which direction the vessel would take; despite earlier disappointments they were ever hopeful. The other vessels headed north towards Denmark, but the tugboats turned westward towards Warnemünde with their barges.

The view was extraordinary. Rügen, with its many mini islands, lay to the east of the convoy. Beyond that they could see the northern tip of Kapp Arkona. There were many small, picturesque fishing villages to see. The water was shallow and beacon lights were all over.

On Tuesday, May 1, the wind started to blow. The *Wolfgang* rolled on the sea.

The police were thinking of the iron in one of the rooms that could easily put a hole in the vessel and sink it, or the possibility that the barge could break in the middle.

The Old Woman

An elderly German woman kept following the Norweger around the barge. During the storm, she stumbled and hit her head on the hatch, remaining motionless for some time. On several occasions the police had to chase her away. The old woman was a kleptomaniac and wore a green criminal triangle, but she came from a good family. One day, she was caught trying to steal from Olav Risøen's backpack. Let it be known that she didn't bother the Norweger again.

The wind died down for a time and the convoy continued to the prisoners' relief.

The *Wolfgang* prisoners were awakened at 05:00 by the anchor being dropped in the Warnemünde outer harbor, where there were many vessels. They saw a ship flying the Danish flag with neutrality markings. After waiting for a time, the *Alder* hoisted its anchor and headed north with the *Wolfgang* in tow.

Warnemünde, the port city of Rostock, was a well-ordered town where the Heinkel Flugzeugwerke airplane factory was bombed earlier. Warnemünde was a beautiful city with many large church steeples. Oberleutnant left for the city with the tugboat while the prisoners waited. An icy bitter wind blew, and the prisoners had to wrap themselves tightly in their blankets.

Suddenly the *Adler* came in full speed and docked by one of the other barges. From there, *Adler* hurried to *Wolfgang*, attached the towline and headed west. *Bussard* also attached a towline to the barge *Vaterland* and followed.

Oberleutnant informed the Norweger that they were now heading directly to Neustadt, which was to be their ultimate destination. He was instructed not to dock at Lübeck. There was now an urgency in his voice. He brought back no provisions or water. Rostock and Warnemünde would surrounder to the Russians on May 2. When the *Wolfgang* left the port of Warnemünde, the Russians were at the city's door.

The landscape west of Warnemünde was impressive. Large beach hotels lined the landscape, and some flew the Red Cross flag over the buildings.

Intense blasts from the beach drew the prisoners' attention. They saw huge pillars of smoke rise into the air and people fleeing in panic. As they continued along the coast, *Adler* turned towards Wismar.

Einar Edvardsen had developed a close friendship with the skipper and his family, and he was permitted to listen to their radio. Edvardsen reported that Russian armored vehicles had broken through all German defenses west of Stettin and were a mere hundred kilometers from Lübeck. The Norweger reasoned it was this advancement they had followed along the coast. Furthermore, Edvardsen reported that Lübeck was liberated by the British, who presumably had tanks surrounding the town of Wismar. How great it was for them to think that the English were so close! Until now, they had believed they would fall into Russian hands and were content to do so; but to be freed by the British was far better! This had never been part of their thinking, but now they were filled with excitement.

Heading for the Bay

As the *Adler* turned into the large and wide Lübeck Bay, a sudden flash lit up the sky, but this time it was lightning not rockets. A sudden sharp gust of wind came rushing across the bay, creating white caps all over the sea, followed by a heavy hailstorm. The prisoners packed their belongings and moved below deck.

Luckily the storm cleared and the weather turned milder. *Adler*, with *Wolfgang* in tow, proceeded to the middle of the bay where there was a row of buoys marking the entrance to Lübeck. Artillery fire from the west of Lübeck could be heard, along with tank cannons between Wismar and Lübeck.

The Germans in Lübeck were in desperation, for every boat that could float was headed out of the bay northward. *Adler* continued along the west side of the bay. Behind the barge, the prisoners saw twenty-five large steamers and a host of smaller vessels heading north. *Adler* towed the *Wolfgang* along the west shoreline and into a small port. It was the city of Neustadt, one of Germany's main submarine stations and marine ports.

Four large warships were moored at the dock, along with a barge moored behind the ships. *Adler*, with *Wolfgang* in tow, moored alongside the barge. The time was 21:00 on May 1. All prisoners who were able came up to the deck and stood shoulder to shoulder, cheering and waving from both barges. Several prisoners on the other barge attempted to get across to *Wolfgang*, but the guards prevented them.

The primary concern for the prisoners was provisions of food and water. The Norweger kept pestering the Oberleutnant about supplies, and a work detail was arranged. The work detail came back with water, but nothing else. Among the sick was Olav Skjerven, who had developed typhus, and Annar Rostad with stomach typhoid; both had a high fever. During the journey, the police occasionally talked with both of them, helping to keep their spirits up.

On the morning of May 2, most prisoners were on deck nestled in their blankets. The body of a gray-haired woman lay on the barge. None of the prisoners would heed her. They just stepped over her and paid her no attention. One prisoner who sprayed the deck straddled over the body and continued to spray the other side.

Men and women sat close beside each other on the edge of barges and did their business or ate. Some mothers nearby were caring for their children.

Hitler is Dead!

Suddenly, there was lively commotion among the prisoners. One Norweger had been on shore and heard a car with a loudspeaker reporting *Hitler ist tot!* (Hitler is dead!) and Rear Admiral Karl Donitz had taken over as his successor. The news did not bring instant excitement among the Norweger; they were used to being disappointed and weren't sure if they should believe the news. Shortly afterwards, they saw warships with the swastika flying half-mast. It seemed strangely quiet on board. Maybe it was true after all!

The commander in Neustadt did not allow the evacuees to dock, but Oberleutnant refused to leave until provisions were provided. The commander said there was no provisions for the prisoners and that there was only enough for themselves.

Adler, with *Wolfgang* in tow, headed out of the harbor at 09:30 with its deck of prisoners. The barge passed many warships of various sizes, including one-man submarines, all with the swastika flying at half-mast.

Adler proceeded into the middle of Lübeck Bay. What on earth could that mean? Irgens tried to find out why they were being towed into the middle of the bay. Irgens had frequent contact with the Oberleutnant and received regular updates. It appeared they were off to secure provisions, but neither the Oberleutnant nor the guards knew where they would secure them from.

Without warning, the skipper came rushing across the deck and screamed that a chicken had been stolen from him. The Poles had gathered in one section of *Wolfgang*, and chicken feathers were found among them. Several SS guards came running to punish the guilty party. The thief was made to stand upright as he was being whipped, then he was shot and thrown into the frigid water.

The gulf narrowed as the barge passed Travemünde, a district of Lübeck. It was approximately 11:00.

Full Evacuation Mode

Travemünde was in full evacuation mode. Several big ships attracted the attention of some former seafarers among the police prisoners. As the barge passed the ships, they saw the overpainted raised letters *Vega* on the bow of a Norwegian ship. The narrow entrance ended at Travemünde, and the barge continued through the strait. The coast was picturesque on both sides, almost like a lush Danish landscape with its flowering cherry and pear trees. Eventually the strait narrowed and the landscape changed. Now there were factories, workshops, floating docks, cranes and ships everywhere on both sides.

At 11:45, aircrafts appeared. From the shore came the shout *"Tiefflieger!"* (Low flying planes!). The planes were British Typhoons flying just above the treetops, therefore they always appeared as a surprise. The prisoners were ordered to lie down flat, and those of the police who were still wearing Italian Badoglio uniforms were made to take them off. There were five to six aircrafts heading towards Travemünde, then they circled back. This was repeated several times, and the planes dropped bombs each time. Had the *Wolfgang* passed Travemünde half an hour later, it would have been right in the midst of the attack. The attack lasted for about fifteen minutes, as the barge continued south towards Lübeck.

A favorite place for the Norweger was at the stern of the barge. It was where they relieved themselves, which was quite a sight! They had to stand on the edge of the deck and hold on to the iron staples. Not everyone was equally proficient at it. The skipper would often come rushing to show them how it was done. The row of heads sticking up over the edge, while their faces mirrored different expressions, was a humorous sight. To master the squat was not that easy, especially when the barge rolled and the sea was rough.

The *Wolfgang* passed through a drawbridge and into a bay. The barge *Vaterland* had passed the *Wolfgang* in the sound, but suddenly the barge turned and headed back towards the *Wolfgang*. A Schutzpolizei on the *Vaterland* shouted at them: *"Zurück nach Neustadt,"* (Back to Neustadt). Immediately, *Adler* turned around with *Wolfgang* in tow, even though they were only one nautical mile from Lübeck. The time was 12:00. They learned from passing ships that there was fighting in the streets of Lübeck and no provisions were left. Oberleutnant decided that he would still make the attempt and headed for shore with *Adler*. Several guards headed to the beach and went inland, while other guards rowed out into the deep and tried their luck at fishing by throwing hand grenades into the water and picking up the dead fish. A few police went to shore and made a fire to cook the fish. The scene was almost like a cookout, until a large steamer created such a large swell it doused the fire. The fire was too close to the water's edge.

The *Thielbek*

On the opposite bank, a large ship named *Thielbek* was anchored with many prisoners on board. A sudden thought hit the Norweger. Had they sailed to this point in order to catch this ship? Would the Germans put them on board the *Thielbek*? Before they could get an answer, they were startled by noises from heavy bombing to the south, in the direction of Lübeck. Huge columns of smoke rose into the air. At that point, they were not aware that two policemen, Arne Sundvor and Alf Andersen, had escaped with the intention of meeting the British army at Lübeck and informing them of the prisoner transport.

At approximately 15:45, *Adler* returned without provisions. Oberleutnant informed them that the English now occupied Lübeck. Instantly, the *Wolfgang* was boarded and set sail back the way they had come. Unfortunately, the drawbridge was closed. There was a continuous stream of vehicles, bicycles and pedestrians proceeding over it. Several ships were also waiting and blasted their horns angrily. The tugboat stuck its nose in land and waited. Finally, the passage was open.

Oberleutnant informed the prisoners that some of the guards had rowed ashore at the bridge and had not returned. *Adler* again went to pick up the guards, leaving *Wolfgang* with its nose stuck into the shore. The guards were on the other side of the bridge. *Adler* went to pick them up and to refuel.

Nine British planes appeared, and the prisoners were commanded to lay flat on the deck. The aircrafts circled and headed for targets closer to Lübeck.

The *D/S Corona* passed the barge. Several Finns recognized the ship as Finnish. They could see the boat had Helsingfors painted over with Kiel. Pillars of heavy smoke rose to the sky beside the barge, and a hefty rumble was heard to both the south and the west. Suddenly there was a powerful explosion only 400–500 meters from the barge. Fire and smoke rose into the air. It turned out the Germans were blowing up their own submarines.

A single German Stork plane came flying overhead. The Stork was a German training plane with long legs. While they were waiting for the tugboat to return, several police sat on a gunnel and recorded what they were seeing, like war correspondents.

Heading for Lübeck Bay

By 18:00, *Adler* had still not returned when a rowboat fully loaded with cardboard boxes appeared. The boxes were heaved on board the *Wolfgang*; they contained Schmalzfleisch (lard meat, Schmalzfleisch is made of 72% pork and 18% bacon along with lard). A second rowboat appeared with several cartons of crackers.

Someone yelled from the shore that the bridge was about to burst. The bridge was about 200 meters above the barge. The guards yelled for the prisoners to go down in the rooms below. Others shouted for everyone to lie down. There was confusion, and no chance to move anywhere. It was again shouted from the shore as the people waved and pointed to the bridge.

Like a miracle, *Adler* appeared. The minutes while attaching the towline and heading outward were suspenseful. Then the bridge exploded! Miraculously, the barge was far enough away and didn't take any damage. *Adler* and *Wolfgang* were the last vessels to leave the sound.

The barge passed a bombed submarine, with only one side of the turret visible above the water. On the banks were soldiers fleeing and civilians running out of their houses with their belongings in hand.

Wolfgang moved briskly with the ebb tide. Behind the barge the traffic subsided. The prisoners passed a huge submarine that had been driven partly onto land with a large hole in the hull. The German naval flag flew at half-mast. The engines could be heard still going. As the barge headed northward, it passed the narrow mouth of the Trave River at Travemünde. On a small island were a number of civilian aircrafts bombed and laying in pieces. A large ship passed the barge with the name *Gertrude Fritzen*. The ship was travelling in the middle of the fairway and taking on water, it was hit by a bomb at mid ship. *Wolfgang* had barely gotten out of the bay when twelve British bombers headed right for them but continued outward towards Lübeck Bay. Earlier in the day, on the *Wolfgang's* journey inward, the barge passed German warships a few kilometers out. Those were obviously the British targets. *Adler* slowed so as not to come within the battle area. Afterwards, the bombers returned and headed towards Travemünde while *Adler* continued at normal speed. As *Wolfgang* got closer to the warships, the British planes returned. The ships opened fire on the aircrafts. The planes dropped bombs all around the area, and *Adler* was forced to zigzag away from the battle area. The move went well! A plane came flying towards them from the west side of the bay. It circled once, and then headed towards the warships where it was met with intense anti-aircraft fire. With a mighty explosion, two rockets fell into the sea. One landed only fifty meters from the port side of *Wolfgang* and the other fell on the starboard side, but a little further away. This was too close. *Adler*, with *Wolfgang* in tow, headed quickly away from the battle area.

Oberleutnant informed Irgens that the course was now set for Flensburg. This was great news! Flensburg is a town situated on the German–Danish border.

A motorboat suddenly appeared and passed near *Wolfgang*, shouting orders to Oberleutnant. Immediately, *Adler* turned and headed in a northerly direction. The Norweger all cheered! They were going in the direction of Flensburg! The prisoners had managed the journey so far, they will most likely survive this night as well.

What the prisoners were watching was the defeat of the last German resistance on the western front. Lübeck fell to the British on May 2, just around dinner time, while *Wolfgang* was in the sound just northeast of the city. That helped to explain the colossal combat operation the prisoners heard and saw all around them; it was the blasting of submarines and bridges.

The prisoners had a ringside seat, on the roof of a German canal barge, as they witnessed a small portion of war history. They were one of the last human transports from the Danzig area and the port of Hela. As the transport moved westward, the Russian army followed on their heels. The prisoners were actually among the last from both the east, and later the west coast, who witnessed the Germans' panicked evacuation from every city and port ahead of the Russian advancement.

They witnessed the German panic in Greifswald, Stralsund, Wismar and Warnemünde area. At Wismar the British came into play, and the prisoners were now between the Russians and the British in their path towards Lübeck.

The Oberleutnant

There arose a new question among the Norweger: How could Oberleutnant embark on such a hazardous expedition towards Lübeck? It was virtually the same as heading into a combat zone. It was thanks to miracles that they survived.

When Oberleutnant was denied provisions in Neustadt, the prisoners were all in a precarious situation. Since they left KZ-Stutthof they had not received anything, other than liver and a dole of margarine in Stralsund. The situation was the same for the Germans on board. Oberleutnant had to get supplies somewhere. Perhaps it appeared that the Lübeck area was the best option? Perhaps he considered taking supplies from the evacuated military warehouses? He may have thought there were a lot of provisions the prisoners could use. The most likely scenario was that the Oberleutnant was not well informed over the military situation. Therefore, he could not foresee the rapid deterioration of events. Perhaps Oberleutnant was so desperate in light of the German civilians' and prisoners' urgent need for provisions? Or maybe he was just plain stupid or misinformed? They pondered these questions. Was the Germans' original intent for the prisoners to be transported to Lübeck and then put on board the vessel *Thielbek*?

Lübeck was the main destination mentioned during their voyage. When the prisoners entered the sound before Lübeck, the *Thielbek* was moored there. British planes, however, attacked the ship and it probably became too "hot" for the ship where it lay. The ship was then towed out while the *Wolfgang* prisoners were left behind. For all appearances, it seemed that was the German plan. The fact was that the *Wolfgang* was not finished with the vessel *Thielbek* yet!

CHAPTER 19 –
Deliverance

The vessels arrived at a small cove just outside Neustadt. Only a small bluff prevented them from looking directly into the city. Several large steamers laid in the bay, close to Neustadt. *Adler*, with *Wolfgang* in tow, set course towards the largest of the ships. The name on the side of the ship read *Cap Arcona*. The barge passed so close that the prisoners could see faces glancing out of the portholes. The faces followed them with their eyes. *Adler* didn't stop. Instead it continued to a ship that was nearest to land, and which the prisoners recognized: the *Thielbek*! The barge *Vaterland* was already moored alongside the ship, and *Adler* made a great arc around *Thielbek* to bring *Wolfgang* alongside *Vaterland*. The time was 21:00. If the prisoners were to board the *Thielbek*, the ship would hopefully take them to Flensburg. On board the *Thielbek* were prisoners from KZ-Neuengamme concentration camp.

On board the *Vaterland*, orders were given to the Jewish women and the Polish prisoners: *"Fertigmachen!"* (Get ready!) and *"Antreten"* (Begin). The prisoners were lined up on the deck with their bundles in hand, ready to enter *Thielbek*. On *Wolfgang* the guards went around and shouted down into the rooms: *"Heraus – alle!"* (All out!). A horrible thought, of being crammed in a tiny space with all the prisoners already on *Thielbek*, passed through the minds of the Norweger.

A rope ladder was dangling high from the side of the ship, but not one crew member was on hand to lower the ladder far enough to be reached from below. The ship seemed deserted and covered in darkness. Ever since the *Wolfgang* arrived, the prisoners hadn't seen a single human being, but a figure appeared on the bow. It was a guard. He peered at them for a moment, then disappeared. There was no one there to arrange for the prisoners to board the ship. It appeared the prisoners were neither expected nor welcome. The whole scene seemed so mysterious. Prisoners on both barges stood and waited for orders, but none came.

Something is Happening

The guards disappeared into their rooms and returned with their belongings. They appeared to be frantic. It seemed they were all departing. The guards went back and forth while whispering to each other. None of them seemed concerned about the prisoners. There was definitely something wrong. The Norweger inquired of several Schutzpolizei, who mentioned orders were given that all German military and civilians should go onboard *Adler*, which came sliding alongside the barge right at that moment. The guards crawled over to *Adler* with their belongings. It caused a stir in particular when the barge skipper and his family boarded *Adler*. Gunnar Jørgensen stopped a German Kapo (No.20) to ask him what was afoot. The Kapo replied that he knew nothing but promised to keep his eyes and ears open and pass on any information. Jørgensen watched the Kapo and saw that he and another German Kapo were discussing something. Jørgensen walked over to listen, and heard one say, *"Ja, ich weiss genau was geschehen will"* (Yes, I know what will happen). The Kapos saw him listening and moved away. Jørgensen saw that No.20 quickly ran down to his room. After a moment he came up again with his pack and boarded *Adler*, which was in a hurry to put some distance between itself and the barges. Three guards didn't manage to get on board *Adler* in time and were left standing on *Wolfgang*. The guards whistled and shouted at the tugboat. *Adler* managed to stick her nose up against *Wolfgang*, allowing the guards to jump on. Andreas Moen and Rolf Henry Berg took advantage of the confusion to smuggle themselves aboard *Adler*, which quickly backed out again. It was as if *Wolfgang* was infected with typhus. A similar scene happened at *Vaterland*.

When Moen and Berg smuggled themselves aboard *Adler*, they didn't notice any other Norwegians among the passengers. The guards were aware they both were prisoners and said *"Wirf sie über Bord!"* (Throw them overboard!). But Moen and Berg said they were Norwegian and therefore Germanic. They were then allowed to travel to Neustadt. At Neustadt, on the night of May 3, they were put in military detention.

A Word of Warning

A German lieutenant aboard *Wolfgang* whispered confidentially to Hjellemo before he jumped over to *Adler*: *"Sie sehen, wie es sich entwickelt hat. Ich möchte nur darauf hinweisen, dass der Dampfer, an dessen Seite Sie stehen, Sprengstoff an Bord hat. Wir haben Aufträge von Bord zu gehen erhalten, aber Sie sind die Norweger und gute Seeleute"* (You see how it has evolved. I just want to point out that the steamer you're alongside has explosives on board. We have received orders to disembark, but you are the Norwegians and good seafarers), he said. *"Leben Sie wohl!"* (Farewell!).

That statement left the police puzzled and dismayed as they discussed it amongst themselves. What on earth could that mean? The prisoners were now left entirely to themselves. Usually that would make them thrilled, but instead it created concern, unrest and misgivings. The way everyone left caused great suspicion that something bad was about to happen. Irgens and Hjellemo had, for some time, been trying to find out what was going on, but without success. Even the most co-operative Schutzpolizei didn't have time to talk, or simply wouldn't. As long as the guards were on board, the prisoners felt safe, but now anything could happen. It was whispered among the Norweger that the barge along with the ship was to be blown up, creating even a greater horror among the prisoners. They remembered the factories, airports, submarines and other things the Germans had already blown up.

The *Wolfgang* skipper, however, had come back onboard. He most likely came on board during the confusion the last time *Adler* stuck her nose in. The skipper picked up some of his things, put them in *Wolfgang's* small rowboat and pulled himself forward along the side of the barge. The *Norweger* called out to stop him from leaving *Wolfgang,* and a few energetic policemen jumped into the boat and dragged him back onboard the barge.

The skipper cursed at the police, but quickly realized that it was no use. Afterwards he was led voluntarily to his quarters. The rowboat was moored alongside the barge. The skipper was to be a hostage. If the prisoners were to be blasted into the air, so was the skipper. Five or six German civilians came up from a room on *Wolfgang*. They had no doubt slept during the earlier 'evacuation'. The Germans signaled, in the dark, to the tugboat *Bussard*. Recognizing the signal, the crew of the *Bussard* stuck her bow in, and the civilians jumped over the rail and onboard the tugboat. When *Bussard* backed out from *Wolfgang*, they called to the prisoners saying they would come back the next morning. Sarcastic laughter from the guards followed the remark. During the confusion, Bjarne Finnebraaten and Kristoffer Sœbø found an opportunity to jump on board *Bussard*. Irgens urged Hjellemo (who spoke fluid German) to follow in order to learn what was happening. Hjellemo also jumped on board the *Bussard*. Sœbø, Finnebraaten, and Hjellemo hid aboard the *Bussard*. As they approached Neustadt, Hjellemo began to speak with a German officer. The officer was aware that the Norwegians were prisoners. Hjellemo asked the officer what was going to happen to the barges, but he replied that he didn't know. *Bussard* docked at a submarine dock in Neustadt. The three Norwegians and the officer proceeded to the military barracks. At the barracks, they spoke further but didn't learn anything new. At night they all had separate rooms.

As *Bussard* was just backing out from *Wolfgang*, there was a violent explosion approximately 300 meters in front of the barge, in a northerly direction. A pillar of fire rose into the air. The explosion was so powerful that the prisoners clearly felt the air pressure. It was a freighter that was blown up. They could see the stern of the ship as it went down. The explosion was followed by an unnatural silence, but then they heard screams and cries for help. *Cap Arcona* shone a couple of spotlight beams out over the bay to assist lifeboats rowing towards the explosion site. The ashes from the explosion sprinkled down on the prisoners.

Explosion in Lübeck Bay

Several screams and cries for help were heard. But *Bussard* was running at full speed in the opposite direction and disappeared into the darkness towards Neustadt. There was no help from them. "What had happened?" the prisoners asked. There were no bombs dropped, or they would have heard planes. Besides, it was dark. Some marine vessels that might have launched torpedoes were seen around, but why wouldn't they shoot at the other vessels as well? Could it have been a mine? Which ship was blown up?

Another question was, why did *Bussard* disappear in the direction of Neustadt with no intention of helping survivors of the unknown ship?

The situation was critical, with both barges tied to *Thielbek* without a single guard on board. The skipper was kept as prisoner. It turned out that the skipper's daughter was also still on board *Wolfgang*.

Abandoned

Alongside the barges loomed *Thielbek*, dark and gloomy. The Norweger assembled to discuss their situation and options. No one would venture to go on board the *Thielbek,* and no one wanted to stay where they were. There was only one option, to get away from this dangerous situation and head for shore. The question was, would this be considered an attempt to escape? If so, they could all face execution. On the other hand, the Germans' abandonment could be understood as leaving them alone to fend for themselves. It was unheard of that the Germans would leave a couple thousand prisoners to fend for themselves without a single guard. It was decided that they would be fools if they didn't take this opportunity. This may be the defining moment they had been waiting for.

Skjolden was a very resourceful ex-naval sailor, and he took command. This was certainly a job for him. Skjolden checked the weather. A light breeze blew towards land to the west. The distance to land was not more than three kilometers, making success highly probable. The ropes were cut, the anchors were lifted and *Wolfgang* started to drift. The prisoners on *Vaterland* understood what was happening and did the same. They cut their mooring and began drifting into *Wolfgang*. *Vaterland* tried to tie up to *Wolfgang*, but that would not do. If this happened, they would risk a mass exodus and overload *Wolfgang*. Any oars and boathooks the prisoners aboard *Wolfgang* could find were used to keep the *Vaterland* at bay. The prisoners aboard *Wolfgang* proved much stronger than the *Vaterland* prisoners. *Vaterland* lacked strong men as well as organization. There were only a few men aboard *Vaterland* who had the initiative and strength to do anything. The others were starving Poles and Jewish women. Skjolden gave orders for as many people as were able to stand up in a row with their blankets outstretched to catch the breeze. The rest were to remain still and either sit or lay down in clusters. *Vaterland* saw what was happening and followed suit. At a distance a ship exploded, and a pillar of fire rose into the night sky. The explosion lit the group holding the blankets. They appeared as silhouettes of bats against the spring sky.

On *Thielbek*, there was no indication of life other than the occasional spotlight shining over the barges.

Wolfgang's small rowboat was manned by four Norwegians and one Finn who helped with the speed and steering. They rowed with their legs in the water, up to their thighs. The rowboat was constantly called back to the barge to rescue prisoners who had either fallen or jumped overboard. Only on one occasion were they able to rescue the poor prisoner. A small cruiser and two torpedo boats patrolled the area and signaled each other regularly. At any moment the barges expected a torpedo to come their way. The minutes seemed like an eternity. A thick mist floated into the bay, and in a few minutes the fog formed a wall that hid the barges from the warships. After the fog was gone, so were the ships. Two German canal barges sailing with 2,000 prisoners on board, and with wool blankets stretched out as sails, would have been an easy target.

Leif Takle and three Finns manned a second rowboat. That rowboat was mainly to keep the barge in the wind and steer it towards the beach.

Pelzerhaken

At 04:00 on May 3, 1945, the *Wolfgang* ran aground on a sandbank twenty-five meters from shore. The beach was long, flat and sandy. They had landed at Pelzerhaken, the same bluff preventing them from seeing into Neustadt earlier. The barge *Vaterland* landed alongside *Wolfgang* as daylight had just broken.

Two Norweger were sent ashore in a rowboat to *orge* a larger rowboat nearby and some rope, enabling *Wolfgang* to be tied to the shore as the tide began to rise. The plan was to pull the rowboat back and forth along the wire. And thus began the strange disembarking. As the sailor he was, Skjolden gave the order: *"Frauen und Kinder zuerst, in Gruppen von zehn"* (Women and children first, in batches of ten). It was as if it was an actual shipwreck. The women were told what was happening, but at first, they didn't understand. When they realized they were free, they all ran about like a flock of hens. It was quite a chore trying to calm them down and separate them into small groups. The women were so weak the police had to help them disembark. Most of the women were not used to such treatment, and when they came ashore they fell weeping on the necks of those who had assisted them. It was a 'hug of death' for some of the policemen. Of the five policemen who helped with the first landing, three died of typhus before they reached home and several others were infected and became seriously ill.

For Skjolden, the evacuation was going too slow. He decided to send several Norweger with boats to speed up the evacuation. On the larger boat were ten men, and on the smaller were four. A couple of men in each boat were given the task to pull the boat towards the barge, while the others standing on the shore pulled the boat back to the beach. This went much faster! Dahlin took command of each group that reached shore and arranged them in small groups along the beach. It was still twilight, but soon the sun would come out. It would then be best if there was as little activity and visibility as possible on the beach.

There were no plans for what to do after everyone had reached shore. Constantly, the prisoners scouted the bay to see if anyone was coming for them. A couple of small naval boats lay a kilometer from the beach, but they didn't bother the evacuees. Not so much as a light beam shone their way. One would think that the noise from disembarking could be heard quite a distance. The sick were now brought to shore. The next concern was finding an adequate place to put everyone.

Seeking Accommodations

At dawn, the prisoners saw glimpses of houses further down the beach and another somewhat further up. An accommodation expedition was sent out. The first house turned out to be full of male Poles. The Poles had come from the *Vaterland*, and they had taken control of the place. They helped themselves to whatever was in the house without consideration of the residents. There was no question about placing the sick there. The expedition to the other house came back and said they were greeted outside by a couple of tough civilian men armed with machine guns. The men wouldn't even talk to the Norweger; they just waved their guns at them.

Frøseth and Dahlin went to a third house that could be seen at a distance. The resident obviously saw them approaching because he met them in the courtyard. He was a man in his forties. He was polite and apologized that he could not receive them. Besides his family, he had ten evacuees from East Poland. Frøseth and Dahlin explained their situation to the man. He recommended they make a call to Neustadt for help. For obvious reasons, that advice did not sit well with them. Dahlin asked if they could get water, and he graciously showed them a pump in the garden. When Dahlin and Frøseth had quenched their thirst, several women came running out of the house. The women felt safer now and clasped their hands in disbelief when they heard that the prisoners aboard the barges had been practically without food and water for eight days.

The women wanted to be helpful and aided in carrying buckets down the road to the courtyard, where the Norweger could come up and take them down to the beach.

Except for a few sick Jewish women and some older Poles still aboard, the evacuation of *Wolfgang* was complete. Evacuation of *Vaterland* did not go well. With a few honorable exceptions, all the men had run away without concern about the remainder. The men had made a few bad rafts that were tied to the stern of the barge. A rope was fastened on board, and one by one they let themselves down to the raft. Occasionally the raft would slide away, and some were left hanging on the rope screaming for the raft to be put back in place. At the front of the barge, they had piled up planks to make a walkway to the shore. One by one they lowered themselves down onto the planks. It went extremely slow, and the planks were submerged in some places. Every now and then someone would get stuck. A woman hung screaming for quite some time until someone took pity on her. Some girls took off their shoes, pulled up their clothes and lowered themselves into the water. The water came no higher than their knees and they could wade to shore.

The beach now became crowded. Some washed, others cooked and still others paced back and forth. The male Poles, for the most part, disappeared inland in small groups. The *Wolfgang* prisoners were given strict orders to stick together on the beach or remain close by, so as not to do anything the Germans could punish them for.

The prisoners who had stayed a little farther inland unexpectedly came down to the beach, followed by a naval officer in full uniform carrying a pistol in one hand. Skjolden explained the situation to him, and the officer agreed that the landing should continue but they should all stick together on the beach. The Norweger pulled themselves over to a grassy slope that stretched down to the sea. A creek, which trickled through the shrubbery and continued down the grassy slope, served as the Norweger border. Several Poles searched the shoreline for firewood for cooking. They were told to make sure they were quiet on the beach. The Poles were quite obstinate now that there were no German rifles holding them at bay.

Ever since it became light, the prisoners kept lookout for tugboats that could come and collect the barges. At 07:00, the steam ship *Thielbek* was spotted and two tugboats, *Bussard* and *Adler*, went out to the ship. The prisoners followed the tugboats intensely in case they came to the beach to get the barges. They did not, and the prisoners were all relieved. The lack of sleep began to take its toll, and many prisoners laid down to get some rest.

Someone shouted *"Soldaten kommen!"* (Soldiers are coming!). Coming down the hill was a long line of marines shouting at the prisoners. The marines formed a long line on the beach while pushing the prisoners in front of them. From the bushes near the Norweger came the Schutzpolizei. *"Antreten ohne Gepäck"* (No luggage) was the roar from all sides. No sooner had the prisoners lined up before the marines roared *"Kein Gepäck! Los – los!"* (No Luggage! Go – go!). The Schutzpolizei standing next to the Norwegian police were their old 'friends' from *Wolfgang*. That meant they were not on the tugboat that went out to *Thielbek* earlier. The police tried to read the faces of the Schutzpolizei to determine the kind of mood they were in. Their faces looked dejected, almost like a hangover. This was not a good indication. The Norweger were lined up, by themselves, on the trail along the edge of the waterfront.

Massacre at Pelzerhaken

As the Norweger stood there, the most grotesque scene they had ever witnessed began to unfold. Several young marines, students from a naval school, had come out on the barge *Vaterland*. Its broadside was closest to the Norweger, and they could easily see what was happening right in front of them. They not only saw the events, but followed them closely as they unfolded. The marines ran from hatch to hatch and yelled *"Heraus!"* (Out!). Prisoners were rounded up and were then hit, kicked and ultimately chased into the sea. This didn't happen fast enough for the marines, who proceeded to run around the deck and kick prisoners off both sides of the barge. The Norweger heard screams and cries for help all around the barge. Many of the prisoners struggled in the water and were too weak to drag themselves to shore. The struggling gradually subsided, until finally they floated like bags in the water. The marines became totally intoxicated with power. They leaned down the hatches and began shooting into the rooms. Screams could be heard everywhere. Those who were able climbed up and tried to get away. In horror, the Norweger witnessed the marines calmly shooting the prisoners as they came up from below. The dead or dying rolled down the deck, with some making it to the edge of the barge only to be shot and kicked headlong into the sea. Even this was not enough! The prisoners who were already in the sea and struggling to get to shore served as target practice for the sailors. An elderly woman and her young daughter ran across the deck to wade ashore; they were shot twice in the neck and then kicked overboard. Another elderly woman had made it into the water and was wading to shore. It took five shots from a marine before she fell face down in the water. A young girl on the shore shouted at her mother and ran to meet her but was stopped by a shot to the head.

While this was happening, Leif Tackle and several other Norwegian police climbed into the large rowboat and rowed to the *Wolfgang* to bring the last prisoners to shore. Trygve Rindahl continued to haul the dinghy to and from *Wolfgang*, putting prisoners on land, when he was confronted by a marine on board *Wolfgang*. The sailor was so furious that he foamed around his mouth and shouted at Rindahl, demanding he come on board *Wolfgang*. Rindahl refused! He was aware of what was happening on the other barge. The marine then aimed his gun at Rindahl. They were just a few meters from each other. There was a minute of eerie silence. Rindahl began speaking German to the sailor and told him that he was Norweger and a Sonderlager prisoner. This seemed to calm the German, and Rindahl continued to shore.

All the marine students then went over to *Wolfgang* and began shooting prisoners still on board. The massacre took almost half an hour. Bullets and ricochets whined about the Norweger ears as they were only ten meters from the sea. The Norweger went down on their knees to avoid getting hit, while Schutzpolizei behind them swore and snarled resentfully. They had become agitated and moved behind the Norweger, using them as a shield. It was clear that they did not like what was happening. During their time as prisoners of Nazi Germany, the police had become accustomed to brutality, but this display was monstrous and beyond anything they could have imagined. The display of brutality made them nauseous. It had now become dead quiet on the beach. The sea was coloured red.

Before the sailors came along, two policemen, Walther Tvedt and Odd Fjælberg, escaped from the beach along with a Norwegian woman, Inga Hobbesland. They were not seen afterwards. The police hoped they had gotten away and survived.

Neustadt

The order *"Abmarschieren,"* (March on) was given at 10:00 and the prisoners began to stroll off the beach. They were all shocked to the core and eager to leave the scene. They had all witnessed mass murder!

The Norweger led the column and struck up a conversation with a Schutzpolizei. The guard told them that, the night before, the guards were in a panic because they learned that a Russian submarine was in the bay. This explained a lot about the Schutzpolizei and SS guards cowardly leaving 2,000 prisoners without even telling them. It was particularly cowardly to take off to Neustadt when people lay drowning and fighting for their lives after the explosion of the unknown ship. The guard further told them they were going to Neustadt and would embark from there for passage to Flensburg. The guard did not speak any further about their journey.

The prisoners marched along the beach until they came to a nearby park and rested. Dahlin sat and watched a couple strolling in the park, not knowing that the next day he would also be strolling in the same way.

While this was going on, Sœbø, who arrived at the marine barracks the morning before, went for a walk in the military field and then down to the sea. From there he could see the prisoner column marching on the other side of the canal. He then saw the German guards drive several prisoners from the rear of the column into the sea, then begin to shoot at them. A prisoner managed to swim across the canal and came ashore near Sœbø.

The prisoner had difficulty getting ashore, and Sœbø went over to offer assistance. The prisoner had been shot through his shoulder and was bleeding. Sœbø tried to talk to him, but the prisoner didn't understand. He spoke a language Sœbø could not understand, possibly Czechoslovakian. After the prisoner was helped ashore, he disappeared. Sœbø stayed in the barracks area until the rest of the Norweger arrived later.

Andreas Moen and Rolf Berg were released from jail in Neustadt and then brought to the football field where they were ordered to wait for the other Norwegians. The Germans told them that the Norwegian prisoners had landed at Pelzerhaken and were en route to Neustadt. From where they were seated, Moen and Berg could see directly down the channel and could see the prisoner columns on the other side. They saw the German guards taking fifteen to twenty prisoners from the rear of the column aside and chasing them into the sea. The guards began to shoot and used them for target practice.

The rest of the prisoners marched through the park and across the bridge over the canal. A group of Jewish women at the back of the column were prevented from going over the bridge. Instead, they were commanded to swim across the canal. When the women came out of the water, the guards used them as targets. Those who witnessed it estimated about fifty people were either shot or drowned.

The Norweger did not witness these atrocities because they were in the front of the prisoner columns. They learned about them later at the football field.

When the prisoners marched through Neustadt, many of its citizens looked at the prisoners with great interest. Several of the children spat on them. One would think that this couldn't be true, but it was!

How many prisoners were murdered on the beach and on the road to Neustadt that morning? They couldn't say for sure, but they believed that at the beach there were 150–170 killed. Most of them were from the *Vaterland*, but there could possibly have been more. The German sailors and SS soldiers continued shooting prisoners during the entire march to Neustadt. It's well known that the weak and the sick who lagged behind were shot. Later, a German resident in the area counted 208 killed on the beach and on the road to Neustadt.

However, after the war it was determined that 400 were killed aboard the barges, on the beach and in the suburbs of Neustadt.

Commandant Hoppe

The prisoners marched right through the city and through a gate where they entered the militarized zone. At 11:00 the prisoners entered a large football field that served as a holding area and were ordered to sit. Most prisoners were so tired they slept. After a while, buckets of good soup arrived to feed the estimated 1,000 prisoners, with more continually coming. At 12:00, while the police were eating their soup, none other than the SS Obersturmbannführer Werner Hoppe, Commandant of KZ-Stutthof, arrived. Hoppe had evidently been promoted since he left the camp. Hoppe had left KZ-Stutthof on April 4, 1945, and was now the supreme leader of prisoner evacuation in the Neustadt area. He had command of *Cap Arcona, Thielbek, Deutschland,* and several other ships, as well as the administration of prisoners on land.

The Commandant spoke with Irgens, who in turn conveyed the message to the Scandinavians that they were going by themselves aboard the ship *Athens*, a freighter down in the harbor. The ship would take the Scandinavians to Flensburg, and from there they would leave for Sweden on a Swedish Red Cross boat. This news triggered spontaneous enthusiasm among the police, but they were still doubtful. They had no reason to believe the Commandant.

Just after 14:00, the prisoners marched down to the docks. The freighter, *Athens*, was docked right in front of them and on the other side of a large, open wharf. Other prisoners came marching on the dock and stopped near the Scandinavians. After a short time, the other prisoners started boarding the *Athens* while the Scandinavians had to stand and wait. This surprised them. They were told earlier they would be the only passengers to board *Athens*. As they suspected, Hoppe's word could not be trusted.

The *Athens*

It began to rain heavily, and the Scandinavians took the opportunity to wash their hands, brush their teeth and fill their water bottles. The rain stopped at 14:30, just as a squadron of British Typhoon fighters came from the direction of Lübeck. Anti-aircraft artillery from *Athens* was the first to react, but the aircrafts continued towards the bay where *Cap Arcona, Thielbek* and *Deutschland* lay. The prisoners could not see the ships because of a long, wooded hill that lay between the ships and the prisoners. The planes ducked behind the treetops, and the prisoners heard the roar of bombs. The planes reappeared and dove again. Explosions and thick black smoke rose above the treetops. The squadron then turned towards the harbor and *Athens* again opened fire from both the front and rear guns. The planes responded with machine gun fire, causing the aft mast flying the German naval flag to be cut in two and fall to the wharf.

As this was happening, prisoners began climbing out of all the possible openings in *Athens* to seek shelter wherever they could find it. Several Scandinavians ended up behind a brick wall, directly by a street that enabled them to see the events happening. The aircrafts took a big turn towards Lübeck, but then swung around and headed back towards the bay where the steamships lay. The planes dove again and dropped several bombs on the ships. An enormous pillar of black smoke rose into the sky and over the treetops. Several times, the aircrafts came flying back over the harbor. Each time, people scrambled off the wharf.

Boarding Athens

There were three different squadrons of British aircrafts that flew over Neustadt and Lübeck from 14:30 onwards. The first squadrons were Typhoon fighter bombers with a new weapon of rocket bombs. Each aircraft had eight such rockets. There was a total of eight aircrafts in each squadron. The second two squadrons were Tempest fighter aircrafts that attacked with machine guns and carried only conventional bombs.

Three small patrol boats left the harbor and motored out towards the smoke columns to rescue survivors. During the ongoing air attacks, prisoners continued to pour out of *Athens*. There was much confusion, with people scrambling in each direction. The planes came back into the harbor several times and continued to drop bombs. By now the guards were gone and nowhere to be seen.

There was no need for the police to be standing on the dock anymore. Taking their packs, they wandered onto a nearby street. A stream of people, consisting of civilians and German military personnel, passed the police and headed into the town. Someone came running and shouted that British armored cars were about to enter the city.

Looking back to the dock, they saw *Athens* burning and ammunition exploding. They feared that *Athens* and other vessels could explode. It was said that the guards on board the *Athens* hoisted the white flag of surrender, but they didn't see this. On the contrary, the Germans on board *Athens* kept shooting at the aircrafts as long as they could. The police moved further up into town and saw streams of people with little clothes on. Others were wounded and bloody and had to be helped by the Red Cross. The police now understood that these were survivors from the steamships, *Cap Arcona* and *Thielbek,* that were brought in by the patrol boats they saw earlier. The patrol boats had returned with survivors and then pulled out again to pickup more. Several policemen went into the city and met people fleeing in the opposite direction, running away from the British. Several police sought refuge in the basement of a large brick house. They felt relatively safe there until they saw a gun-waving German stand in front of them and shout *"Heraus!"* (Out!). The police tried to explain they only sought shelter, but it was no use. They were driven out on the street again. A separate group of police sought refuge in a basement of a private house, where they dug themselves into a pile of coal. They intended to remain there until the English had taken over the city.

An SS soldier threw his machine gun and ammunition belt behind a bin and turned to go. They looked at each other briefly. The soldier just shrugged his shoulders then walked away.

The police walked from street to street and finally came to the main road from Lübeck. On the street were hundreds of Jewish women and other prisoners. A group of Scandinavians also gathered in a small space. Other police members began trickling in, and they were united once again.

Liberated

Then at 17:35, someone yelled: *"Panzer kommen!"* (Tanks coming!). Two small British tanks came down the main street. Each tank was manned by three men, one stood behind and steered, and the other two lay on top, each with a cigarette dangling from their mouth and a finger on the trigger of a machine gun. It was an astonishingly relaxed entry.

Celebration broke out as they passed by. There was shouting and waving. The Jewish women were hysterical and sobbed loudly and embraced everyone they met. Scandinavians shouted *"Hurrah!"* and waved. There was confusion, but now in a completely different sense. People embraced each other, shook each other's hands, slapped one another on the shoulders, and congratulated each other with enthusiasm. Everywhere there were smiles of joy. The British remained nonchalant and threw out cigarettes and chocolates.

Some German civilians stood in the windows and stairs and viewed the activities from a distance. As far as the police could see, the German civilians took the situation calmly. From several windows, civilians threw out sandwiches, which the Russian and Polish prisoners fought over. It was truly a scene of conflict. The British looked on and analyzed the grim spectacle without a word. An English non-commissioned officer confided in Olaf Walle, "I didn't think things were that bad". When Ole Bakke saw the British tanks coming, he pulled out a Norwegian flag he had received from home and waved it. Afterward, a man in an English uniform came up to Bakke and began talking to him in English. When he realized that Bakke was not particularly good in English, the man started to speak to him in Norwegian. It was Marius Eriksen, the alpine skier and later movie star in the 1950s.

There were several British tanks along with a few military vehicles, but few British soldiers. The main regiment would follow shortly. German troops had left the city. It was now declared 'open'.

It was hard to believe that they were now free! The police had looked forward to this moment for so long, but this time they needed to be sure. They had been disappointed so many times in the past. They were also emotionally drained from the harrowing events of the past twenty-four hours and couldn't immediately react. After the police shook hands and clapped each other on the shoulders, they began to look for other Norwegians. Small clusters of Scandinavians were found throughout the city, and they all agreed to gather at the football field they had left earlier. They would remain there until further notice.

Irgens went to negotiate with the British. The Scandinavians were prepared to spend the night at the football field. Lorentzen and Dahlin walked around the football field – one could call it 'victory laps' – and eventually walked into the city. Neustadt had disintegrated into a chaos of plundering. Many ex-prisoners were drunk, as they couldn't handle the alcohol. Many also died later from overeating. They were unable to control themselves when there was an abundance of food.

The police were good at *orge*, and several set out to *orge* food, among other things. Olav Risøen had *orged* bottles of wine that they circulated.

To the delight of the police, the British soldiers rounded up the German military personnel.

The number of police members had reduced by five. Arne Sundvor and Alf Andersen had escaped to Lübeck and Odd Fjælberg, Walther Tvedt and Inga Hobbesland were wandering around somewhere. The Norwegian police members now totaled 219. Not included in the tally were police missing during the evacuation and the sick, together with Herman Heggenes and Eivind Luthen, who did not come with the police during the evacuation.

CHAPTER 20 –
Norway House

After a surprisingly short time, Irgens came back with the news that the English commander, Major Rustin, had delegated the submarine administrative center to the Scandinavians. The center consisted of a main building, Stabsgebäude (staff building), which the police immediately renamed Norway House. There were also two adjacent buildings, Offiziersheim (officer's home) and Schulgebäude (school building). Norway House was a large brick building with three floors. One policeman cut big fancy letters out of tin strips to read NORWAY HOUSE and put them at the front door. The British gave an approving smile, but it irritated the Germans greatly. The large foyer in Norway House displayed a model of a submarine in a glass case. On either side of the model sat a smaller submarine model. Offiziersheim had been the residence of the submarine officers. It contained a dining room, coffee room, lounges, and a well-stocked wine cellar.

The largest number of Scandinavians was the Norwegians, therefore they moved into Norway House and the Offiziersheim. Pettersen, Grønnevik, Ulfsrud, Annar Rostad and Skjerven were sick and hospitalized in Neustadt. The Finns, Danes and Balts moved into Schulgebäude.

When the Scandinavians first moved into the buildings, it was chaotic. It seemed the Germans had prepared to evacuate but were forced to leave in a hurry. The Norwegians created a renovation work detail at Norway House, with John Trøen as chief. The work detail cleaned up everything in the hallways. Only the glass cases with submarine models were left on the main floor. A small room was set aside for food distribution. John Ljosland was in charge, with bread, butter, and cheese at his disposal. The old kitchen in Offiziersheim was to operate as before, with its German laborers and a German naval officer as the leader, but the English supervising. An English supervisor constantly asked the Norwegians how the food tasted.

The kitchen delivered various food and soups to all prisoners. The different barracks picked up their containers and further distributed the food. Apart from bread, there was plenty of everything. The town of Neustadt was required to pay for the food.

Wine Cellar

It was rumored that there was a wine cellar in the Offiziersheim. Several police found their way to the cellar and returned with not only bottles, but cartons of wine and spirits. Of particular interest was a carton of Rhine wine. The Rhine wine, a Chateau Cassaduo vintage 1937, had been stolen in France by German soldiers.

The English did not hinder the procurement. On the contrary, they encouraged it. The English clearly understood what the prisoners had been through. It was clear that the liberation had to be celebrated! Stockpiles of cheese, barrels with real butter, sugar bags and much more was discovered outside the city. There was certainly an adequate supply of food for hungry prisoners when they came to town aboard the barges on the night of May 1. The city authorities were just not interested in helping.

The first morning of freedom was Friday May 4, 1945. The prisoners had stayed on the barge *Wolfgang* for six days.

Sitting in Norway House in Neustadt, the police tried to reconstruct and write down the details of the dramatic climax of their experiences and the end of their Baltic Sea voyage.

Athens was still burning down at the wharf. There were constant explosions from ammunition stored aboard the ship. The ship was hit by several rocket bombs, but it still didn't sink. They later learned that the anti-aircraft guns on board the *Athens* continued to shoot at the British planes. The shooting continued even after British tanks were in the area. This led to a shootout between *Athens* and the British, resulting in the fire on board. The shooting and explosions caused panic among the prisoners who were still on board. They struggled to get off the ship and some jumped into the sea, but most drowned. Others jumped onto the wharf and injured themselves. The police realized that if the British aircrafts had come a few minutes later, they would have been on *Athens* as well. The ship, with its ammunition, presented a dangerous threat because of its proximity to Norway House and other buildings. The ship was only 200 meters from Norway House. Later that day, *Athens* was towed out into the bay.

The wrecks of *Cap Arcona*, *Thielbek* and *Deutschland* lay out in the bay. *Cap Arcona* lay on her side on the bottom, with eight meters showing above the surface of the water. *Deutschland* was still able to slowly sail out of the bay. *Thielbek* was sunk. Inside the wrecks were thousands of corpses.

In one day, the police had avoided boarding three ships – the *Cap Arcona*, *Thielbek* and *Athens*. They avoided boarding all three at the last minute. If any of these boardings had been completed, the result would have been dire for many of them, if not all.

Neustadt in Chaos

The town of Neustadt was in total chaos that night, but also within the barracks area. Things were bound to go wrong when 4,000–5,000 starving prisoners were unleashed with the feeling of freedom and the urge to retaliate against the Germans. There were reports of stores looted and private homes burglarized. At the station, some rail cars containing sacks of sugar and cartons of butter and cheese were broken into. Some prisoners were too weak to carry the cheese, so they rolled it in front of them. Armed ex-prisoners had also rounded up Germans. By all accounts, they shot sixty Germans in the harbor after having flogged them in the streets. The prisoners felt it was justified revenge for the fifty to sixty prisoners driven into the canal and shot the day before. Outside the city, there had been considerable looting, especially by the Poles and Russians, who had broken into wherever they could. This could not continue!

Major Rustin sent for Irgens and asked if he could arrange for the Norwegian police to restore law and order with detail of no less than fifty men. There was no objection to his request, and there was no difficulty in setting up command of a hundred men under Skjolden's command. The police were issued older Italian rifles and uniforms, along with black 'Monty-caps'. Their task was to patrol the old town and the barracks area.

As a general-duty officer, Skjolden was granted the use of a car. With his customary modesty, he took the best car he could find.

The police protected the German civilian population and the German military from further abuse. They had to fire warning shots several times to keep ex-prisoners from plundering and seeking revenge.

Irgens spent much of his day with the English, Lorentzen with arranging guard patrols, and Dahlin with office work.

The police wanted to change their clothes from the hated Badoglio uniforms to something more appropriate, but all clothing stores in the city were already plundered. Norway House was full of German marine uniforms. A policeman could appear in a smart lieutenant jacket and civilian pants, another with gold edged officer hat and denim pants and still another in full uniform. Most of the police went for more practical clothing and preferred not to be mistaken for German. During their patrol rounds, the police travelled in either a car or motorcycle.

The celebration of freedom continued the whole day. Supplies in the wine cellar fit right in with the festivities. It turned out that one policeman was under the influence and unshaven when he patrolled the streets. This was not good! Having been a prisoner for a long time and then released, one was allowed to be "under the influence", but not unshaven!

The police's old friends, the Schutzpolizei from *Wolfgang*, expressed deep concerns for their own safety.

They were unarmed and expected to serve as police officers, but they were afraid to go out alone and asked for Norwegian police escorts. Their old friend, Oberleutnant, asked for protection against prisoners who would intrude on where he and the other Schutzpolizei from *Wolfgang* were living. He expressed deep concerns for their safety. In reality, the Oberleutnant was a "decent sort" and well liked.

Cap Arcona and *Thielbek* Tragedies

It became the general consensus that the Norwegians would make the decisions. They entertained all kinds of inquiries and requests, and their office became the Scandinavian headquarters.

That morning, three rescued Czechs appeared. The police were given the task to talk to them. The Czechs' spokesman, named Koubek, informed them that he was the supply manager for *Cap Arcona* and *Thielbek*. He had managed to swim ashore to the same beach, Pelzerhaken, where the barges had landed the morning before. He said there were 2,000 detainees on *Thielbek* and 6,000 on *Cap Arcona*. Being the supply manager, the police had no reason to doubt him. Of the approximately 8,000 prisoners, only 550 were rescued, said Koubek. The *Deutschland* had 2,500 prisoners on board, but he was not aware of how many were rescued. Unbelievable! The police expressed surprise that the British planes had bombed and shelled the ships, but noticed that the Czechs became silent. The Czechs would not tell more. It was clear to the police they were uncomfortable with discussing the incident. They promised to come back with some *Deutschland* survivors in order to gain more information.

Sometime later, the police were informed that two representatives from the Red Cross were waiting outside. It was a Swedish physician from Gøteborg, Dr. Hans Arnoldson, and a Norwegian doctor, Bjørn Heger. They had come directly from Lübeck by car and said they had contact with two policemen who escaped from "the cooking place", Arne Sundvor and Alf Andersen. When the doctors first found them, they were wearing the Italian Badoglio uniforms. Later, the two were elegantly dressed in civilian clothes with their own car and driver. The doctors mentioned that Sundvor and Andersen had arrived in Lübeck without much difficulty. The two had made their way to the Swedish embassy, where they met Dr. Arnoldson and the Norwegian Seamen's Chaplin from Hamburg, Conrad Vogt-Svendsen. While they dined together, the policemen told of the barges on the way to Lübeck. The four took Vogt-Svendsen's car and drove directly to "the cooking place" on the beach. At the site, they were informed by an older German civilian that the barges had been towed away half an hour earlier. The four returned to the

Swedish embassy to report just as the English were disarming German soldiers outside the embassy. Vogt-Svendsen later wrote:

> *When we came out of the embassy again, British troops appeared in the street. Flocks of German soldiers and SS streamed towards them to surrender. We helped with willing hands. The Swedes stood as sympathetic and neutral onlookers, watching us stack weapons in piles. Two hours after Andersen and Sundvor were beaten for the last time by their German guards, they disarmed the SS men as if they'd never done anything towards them. An SS car with an officer behind the wheel moved past. Police constable Sundvor stopped him. "Where are you going?" he asked. "To find a place where I can surrender," the officer replied.*
>
> *"This is Norwegian police, and you can surrender to us. Get them out of the car, you won't need it anymore." Sundvor said. The officer looked a little disoriented but jumped out.*

Vogt-Svendsen mentioned they had secured suitable transportation to Travemünde from the British commander in an effort to stop the barges there. As soon as arrangements were made, they went past both the English and German checkpoints. In Travemünde, they learned that the barges had passed ten to twenty minutes earlier. They were made aware that British aircrafts bombed and shot at virtually all the boats outside Lübeck. Therefore, they turned to an English tank division commander to notify the planes of the barges with prisoners on board. The commander referred them to the regiment commander just west of Lübeck. From there, they made contact with the English Colonel Harding, who forwarded the information to the British Air Force (RAF) regarding the barges. He assured them that the message arrived at the RAF headquarters, but he didn't know if the message got through to the British planes already in the air.

The doctors told the police their mission was to travel around Germany and trace the whereabouts of Scandinavian prisoners to get them out of the country. They began their journey on March 8 and had since been on a continuous journey around Germany to different KZ-camps. They had succeeded, along with the White Buses, in collecting around 8,000 Scandinavian prisoners from KZ-Neuengamme and transporting them to Sweden. They had been through most of the KZ camps in Germany.

When the two were in KZ-Sachsenhausen, Olaf Borgen came knocking asking for help. Borgen had journeyed from Danzig, through Germany, to KZ-Sachsenhausen by himself without speaking any German. He was very much alive and already in Sweden.

Role Reversal

The police's first priority was to send word home that they were safe. The doctors promised to send information via London Radio. The police were also interested in knowing when they would be able to leave Neustadt and go home, but the doctors could not say anything about that. It could take eight days or perhaps months, they said. That information was certainly not encouraging.

Irgens met with the barrack leaders to update them on the information given by the doctors, along with various internal issues to be discussed. Dahlin was appointed "house chief" for Norway House, Kåre Enge for Offiziersheim and a Finnish prisoner, Johanson, for Schulgebäude.

Out in the yard, German officers and soldiers were put to work digging. The Norwegians were pleased to see the Germans humiliated and put in the same situation they had been in. The police had been pushed around by the master race on numerous occasions.

A former Polish prisoner had been watching the Germans digging. The ex-prisoner hadn't had time or opportunity to change his clothes and was still in his striped prisoner uniform. But unlike during his captivity, he was well fed and satisfied and otherwise happy with what he was able to observe. When a German officer couldn't handle the spade well enough, he went over to the officer and, taking the spade out of his hands, demonstrated how it should be done. *"Also, mein Herr – also"* (So, my lord – so), he commented. After the demonstration there was a brief pause, then the ex-prisoner broke out with *"los – los"* and gave the German a smack on the back of the neck; the officer tumbled forward. The British were amused at the incident, as were many others. The Pole left the place with his head high and much happier than he had been for a long time. The British made it clear why the Germans were digging in a large open area. It was to be a common grave for dead prisoners, including those who were shot in the canal and at Pelzerhaken where the barges landed. The Germans had to retrieve the bodies themselves, and then bury them.

Previously, members of the Norwegian police had escorted British officers to the landing spot at Pelzerhaken where the barges laid, then boarded them. The English filmed it all. They stated that this was one of the most sinister things they had seen in Germany.

Alternate Route Home

On May 5, 1945, many of the Norwegians woke up with hangovers. It was, of course, due to too much smoking and drinking. Their meals consisted mainly of canned peaches and cream, with French Rhine wine. The wine was so good that everyone stopped by for a taste. For this reason, there were many "tastings" between meals. The two doctors from the Red Cross also sampled the wine. They were not used to such good wine either.

Around noon, Captain Einar Sørensen from Kristiansand paid a visit to Norway House. Sørensen was a former prisoner of war in Germany but had escaped to Sweden. He then traveled back to Germany, this time as a liaison officer in the British service, to search for Norwegian prisoners and help facilitate their return. Feeling that Captain Sørensen should be made aware of them, the police mentioned Walther Tvedt, Odd Fjælberg and Hobbesland, who had all disappeared upon landing at Pelzerhaken on the morning of May 1.

The captain believed it was impossible to get private messages sent home via London and advised the police to try to make it north on their own. This option, in fact, had been seriously considered. He went on to say that there were barrier zones created everywhere, including at the Kiel Canal. He warned them that they would risk being stopped and sent to some camp where they may not be treated as well as in Norway House.

The police followed closely as the war unfolded. The day before, Kiel and Flensburg were declared "open cities", and Allied troops crossed the Danish border. German troops surrendered in the Netherlands, northern Germany and Denmark on May 4, becoming effective at 12:00 on May 5. The news triggered tremendous excitement among the Danes, and they partied late into the evening.

What concerned and greatly distressed the Norwegians was not hearing any reports on the progress of the war in Norway. No matter how intensely they followed the war events, there was no news about Norway. Would the battle between the 300,000–400,000 German troops and the Allied forces not be newsworthy? The police knew from experience what such a conflict would mean to the suffering and misery of the civilian population.

On Sunday, May 6, 1945, the barrack chiefs met with Major Rustin. Representatives of fifteen to twenty nationalities were also in the meeting. The barrack chiefs were given instructions on accommodation, cleaning, counting, meal tickets, and much more. There would also be an area in the barracks earmarked for ex-prisoners to consult with the doctors between 14:00 and 16:00.

The arrangement turned out to be necessary, as all who were healthy were required to take their turn at patrolling. There was a high percentage who were sick, which made it difficult to provide a full team of guards. A list of the sick was to be given to Major Rustin, but this proved difficult because people constantly moved from room to room and building to building. There was also a list of all freed Norwegians, Danes, Finns, and Balts given to Arnoldson and Heger. The two doctors were not concerned about the liberated prisoners, but about those missing.

Prolonged Stay

The two doctors informed the police to expect a prolonged stay in Neustadt. They reported that the directions for being sent home were war prisoners first, then civilian internees, and finally KZ prisoners. It could take up to ten or eleven months for KZ prisoners to be sent home. This sounded very bleak indeed to the Norwegian police.

Monday, May 7 came without the Norwegians hearing any further news about the situation in Norway. The three 'house chiefs' were summoned by Major Rustin, who informed them that typhus had broken out in the barracks and that the camp was under quarantine. No one was permitted to go in or out of the gate and all prisoners would be deloused.

That same day, Brezina, Koubek, and Dr. Døslik, all from Prague, came for a meeting with the Norwegian police. Dr. Døslik had been chief physician aboard *Deutschland*. They stated that so many strange things had happened in connection with the *Deutschland* tragedy, but could not comment further. The police took their names and addresses in case the Red Cross needed more information from them later.

An English lieutenant made a request for three interpreters to assist the English in Travemünde. The volunteers would receive wages, room and board. Skjolden, John Bœvre, Gisle Ianke and Thorleif Eide were elected on Dahlin's recommendation. It proved amusing to the Norwegians that very few Englishmen spoke German, but they assumed the Norwegians were fluent in both English and German. There was a constant need for interpreters. Einar Edvardsen was permanently employed as an interpreter with Major Rustin.

Norway is Liberated!

At 14:00 on May 8, 1945, the radio announced that German soldiers in Norway had capitulated and it was now armistice in Europe. The news triggered spontaneous enthusiasm and congratulations.

"Fortress Norway" was the German term for the heavy defence and fortification system of Norway during the occupation by Nazi Germany. Reichskommissar Josef Terboven thought that these fortifications would serve effectively as a last perimeter of defense of the Third Reich in the event of Allied victory on the continent. It turned out that they kept German troops away from mainland Europe and thus helped to end the war more quickly

At 20:00, all the Norwegians gathered in the park. Irgens gave a small well-spoken speech. Afterwards, Walle led in three verses of the Norwegian national anthem *"Ja vi elsker dette landet"* (Yes we love this country).

From about 20:30 they heard Norwegian programs over Swedish radio.

It was strange for the police to sit and listen to tributes to Norway, to those who suffered and to those who remained behind, while they were not mentioned. They felt they had been written off, forgotten. It was a bitter pill to swallow.

Earlier that same day, May 8, Dr. Heger informed the Norwegians that a telegram with a notice of their mission in Neustadt was sent to London the day before. It was a welcome message for the police that morning. Though truth be told, no notification was forwarded to Norway.

During the afternoon they listened to Churchill's speech and in the evening King Haakon's speech.

The following morning, the police turned on the radio to hear if there were any messages about them, but there were none. There was news about everything else, including the imprisonment of Vidkun Quisling and his ministers and the arrest of Nasjonal Samling members all over the country. But that was the extent of the news, nothing about the police.

Major Rustin, accompanied by several officers, stopped by Norway House later that evening. They looked in on some of the rooms and expressed how very neat and orderly they were. Rustin gave Irgens a copy of an English magazine article that highlighted the memorial ceremony for President Roosevelt. The magazine showed King Haakon VII shaking hands with the Lord Major (mayor) of London, with Crown Prince Olav and Major Østgård in the background.

A Finnish woman, Marie Altonen, lived in a room in Norway House with her little girl, Leah. Staying with her was an Estonian woman who had also given birth to a girl in KZ-Stutthof in January 1945. On this particular morning, the Estonian woman came to the administration office to say her baby had died during the night.

Dahlin was commissioned to arrange the funeral for the child. He arranged for Johannes Braaten to make a small casket, which he covered with white paper and embellished with blossoming cherry branches. Carl Frøseth was instructed by Dahlin to make the necessary arrangements with the British. Frøseth arranged for a Chaplin, a British captain, to perform the funeral the next day at 12:00. The child was to be buried in a simple grave in the open space in front of Norway House. This was a public burial place, next to where the murdered prisoners were buried a few days earlier.

Tore Jørgensen

Funeral for Linda

At 12:00 the funeral began at Norway House. First came the English Chaplin and next the Finn carrying the baby in her small coffin. Linda Salura was born on January 24, 1945, in KZ-Stutthof and died on May 9, 1945, in Neustadt. After the coffin came the Estonian mother, and lastly a Norwegian police officer. After a short service the German prisoners, who had dug the grave, filled it again.

The Chaplin was extremely interested in the Norwegian police experiences and received an oral account of the time from KZ-Stutthof until now. He asked to have the main features summarized in written form.

In the afternoon, hot water was made available in the Offiziersheim. This meant that everyone should report to the sidewalk in front of Norway House for delousing. The Englishmen showed up with a small motor connected to a box of lice powder and a hose. The powder was sprayed over the sleeves, down their backs and chest, and to the crotch trouser waistband. It caused great cheers among the women who were to follow. Some of the British lifted their kilts. Afterward, they were all painted with a blue spot on the neck to indicate they had been deloused. The process was quick but effective.

May 10 was a kind of commemoration day for the police. It had been one week since their dramatic experience on the barge at Pelzerhaken during and after landing, and later the liberation.

It was obvious that the Norwegians had the favor of the English. Constantly, even at odd times, a soldier would come and request for Irgens to meet with Major Rustin to exchange opinions. The previous night, Irgens had just been with the Major when he was requested to return. Irgens was told the Major wanted him to be a film sensor for the German films. Anything that smelled of Nazi propaganda was to be edited. Irgens was asked to create a committee with a couple of police officers, and he chose Backer and Frøseth for the job.

The weather had become spring-like; several of the police went to the park to sunbathe. It was an attractive little park that stretched between Norway House, Schulgebäude, and a stone staircase leading down to the beach. Right below them was a wooden pier with a bathhouse at one end. The view across the Bay of Lübeck and east towards Weimarlandet was pleasant. It was ironic to think the park was previously frequented by German naval officers dressed in gold studded uniforms. The officers had been replaced by ex-prisoners of various nationalities who now strolled the area.

In the park, the police saw people washing clothes. Some were out fishing, with others frying the fish. In other places, people were playing cards or simply sunbathing.

Dr. Heger, together with two Norwegian sailors, told the police that their message over the radio never reached London.

They did emphasize that a large Swedish steamship now in Gøteborg, *Jamaica*, was cleared to come to Neustadt and could pick up the police. If the ship did come, it needed four to five days to unload its cargo. None of the visitors knew anything for sure, but they doubted that any boat would be dispatched before four or five weeks. A departure from Neustadt seemed to be in the distant future.

The police had also discussed a problem amongst themselves that had plagued them for some time: their relationship with the English. How far did their obligations go? The police were required to be in service for the English, and of course they were not opposed to that, but it seemed they had become errand boys.

At one point, Major Rustin suggested they be equipped with English uniforms. The police feared that they could be, or were, mobilized for British service. One must not forget that the police had just regained their freedom. Moreover, most of the police were not medically fit to serve for a long time. Because of their concerns, Irgens – along with Dr. Heger, W. Bulukin and Vogt-Svendsen – went to see Major Rustin and confer with him.

Upon his return, Irgens seemed somewhat confused. Bulukin had stated to Major Rustin that the Scandinavians would be traveling that same night on twelve Red Cross trucks obtained in Lübeck. Rustin had been dumbstruck and did not know what to say, but graciously accepted it. He expressed his regret that the Norwegians were going, but stated he was very happy for them, especially their leaders. The Major was simply taken by surprise. So were the other bystanders. Bulukin gave notice that the police should be ready to leave at 20:00.

Sevi Bulukin

At first, the police didn't know what kind of a man Wsevolod Walentinowitch "Sevi" Bulukin really was. Bulukin proved to be one of the practical leaders of the White Buses that traveled around war-torn Germany to bring Scandinavian prisoners back home. He had been on several trips to camps in Germany, Austria, and France and was a skilled organizer and improviser. Bulukin was the leader of the newly created Norwegian Relief Corps, and later became the head of the newly established Norwegian Consulate in Hamburg. Interestingly, just one day after organizing the police's return, Bulukin started on another journey. This time he would travel through the demarcation zone and into the Russian-occupied German territory to try to reach the Norwegian officers who were still in Luckenwalde, just south of Berlin. Bulukin spoke fluent Russian.

Captain Sørensen arrived with 200 sets of underwear that he had managed to *orge* from a business in Lübeck. He also brought cigarettes with him. When he heard about the arrangement with the trucks and buses, he was shocked. Sørensen said that, in the first place, the vehicles would not be ready before 22:00; secondly, the police were taking a big risk. The blockade of the various zones still applied.

Nevertheless, the police were prepared to take their chances. They had been in even worse situations before. When the news became general knowledge among them, the police celebrated with food and drink. Each could carry all their personal belongings in a small backpack. On the other hand, carrying all the food, bottles of wine, and souvenirs they wanted to take along was tricky.

By 20:00, and then 21:00, nothing was happening.

On May 11, the police awoke still in Neustadt. All patrol missions had been canceled due to their imminent departure. That left the police with nothing to do but sit out in the sun and enjoy the glorious weather while hoping the buses and trucks would arrive soon.

Going Home at Last

Then at 10:00, the call came: *"Bilene kommer!"* (The cars are coming!). At 12:00, large trucks and several private cars turned into the square in front of Norway House. Painted in large letters on the sides of the vehicles was International Rouge Croix (International Red Cross). Dr. Arnoldson, Dr. Heger, and Sørensen were in one of the private vehicles, and Sundvor and Andersen were in another.

One of the trucks was designated as an ambulance and lined with mattresses over the floor.

During the confusion that arose with the police leaving, other ex-prisoners used the opportunity to sneak into Norway House to steal from the police. Several packages went missing.

All Scandinavians and Balts were to leave. Irgens appointed Dahlin to be the transport manager. He arranged for thirty persons in each car. There was too much luggage and some of the additional items had to be left behind. Some tried to bring radios, typewriters and uniforms. One even tried to bring an old wall phone, and another a bucket of paint.

As they were boarding the vehicles, Øyvind Lunde stood on one of the trucks and sang *"Norge mit Norge"* (Norway my Norway). Now they were actually going home!

The vehicles were so crowded that some had to sit on the roofs of the trucks. One after another, they ran in again to retrieve something they had forgotten; most returned with two to three wine bottles.

After this, the convoy moved and headed homeward with 214 Norwegian police officers, 5 Norwegian civilian men, 4 Norwegian women and several Danes, Finns and Balts. At 12:10 on May 11, 1945, they left Neustadt.

The last thing they saw was rays of sunlight reflecting from the letters:

NORWAY HOUSE

Glossary

A

Alexanderplatz: A large public square and transport hub in the central Mitte district of Berlin. The square is named after the Russian Tsar Alexander I. Alexanderplatz is one of Berlin's major commercial areas, housing various shopping malls, department stores, and other large retail locations.

Arbeidstjenesten: A compulsory service for young people for social dedication. The purpose was partly to get work done that could hardly be done by the ordinary labor force in times of crisis, and partly to counteract unemployment and create greater solidarity between young people.

Askvig, Carl Bernhard (1885–1954): A Norwegian police officer and Nazi collaborator during the German occupation of Norway from 1940 to 1945. He helped escort the invading Germans into Oslo. He was appointed chief of police in Oslo in April 1940, after Kristian Welhaven. Askvig was later given the title of "police president". He was a central figure in the Nazification of the Norwegian police, together with Jonas Lie.

B

Badoglio, Pietro (1871–1956): An Italian soldier and politician. He was a member of the National Fascist Party and fought alongside his nation's troops under Benito Mussolini in the Second Italo-Abyssinian War; his efforts gained him the title Duke of Addis Abeba. He eventually signed an armistice with the Allies. On October 13, Badoglio and the Kingdom of Italy declared war against Nazi Germany. He was never tried for war crimes by the Allies because he helped them in the invasion of Italy. The Badoglio uniforms worn by the Norwegian police prisoners at KZ-Stutthof were regarded as "traitor uniforms" by the Germans.

Birger, Trudi (1927–2002): Born into a wealthy Jewish family, Trudi Birger's childhood in Frankfurt was abruptly interrupted in 1934 by the advent of Nazism. With the persecution of Jews starting, her family lived in hiding for several years before being captured and sent to KZ-Stutthof. Trudi managed to survive, as she tells in her autobiography. After the war, she married and moved with her husband to Israel, where she worked as a microbiologist.

Brigadeführer (brigade leader): A paramilitary rank of the Nazi Party (NSDAP) that was used from 1932 to 1945, mainly known for its use as an SS rank. As an SA rank, it was used after briefly being known as Untergruppenführer in late 1929 and 1930. The rank was first created due to an expansion of the SS and assigned to those officers in command of SS-Brigaden. In 1933, the name SS-Brigaden was changed to SS-Abschnitte; however, the rank of Brigadeführer remained the same. Originally, Brigadeführer was considered the second general officer rank of the SS and ranked between Oberführer and Gruppenführer. This changed with the rise of the Waffen-SS and the Ordnungspolizei. In both of those organizations, Brigadeführer was the equivalent to a Generalmajor and ranked above an *Oberst* in the German Army or police. The rank of Generalmajor was the equivalent of brigadier general, a one-star general in the US Army.

C

Courland Peninsula: An area where a group of Nazi German forces from the Reichskommissariat Ostland was cut off and surrounded by the Red Army for almost a year, lasting from July 1944 until May 1945. When they were ordered to surrender to the Soviet command on May 8, they were in 'blackout' and did not get the official order before May 10, two days after Germany's capitulation. It was one of the last German groups to surrender in Europe

D

Dunkirk, Battle of: A battle fought in Dunkirk (Dunkerque), France, during the Second World War between the Allies and Nazi Germany. As the Allies were losing the Battle of France on the Western Front, the Battle of Dunkirk was the defense and evacuation to Britain of British and other Allied forces in Europe from May 26 to June 4, 1940.

E

Eilifsen, Gunnar (1897-1943): The Chief of Police of the Oslo Police Department of Civil Crime. In 1943, during the Nazi occupation of Norway, he was executed for disobedience when he refused to arrest three girls who did not show up for forced labor. Eilifsen's execution initiated the Norwegian police and civil servants' arrests all over the country, under the code name Aktion Polarkreis. A retroactive law was hurriedly passed after his execution, and that law was subsequently referred to as *Lex Eilifsen*.

Einsatzgruppen: Schutzstaffel (SS) paramilitary death squads of Nazi Germany responsible for mass killings, primarily by shooting, during World War II (1939–45) in German-occupied Europe. The Einsatzgruppen had an integral role in implementing the so-called 'Final Solution to the Jewish Question' (Die Endlösung der Judenfrage) in territories conquered by Nazi Germany. They were involved in the murder of much of the intelligentsia and cultural elite, including members of the priesthood. Almost all of the people they killed were civilians, beginning with the intelligentsia and swiftly progressing to Soviet political commissars, Jews and Romani people as well as actual or alleged partisans throughout Europe.

Epp, Gerhard: A Mennonite builder who used slave laborers from KZ-Stutthof to build factories near the camp. He served as a general contractor to the SS and assumed responsibility for constructing all buildings on the premises. The EPP Work Detail was to build barracks for German factories around KZ-Stutthof.

F

Fehlis, Heinrich (1906-1945): An SS officer during World War II, most noted for his command of the Sicherheitspolizei and Sicherheitsdienst in Norway during the occupation of Norway by Nazi Germany. Fehlis was active in the Einsatzgruppen during Operation Weserübung (invasion of Norway and Denmark). In November 1940, he took command of the SD and Sicherheitspolizei for Norway and Oslo, reporting to Reinhard Heydrich in Berlin and Josef Terboven in Norway.

Feldgendarmerie: A type of military police unit of the German Empire and Nazi Germany's armies from 1810 until after World War II.

G

Germanic peoples: A historical group of people living in Central Europe and Scandinavia. Since the 19th century, they have traditionally been defined by the use of ancient and early barbaric Germanic languages and are thus equated at least approximately with Germanic-speaking peoples, although different academic disciplines have their own definitions of what makes someone or something 'Germanic'. The Romans named the area in which Germanic peoples lived Germania, stretching West to East between the Vistula and Rhine rivers and north to south from Southern Scandinavia to the upper Danube. In discussions of the Roman period, the Germanic peoples are sometimes referred to as Germani or ancient Germans, although many scholars consider the second term problematic, since it suggests identity with modern Germans. The very concept of "Germanic peoples" has become the subject of controversy among modern scholars, with some calling for its total abandonment.

H

Haakon VII (1872-1957), born **Prince Carl of Denmark:** The King of Norway from 1905 until his death in 1957. Originally a Danish prince, he was born in Copenhagen as the son of the future Frederick VIII of Denmark and Louise of Sweden. Prince Carl was educated at the Royal Danish Naval Academy and served in the Royal Danish Navy. After the 1905 dissolution of the union between Sweden and Norway, Prince Carl was offered the Norwegian crown. Following a November plebiscite, he accepted the offer and was formally elected King of Norway by the Storting. He took the Old Norse name *Haakon* and ascended to the throne as Haakon VII, becoming the first independent Norwegian monarch since 1387. Norway was invaded by Nazi Germany in April 1940. Haakon rejected German demands to legitimize the Quisling regime's puppet government and refused to abdicate after going into exile in Great Britain. As such, he played a pivotal role in uniting the Norwegian nation in its resistance to the invasion and the subsequent five-year-long occupation during the Second World War. He returned to Norway in June 1945 after the defeat of Germany.

Håkonshallen: A medieval stone hall in Bergen. It was first built as a royal residence and banquet hall under Håkon Håkonsson's Norway rule (1217–1263). The first time the hall is known to have been used was during Håkon's son Magnus' (later known as Magnus Lagabøte) wedding on September 11, 1261.

Hauptscharführer (head squad leader): A Nazi paramilitary rank used by the Schutzstaffel (SS) between the years of 1934 and 1945. The rank was the highest enlisted rank of the SS, with the exception of the special Waffen-SS rank of Sturmscharführer.

Hauptsturmführer (head storm leader), originally Sturmhauptführer (storm chief leader): A Nazi Party paramilitary rank that was used in several Nazi organizations such as the SS, NSKK and the NSFK. The rank of Hauptsturmführer was a mid-level commander and had equivalent seniority to a captain (Hauptmann) in the German Army and the equivalency of captain in foreign armies.

Heinkel Flugzeugwerke: A German aircraft manufacturing company founded by and named after Ernst Heinkel. It is noted for producing bomber aircraft for the Luftwaffe in World War II and for essential contributions to high-speed flight, with the pioneering examples of a successful liquid-fueled rocket and a turbojet-powered plane in aviation history. Both Heinkel designs' first flights occurred shortly before the outbreak of World War II in Europe.

Heydrich, Reinhard Tristan Eugen (1904–1942): A high-ranking German Nazi official during World War II and one of the principal architects of the Holocaust. Historians regard him as the darkest figure within the Nazi elite; Adolf Hitler christened him 'the man with the iron heart'. He was the founding head of the Sicherheitsdienst (SD), an intelligence organization charged with seeking out and neutralizing resistance to the Nazi Party via arrests, deportations and killings. He helped organize Kristallnacht, a series of coordinated attacks against Jews throughout Nazi Germany. Heydrich sought to eliminate opposition to the Nazi occupation by suppressing Czech culture and deporting and executing Czech resistance members. Heydrich was attacked in Prague on May 27, 1942 by a British-trained team of Czech and Slovak soldiers sent by the Czechoslovak government-in-exile to kill him in a sting code-named Operation Anthropoid. He died from his injuries a week later. Intelligence falsely linked the assassins to the villages of Lidice. Lidice was razed to the ground, and all adult males executed. All but a handful of its women and children were deported and killed in Nazi concentration camps.

Himmler, Heinrich Luitpold (1900–1945): Reichsführer of the Schutzstaffel (Protection Squadron; SS) and a leading member of the Nazi Party (NSDAP) of Germany. Himmler was one of the most powerful men in Nazi Germany and a leading architect of the Holocaust. From 1943 onwards, he was both Chief of German Police and Minister of the Interior, overseeing all internal and external police and security forces, including the Gestapo (Secret State Police). He controlled the Waffen-SS, the military branch of the SS. Due to his lifelong interest in occultism, Himmler interpreted Germanic Neopagan and Völkisch beliefs to promote the racial policy of Nazi Germany and incorporated esoteric symbolism and rituals into the SS. Himmler formed the Einsatzgruppen and built extermination camps. As overseer of the Nazi genocidal programs, Himmler directed the killing of some 6,000,000 Jews, between 200,000 and 500,000 Romani people and other victims. The total number of civilians killed by the regime is estimated at eleven to fourteen million people. Most of them were Polish and Soviet citizens.

Hoppe, Paul-Werner (1910–1974): An SS-Obersturmbannführer (lieutenant colonel) at KZ-Stutthof concentration camp and commandant from September 1942 until April 1945. In April 1941, he was given command of an infantry company, and in the spring of 1942 he received a severe leg wound in fighting the Red Army. After convalescing, he was assigned to KZ-Auschwitz as head of a guard detachment. In September 1942 he was promoted to SS-Sturmbannführer and Commandant of KZ-Stutthof camp. As the Soviets advanced westward, it was decided to evacuate KZ-Stutthof. Hoppe evacuated the camp on January 25, 1945. The evacuation began an hour later under the command of SS-Hauptsturmführer Theodor Meyer and referred to as the "Death March".

K

Kapo or **prisoner functionary** (German: Funktionshäftling): A prisoner in a Nazi camp assigned by the SS guards to supervise forced labor or carry out administrative tasks. Also called 'prisoner self-administration', the prisoner functionary system minimized costs by allowing camps to function with fewer SS personnel. The system was designed to turn victim against victim, as the prisoner functionaries were pitted against their fellow prisoners to maintain their SS overseers' favor. If they were derelict, they would be returned to ordinary prisoners' status and be subject to other Kapos. Many Kapos were recruited from the ranks of violent criminal gangs, such criminal convicts were known for their brutality toward other prisoners. This brutality was tolerated by the SS and was an integral part of the camp system. Kapos were spared physical abuse and hard labor, provided they performed their duties to the SS functionaries' satisfaction. They also had access to certain privileges, such as civilian clothes and a private room. After World War II, the term was reused as an insult; according to *The Jewish Chronicle*, it is 'the worst insult a Jew can give another Jew'.

Konzentrationslager (KZ) (Concentration camp): The labor and extermination camps of the Nazi regime. In a broader sense, the word is used for an internment camp. The concentration (KZ) camps were established in the German Reich and occupied territories by the NSDAP. In the end, there were around 1,000 concentration and sub-camps, as well as seven extermination camps. They served to murder millions of people, eliminate political opponents, exploit through forced labor, perform medical experiments on people and intern prisoners of war. The camp system was an essential element of the Nazi rule of injustice. Large branches of German industry benefited directly or indirectly from it.

L

Lebensborn (Fount of Life): An SS-initiated, state-supported registered association in Nazi Germany with the goal of raising the birth rate of Aryan children of persons classified as 'racially pure' and 'healthy', based on Nazi racial hygiene and health ideology. Lebensborn provided welfare to its mostly unmarried mothers, encouraged anonymous births by unmarried women at their maternity homes and mediated adoption of these children by likewise racially pure and healthy parents, particularly SS members and their families. The Cross of Honor of the German Mother was given to the women who bore the most Aryan children. Abortion was legalised by the Nazis for disabled children, but strictly punished otherwise. Initially set up in Germany in 1935, *Lebensborn* expanded into several occupied European countries with Germanic populations during the Second World War. It included the selection of 'racially worthy' orphans for adoption and care for children born from Aryan women who had been in relationships with SS members. It originally excluded children born from unions between common soldiers and foreign women, because there was no proof of 'racial purity' on both sides. During the war, many children were kidnapped from their parents and judged by Aryan criteria for their suitability to be raised in Lebensborn homes and fostered by German families.

Lidice: After the assassination of Reinhard Heydrich, Adolf Hitler ordered that every adult male, and some fifty-two women, in the small village of Lidice, Czechoslovakia, be killed. All surviving women and children were then deported to concentration camps or found suitable to be 'Germanized' and sent to the greater Reich. The Nazis then proudly proclaimed that the village of Lidice, its residents and its very name will be forever blotted from memory.

Lie, Jonas (1899–1945): A Norwegian councillor of state in the Nasjonal Samling government of Vidkun Quisling in 1940, then acting councillor of state 1940–1941 and Minister of Police between 1941 and 1945 in the new Quisling government. In the tradition of his father and grandfather, Lie was also a writer in his own right. During the 1930s, he produced several popular detective novels under the nom de plume Max Mauser. In 1942, he also published *Over Balkans syv blåner*, an account of his service with the Leibstandarte Adolf Hitler in the Balkans.

M

Meyer, Theodor Traugott: An electrician by profession, he joined the NSDAP in 1931. From April 1938, Meyer worked as a camp engineer in the Dachau concentration camp, a position he held until the end of December 1940. At the beginning of January 1941, Meyer was transferred to the Ravensbrück concentration camp as a protective custody camp leader. Under camp commandant Paul Werner Hoppe, Meyer became an adjutant and protective custody camp leader of Stutthof concentration camp beginning in January 1942. During the evacuation of Stutthof in January 1945, Meyer, again under Hoppe, became an adjutant and protective custody camp leader of the Wöbbelin concentration camp. In the second Stutthof trial, Meyer was sentenced to death and executed by hanging on October 22, 1948.

Mitte: The first and most central borough of Berlin. The borough consists of six sub-entities: Mitte proper, Gesundbrunnen, Hansaviertel, Moabit, Tiergarten and Wedding. Mitte encompasses Berlin's historic core and includes some of the most important tourist sites of Berlin.

N

Nasjonal Samling (NS): A Norwegian far-right party active from 1933 to 1945. It was the only legal party in Norway from 1942 to 1945. It was founded by former minister of defense Vidkun Quisling and a group of supporters. The party never gained direct political influence, but it made its mark on Norwegian politics nonetheless. Even though it never managed to get more than 2.5% of the vote and failed to elect even one candidate to the Storting (Parliament), it became a factor by polarising the political scene. The established parties in Norway viewed it as a Norwegian version of the German Nazis and generally refused to cooperate with it in any way. A significant trait of the party throughout its existence was a relatively high level of internal conflict. Antisemitism, anti-Masonry, differing views on religion and the party's association with the Nazis and Germany were hotly debated and fractioned the party. Strong belief in Norse Paganism, Romantic nationalism and totalitarianism dominated NS ideology. It also relied heavily on Nordic symbolism, using Vikings, pre-Christian religion and signs in its propaganda and speeches.

Nava Jack: A rock and sand mixture for use as base, foundation or pathway.

Nielsen, Martin: (1900–1962): A Danish politician, managing editor, member of parliament for the Communist Party of Denmark and Holocaust survivor. Before his election to the Danish parliament (Rigsdag), he was a dairyman and farmworker. In June 1941, Danish police arrested Martin Nielsen and around 300 other members of the Communist Party of Denmark (DKP). On October 2, 1943, he was one of 150 communists deported to Stutthof concentration camp, on the ship Wartheland via Swinemünde and by cattle car. On January 25, 1945, Nielsen was marched from Stutthof. On March 10, 1945, he was liberated by the Red Army, which sent him (part of the way on foot) to Moscow, from where he was repatriated.

O

Oberleutnant (OLt): The highest lieutenant officer rank in the armed forces of Germany (Bundeswehr), the Austrian Armed Forces and the Military of Switzerland.

Oberscharführer (senior squad leader): A Nazi Party paramilitary rank that existed between 1932 and 1945.

Obersturmbannführer (senior assault unit leader): A paramilitary German Nazi Party (NSDAP) rank used by both the SA and the SS. It was created in May 1933 to fill the need for an additional rank above Sturmbannführer as the SA expanded. It became an SS rank at the same time. An Obersturmbannführer was junior to Standartenführer and was the equivalent to Oberstleutnant (lieutenant colonel) in the German Army. The insignia for Obersturmbannführer was four silver pips and a stripe, centered on the left collar of an SS/SA uniform. The rank also displayed the shoulder boards of an Oberstleutnant and was the highest SS/SA rank to display unit insignia on the opposite collar.

Oradour-Sur- Glane: On June 10, 1944, the village of Oradour-Sur-Glane in Haute-Vienne in Nazi-occupied France was destroyed when 642 of its inhabitants, including non-combatant women and children, were massacred by a German Waffen-SS company.

Organisation Todt (OT): A civil and military engineering organization in Nazi Germany from 1933 to 1945, named after its founder, Fritz Todt, an engineer and senior Nazi. The organization was responsible for an extensive range of engineering projects in Nazi Germany and occupied territories. It became notorious for using forced labour. From 1943 until 1945, during the late phase of the Third Reich, OT administered all concentration camps' constructions to supply forced labor to industry.

P

Paper Clip Resistance: In the autumn of 1940, students at Oslo University started wearing paperclips on their lapels as a non-violent symbol of resistance, unity and national pride. Symbols related to the royal family and state had already been banned, and they wanted a slick way of displaying their rejection of the Nazi ideology. In addition to wearing a single paperclip, paperclip bracelets and other types of jewelry were fashioned as well, symbolically binding Norwegians together in the face of adversity.

Q

Quisling, Vidkun (1887-1945), Norwegian politician, whose collaboration with the Nazis during World War II (1939-1945) made his name synonymous with traitor. In the 1930s he founded Nasjonal Samling (National Union), a Fascist party that received subsidies from Germany. During a visit to Hitler in Berlin in the winter of 1939-40, Quisling had pointed out how valuable it would be for Germany to occupy Norway. Immediately after the invasion, on the morning of April 9, 1940, he proclaimed himself the new head of the government and ordered the Norwegian armed forces to stop battling the Germans. But Quisling's intervention backfired and stimulated the resistance. Thus, the occupying power quickly realized that — for the time being — Quisling did not serve their interests and they chose to base their administration of the country on a certain degree of give-and-take with the existing civilian authorities. Hitler appointed Josef Terboven as Reichskommissar who in turn appointed Quisling to a token role as prime minister in 1942 and throughout the war he collaborated with the Nazis. Terboven and Quisling constantly battled. Quisling was tried and executed after the war.

R

Rediess, Friedrich Wilhelm (1900–1945): At the onset of World War II, Rediess was responsible for implementing German racial laws in Prussia, overseeing the deportation of Jews from East Prussia. Rediess was then given the task of eradicating 1,558 Jewish deportees deemed mentally ill. He borrowed "gas vans" and personnel from other SS units, offering a bounty of ten Reichsmark for each Jew killed. It took nineteen days to accomplish these killings, after which Rediess reneged on the payment. Following the German invasion of Norway, Rediess was transferred there to work with Reichskommissar Josef Terboven. In March 1941, citing reports of large numbers of Norwegian women impregnated by German soldiers, Rediess implemented the German Lebensborn program in Norway. This program encouraged the production of 'racially pure' Aryan children, usually sired by SS troops. Ultimately, 8,000 children were born under this program's auspices, making Norway second only to Germany in registered Aryan births during World War II.

Reichsarbeitsdienstlager (RAD): An organization in the National Socialist German Reich. The Reich Labor Service law was enacted on June 26, 1936. 'All young Germans of both sexes are required to serve their people in the Reich Labor Service: The Fuehrer and Reich Chancellor determines the number of annually convened conscripts and sets the length of service.' First, young men (before their military service) were called up for six months for labor service. From the beginning of the Second World War, the Reich Labor Service was extended to include young women.

Reichsführer-SS (Reich Leader-SS): A special title and rank that existed between the years of 1925 and 1945 for the commander of the Schutzstaffel (SS). Reichsführer-SS was a title from 1925 to 1933, and from 1934 to 1945 it was the highest rank of the SS. The longest serving and most noteworthy office holder was Heinrich Himmler.

Reichskommissar: After the Norwegian king and his government fled during the German invasion of the country and the failure of a coup d'état by Vidkun Quisling, Hitler appointed a Reichskommissar für die besetzten Norwegischen Gebiete (Reich Commissioner for the occupied Norwegian territories) on April 24, 1940. The office had two consecutive Reichskommissars with extensive authority. The first, from April 24, 1940, to May 7, 1945, was Josef Terboven, NSDAP. He took up residence in the Crown Prince's manor at Skaugum. Answerable only to Hitler, Terboven initially tried to negotiate with the Norwegian Storting (Parliament) to establish a civilian administration which would be willing to sign a peace treaty with Germany. After the collapse of these negotiations, on September 25, 1940, Terboven proclaimed the deposition of King Haakon VII and his cabinet-in-exile and outlawed all political parties except the Norwegian fascist party Nasjonal Samling. Terboven committed suicide during the night of May 8, 1945, just before the surrender of the German forces in Norway became effective. From May 7, 1945, to May 8, 1945, Franz Böhme was commander-in-chief of German military forces in Norway. Böhme assumed

Terboven's responsibilities as acting Reichskommissar until Allied forces took control and had him arrested.

Reichsmark (RM): The currency in Germany from 1924 until June 20, 1948, when it was replaced with the Deutsche Mark. The Reichsmark was subdivided into 100 Reichspfennig. The Mark is an ancient Germanic weight measure, traditionally a half pound, later used for several coins, whereas *Reich* comes from the German nation-state's official name from 1871 to 1945, Deutsches Reich.

Reichstag fire: The burning of the Reichstag (parliament) building in Berlin on the night of February 27, 1933 was a crucial event in establishing the Nazi dictatorship. It is widely believed to have been contrived by the newly formed Nazi government to turn public opinion against its opponents and assume emergency powers. On February 28, 1933, the day after the fire, Hitler's dictatorship began by enacting a decree 'for the Protection of the People and the State', which dispensed with all constitutional protection of political, personal and property rights.

Riisnæs, Sverre Parnelius (1897–1988): A Norwegian jurist and public prosecutor. He was a member of the collaborationist government Nasjonal Samling during World War II. Riisnæs was an important public prosecutor in inter-war Norway and had contacts in the international policing community. He was the public prosecutor in the famous case against Per Imerslund and other Norwegian Nazis who had broken into the home where Leon Trotsky had been staying before his deportation from Norway to Mexico. Riisnœs was appointed councillor of state in the Nasjonal Samling (NS) government 1940–1941 and was one of nine Norwegians signing the declaration on January 31, 1942, which disbanded the Parliament of Norway and directed Quisling to formally take over the powers of government. He served as the Minister of Justice from 1941 to 1945. As Minister of Justice, Riisnæs was responsible for changing the Norwegian legal system to legitimise the Nazi actions and authorized the persecution of those who would not cooperate with the German occupiers. Riisnæs held public speeches against Norwegian Jews. After collapse of the Quisling government at the end of the war, Jonas Lie, Henrik Rogstad and Riisnæs retreated to an NS gathering place outside of Oslo. Surrounded by the Home Front guard forces, Lie died, probably of natural causes, and Rogstad committed suicide. Riisnæs surrendered without a struggle. After the war he was charged with treason, but his trial was suspended based on the defence that he was mentally ill. Riisnæs was hospitalized for this illness in the Reitgjerdet Hospital from 1948 to 1960. In 1974 he emigrated to Sicily, Italy, and later to Vienna. He returned to Oslo in 1985, where he lived for three years in a nursing home until his death. To this day, there are questions whether he feigned mental weakness.

S

Scharführer (squad leader): A title or rank used in early 20th Century German military terminology. In German, Schar was one term for the smallest sub-unit, equivalent to (for example) a 'troop', 'squad' or 'section'. The word führer simply meant 'leader'.

Schellenberg, Walter Friedrich (1910–1952): A German SS-Brigadeführer who rose through the SS ranks to become the head of foreign intelligence. In 1940, he was sent to Portugal to intercept the Duke and Duchess of Windsor and persuade them to work for Germany. The mission was a failure.

Schutzpolizei: The State (Reich) protection police of Nazi Germany. Schutzpolizei is the German name for a uniformed police force. State police departments were in charge of protection, criminal investigations and administration. Policemen had to have previous military service, good physical and mental health, be of Aryan descent and be Nazi Party members. They also had to be members of the SS. Promotion for officers was determined by merit and seniority. Pay for policemen was higher than the average industrial worker.

SS-Oberst-Gruppenführer: The highest commissioned rank (from 1942 to 1945) in the Schutzstaffel (SS) – with the exception of Reichsführer-SS, held by SS commander Heinrich Himmler. The rank is translated as 'Supreme group leader' and alternatively translated as 'colonel group leader'.

Sturmbannführer (assault unit leader): A Nazi Party paramilitary rank (equivalent to major) used in several Nazi organizations, such as the SA, SS and the NSFK. The rank originated from German shock troop units of the First World War.

T

Telavåg: During the occupation of Norway by Nazi Germany, Telavåg played an essential role in the secret North Sea boat traffic (Shetland Bus) between Norway and Great Britain. The village was the 'Telavåg Tragedy' scene in the spring of 1942, during World War II. Reichskommissar Josef Terboven personally oversaw the Nazi reprisal, which was quick and brutal. On April 30, as the villagers watched, all buildings were destroyed, all boats were sunk or confiscated and all livestock was taken away. All men in the village were either executed or sent to the Nazi concentration camp at Sachsenhausen. Of the seventy-two who were deported from Telavåg, thirty-one were murdered in captivity. Women and children were imprisoned for two years. Eighteen Norwegian prisoners (unrelated to Telavåg) held at the Trandum internment camp were also executed as a reprisal.

Terboven, Josef Antonius Heinrich (1898–1945): A Nazi leader most known for his brutal leadership during Norway's Nazi occupation. Terboven was made Reichskommissar of Norway on April 24, 1940, when it became apparent that a more authoritarian administration was needed. Terboven was much hated among Norwegians and earned little respect among his allies. He committed suicide a little past 23:00 on May 8, 1945, by detonating dynamite in his bunker hideout.

U

Unterscharführer (junior squad leader): A paramilitary rank of the Nazi Party used by the Schutzstaffel (SS) between 1934 and 1945. The SS rank was created after the Night of the Long Knives. That event caused an SS reorganisation and the creation of new ranks to separate the SS from the Sturmabteilung (SA).

Untersturmführer (Junior storm leader): A paramilitary rank of the German Schutzstaffel (SS) first created in July 1934. The rank can trace its origins to the older SA rank of Sturmführer which had existed since the founding of the SA in 1921.

V

Valkendorftårnet: A building named after Christoffer Valkendorf. In Magnus Lagabøte's time in the 1270s, a castle was a ring wall tower with a moat and drawbridge, where the king had a chapel decorated. The chapel had cross vaults, and the east and south walls' interior remains to show where there were Gothic window openings. It burned in 1513 and was rebuilt in 1514–23. After an explosion in the gunpowder chamber in the 1530s, the building was partially restored by Valkendorf towards the end of the 1550s.

W

Wehrmacht (defence force): The unified armed forces of Nazi Germany from 1935 to 1945. It consisted of the Heer (army), the Kriegsmarine (navy) and the Luftwaffe (air force). The designation 'Wehrmacht' replaced the previously used term Reichswehr and was the manifestation of the Nazi regime's efforts to rearm Germany to a greater extent than the Treaty of Versailles permitted. After the Nazi rise to power in 1933, one of Adolf Hitler's most overt and audacious moves was to establish the Wehrmacht, a modern offensively capable armed force, fulfilling the Nazi regime's long-term goals of regaining lost territory as well as gaining new territory and dominating its neighbours. This required the reinstatement of conscription, and massive investment and defense spending on the arms industry. The Wehrmacht formed the heart of Germany's politico-military power. In the early part of the Second World War, the Wehrmacht employed combined arms tactics (close-cover air-support, tanks and infantry) to devastating effect in what became known as

Blitzkrieg (lightning war). Its campaigns in France (1940), the Soviet Union (1941) and North Africa (1941/42) are regarded by historians as acts of boldness. At the same time, the far-flung advances strained the Wehrmacht's capacity to the breaking point, culminating in its first major defeat in the Battle of Moscow (1941). By late 1942, Germany was losing the initiative in all theaters. The German operational art proved no match to the war-making abilities of the Allied coalition, making the Wehrmacht's weaknesses in strategy, doctrine and logistics readily apparent.

Welhaven, Kristian (1883–1975): A Norwegian police officer. He was chief of police of Oslo for 27 years, from 1927 to 1954. He was a leading force in establishing an organized Norwegian intelligence service before World War II, and in re-establishing it after the war. During the war years Welhaven was arrested by the Germans and imprisoned in both Norway and Germany, before spending the remainder of the war as a civilian internee in Germany. At the outbreak of World War II, Welhaven was made head of a commission set up to plan the evacuation of the population of Oslo in case of war. When the German invasion of Norway came on April 9, 1940, attempts were made to evacuate people but in the chaos of the invasion the organization fell through and Welhaven called off the evacuation. During the occupation, Welhaven refused to cooperate with the German occupiers and the Norwegian Nazi collaborators. Welhaven was removed from his position by the Germans on September 23, 1940 and replaced with the Nazi-loyal Bernhard Askvig. After the war, Welhaven worked with rebuilding the police force of Oslo, being its leader until his retirement in 1954. He used his influence to ensure that the post-war purge of the Norwegian police force was as gentle as possible. Welhaven was decorated as a Commander of the Royal Norwegian Order of St. Olav in 1947, and also of the Danish Order of Dannebrog and the Swedish Order of Vasa and Order of the Polar Star.

Printed in Canada